Lost Aviation Collections of Britain

Front cover:
The wonderful collection at Colerne bowed out in style – see Chapter 6.

Rear cover:
Colour, clockwise from top left: Southend's Beverley arriving – see Chapter 7; Ormond Haydon-Baillie's fateful P-51D Mustang – see Chapter 12; Lasham's Ambassador – see Chapter 9; Lancaster G-ASXX at Biggin Hill - see Chapter 5; *and centre:* Finningley's Avro 707 – see Chapter 6. *Black and white:* Richard Nash and his Sopwith Camel – see Chapter 1.

Lost Aviation Collections of Britain

A tribute to the UK's bygone aviation museums and collections

Ken Ellis

Special *Wrecks and Relics* 50th Anniversary Edition

Crécy Publishing Limited

Lost Aviation Collections of Britain

First published in 2011 by Crécy Publishing Limited

Copyright © Ken Ellis 2011

A CIP record for this book is available from the British Library

ISBN 9 780859 791595

Printed in Malta by Gutenberg Press Ltd

Crécy Publishing Limited
1a Ringway Trading Estate, Shadowmoss Road, Manchester M22 5LH
www.crecy.co.uk

1961-2011

A small gathering of Colerne inmates, used as a fund-raising souvenir postcard. Top to bottom: Javelin FAW.4 XA634, Heinkel He 162A-2 120227, prone-pilot Meteor F.8 WK935, Messerschmitt Me 163B-1 191904, Hunter F.2 WN907, Auster 'Antarctic' WE600, Spitfire II P7350. *via Roy Bonser*

For
Roy Bonser and Peter Green

Contents

Note: The numbers given with the locations in the contents listing correspond to numbers on the map.

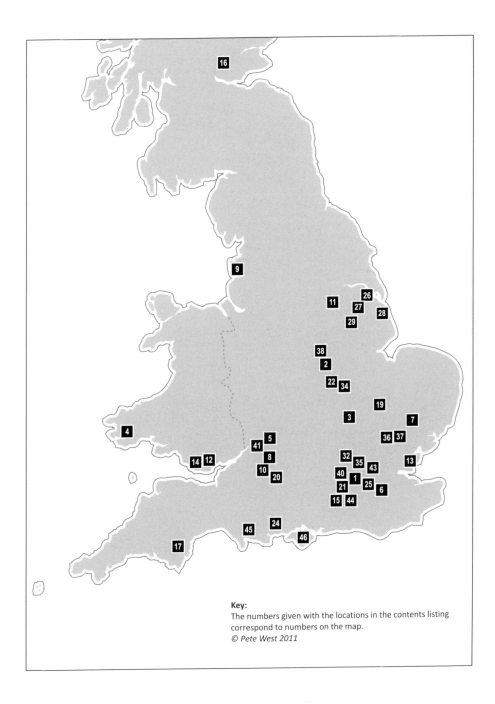

Key:
The numbers given with the locations in the contents listing
correspond to numbers on the map.
© Pete West 2011

Graham Warner in front of the second Blenheim at Duxford for the launch of his book 'Spirit of Britain First', 1996.

Foreword

Very many aviation enthusiasts, especially those anxious to preserve this country's rich aviation heritage, look forward with keen anticipation to the latest edition of Ken's evergreen *Wrecks & Relics*. For many years it has provided a deep, rich, mine of information on the location and status of all the old airframes and major aircraft components scattered throughout these islands. This has encouraged and inspired hundreds of teams, organisations and individuals, both amateur and professional, to work to conserve or restore many rare, often historically important, aircraft that would otherwise have just faded away and been lost forever.

The sheer scale of the amount of research, investigation, checking and updating required by each one of the thousands of entries in such comprehensive volumes I find hard to grasp. Yet it all fell on the shoulders of Ken Ellis, for although assisted by many willing informants, he had to pull together this mass of information, present it in a readily accessible form, and ensure the accuracy of all the entries. Throughout this period Ken also carried the heavy and demanding responsibility of being editor of *FlyPast*, steadily improving both the quality and quantity of the contents, plus being heavily involved in several other Key Publishing aviation titles.

I used to devour each volume of *Wrecks & Relics* avidly from cover to cover, especially as I was building my own British Aerial Museum collection whilst we were restoring the Blenheim to fly at Duxford (see Chapter 16). In their pages I found the two Beech 18s left at Prestwick by a defunct Canadian survey company, both were rescued, restored and are currently airworthy; the Messerschmitt Bf.109E now in the Imperial War Museum's Battle of Britain Hall, a DHC Chipmunk and the airframe of the second Blenheim that we rebuilt to flying condition following the loss of the first at Denham in 1987.

Having described the first restoration in *The Forgotten Bomber* I then wrote about the second in *Spirit of Britain First*. I inscribed Ken's copy with: 'To Ken, who inspired me to turn Wrecks and Relics into flying aircraft'. Ken is a true aircraft enthusiast and I'm sure he has inspired very many others. We all owe him a great debt.

Graham Warner MBE
Storrington, Sussex

Introduction

I were but a lad 'appen when the first edition of *Wrecks & Relics* was published in 1961, but it was to have a major effect on me, even if I didn't know it. Half a century on, I can't seem to shake it off! What to do to mark the looming 50th anniversary of what has certainly become an institution has long since puzzled me. I'd like to claim that the idea for this book was mine, but no. It was Crécy Publishing's genial Jeremy Pratt that schemed up this special edition. I was more than happy to steal it from him and I hope it meets his expectations!

Lost Aviation Collections of Britain is a selection of major collections or sources of historic aircraft over the decades that are no longer with us... have ceased to be... demised... snuffed it – best stop that before it spreads! It begins long before *W&R* did, with Richard Nash and the colleges at Loughborough and Cranfield. From 1974, *W&R* surveyed happenings every two years and for bodies that were in existence during that era I have found it very instructive to knit together their past instead of presenting it as 24-month gobbets. There will be voices saying 'Why didn't X go in?' 'Or what about Y?' The choice is mine and to those groups, museums or organisations large or small that didn't make it I would apologise, but of course to be in this book they must no longer be with us, so I can't!

Is *Lost Aviation Collections of Britain* all about failure? In some cases yes, though all of the pages chart endeavour of one form or another in those heady formative years of trying to secure Britain's aviation heritage. There's plenty of enthusiasm to be found herein, but so often such zeal goes hand-in-hand with naivety. There is much passion also, and the cash required to support these fervours. In quite a few instances the driving force is robbed from us through illness, or flying accident. That is not failure; that's fate. If there is an over-riding message in these chapters it is that Britain has been extremely lucky in the variety and scope of our amazing aviation past that has managed to survive and prosper.

Four of my case studies got through to the 21st century before folding. I was tempted to include the collapse of the RAF Millom and Militaria Museum in Cumbria during 2010, but the final auction of its chattels was only held on 27th January this year and the wounds are too raw for analysis at this point. All being well, I'll get my first chance in 2012 when the 23rd edition of *Wrecks & Relics* is due – just in time to take your mind off the Olympics! Even as I put this into the PC, there are stirrings of one, perhaps two, more organisations on the brink...

Notes

The tables of aircraft are designed to provide an at-a-glance view of the extent of each collection. They are arranged by type and details including the year built and roughly (or occasionally precisely!) when it arrived are given. The potted histories are in *reverse* order – ie last location/user is given *first*. Regular *W&R* readers will have no problems with these and again, I should point out that no attempt was made to make these encompass *every last* moment of an airframe's career – there just isn't the space! What *is* presented is the provenance to the point of arrival in the organisation in question and its fate or current whereabouts. If you seek more, then it is time to refer to your library of past editions! As with *Wrecks & Relics* itself, 'ownership' or 'custodianship' of airframes in this book is not to be inferred as definitive.

The *Ones That Got Away* features serve as reminders that types as well as collections slip the net. Again, the choices are personal and therefore quite random! Origination of the images reproduced within is given where it can be defined, otherwise all come from my own collection.

Acknowledgements

First and foremost, thanks go to everyone who has ever contributed, large or small to *Wrecks & Relics*. Without such input the books would be wafer-thin and never have clocked 50 years. A lot of the people I'd like to thank are no longer with us and I try and pay tribute to as many as possible.

Directly helping with this tome were the following: David Allan of the Ian Allan Group Ltd for kind permission to publish the appropriate front covers, Brian Cocks, purveyor of fine books and sound advice; Howard Heeley of the Newark Air Museum, Watson J Nelson for reality checks, Brian Pickering of Military Aircraft Photographs, Nigel Price, the Editor of *FlyPast*, for shed-loads of patience flowing in my direction; Michael Shaw for his exhaustive investigations; Dick Richardson, now running Popham aerodrome, but latterly with Charles Church and Strathallan; Steve Vizard of Airframe Assemblies.

All of the team at Crécy Publishing Ltd, especially to designer Rob Taylor and to the ever-understanding Gill Richardson. To Graham Warner for his foreword and encouragement over many years – the world needs more of his kind... And to Roy Bonser and Peter Green for their friendship and inspiration. Many thanks go to Pam and the quadrupeds, Rex and Relix, for putting up with a manic retrospective recluse in the house.

Ken Ellis
People's Republic of Rutland
May 2011
Myddle Cottage, 13 Mill Lane, Barrowden, Oakham, LE15 8EH
wrecksandrelics@kenavhist.wanadoo.co.uk

CHAPTER 1

Horseless Carriages
Nash Collection
1934 to 1953

Richard Ormonde Shuttleworth gained fame as a collector of historic vehicles and aircraft in the 1930s. As such he was ahead of his time in realising that aeronautical heritage, although comparatively 'new', needed conserving before precious pioneer airframes slipped the net. His lasting memorial is to be found on the hallowed turf of the former family estate at Old Warden in Bedfordshire where the exceptional collection that bears his name flourishes.

But Mr Shuttleworth was not alone in that decade, there was *another* Richard with similar vision and determination, but he is largely forgotten. This was racing driver Richard 'Dick' Grainger Jeune Nash who amassed an incredible fleet of bicycles, cars and flying machines at Brooklands, Surrey. Dick also has an impressive tribute to his endeavours – take a tour through the halls of the Royal Air Force Museum at Hendon in north London and airframes from his International Horseless Carriage Corporation comprise some of the most important exhibits.

The enquiring after, the hunting down and clinching the deal was the bit that mattered to Mr Nash, but he did develop a side-line to provide some income to help with his passion. A telephone call to Byfleet 653 would reach his office at the Brooklands motor racing track and a quote for borrowing an aeroplane, or a Rolls-Royce, for a special event or a film would be forthcoming. Adverts explained exactly what the International Horseless Carriage Corporation did: "Specialists in the hire of early types of mechanical vehicles for films, theatres, advertising, showrooms, aviation displays and exhibitions." The scope that awaited clients was: "Bicycles 1819 to 1900, horseless carriages 1895 to 1914 and aeroplanes 1903 to 1918." As such, Dick Nash's operation was the forerunner of the present-day Aces High, the aviation film, airshows and events specialist founded by Mike Woodley in 1979 and these days based at Dunsfold in Surrey. Like Mr Shuttleworth, Mr Nash had incredible foresight and the nation is in his debt.

Above: Line-up at Hendon in July 1951 for the '50 Years of Flying' exhibition organised by the Royal Aero Club and supported by the 'Daily Express'. Left to right: Caudron G.3, Avro 504K 'H2311', SE.5a 'B4563', Camel 'H508', all of the Nash Collection. To the right is the tail of Sopwith Camel N5912. All are now on display at the RAF Museum, Hendon.

What might have been

At Hendon the pair of Blériots, the Avro 504, Caudron, Camel, SE.5a and Fokker D.VII are all jaw-dropping exhibits. Then there is the 'Farman' held at the RAF Museum's Michael Beetham Conservation Centre at Cosford, Shropshire, the Sopwith Baby floatplane displayed at the Fleet Air Arm Museum, Yeovilton, Somerset, painstakingly constructed around surviving components and a second Avro 504 on loan in Manchester. That's nine gems and the basis for a reconstruction that was bequeathed to the nation.

What is all the more remarkable about Mr Nash and his International Horseless Carriage Corporation is what *might* have been. World War Two curtailed his foraging and it put paid to *half* of his aeronautical treasures. Establishing just *what* Dick Nash had in his premises at Brooklands has always been a matter of conjecture, because documentary and photographic evidence is thin on the ground. Post-war, Mr Nash was a regular letter writer to aviation magazines and these form the basis of our understanding of the composition of the fleet. Sadly, some pundits have leapt to the wrong conclusions, because some of what Dick Nash wrote was about his 'shopping list'. With a remit of the era of the Wright brothers (1903) to the Armistice (1918) he had a SPAD and a Nieuport in his sights, for example, but there is no evidence he ever attained them, though some sources quote otherwise.

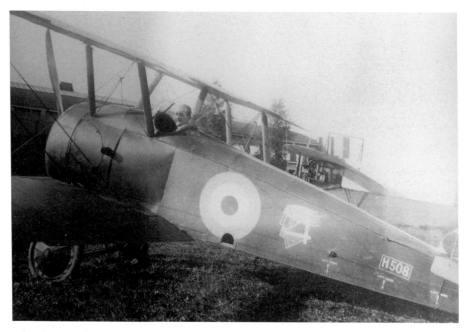

Dick Nash seated in his Sopwith Camel 'H508', complete with somewhat crude Red Indian's head as adopted by the French 4th Lafayette Escadrille. This presumed to have been taken at Brooklands, circa 1937-1938. Note the Blériot behind.
Peter Green collection

Ignoring the survivors, according to Mr Nash by the outbreak of World War Two, he had the following mouth-watering morsels: Wright glider of 1903, Wright biplane of 1908, Antoinette monoplane of 1910, Deperdussin of 1911, Fokker 'monoplane' (*assumed* to be an E.III) of 1916 and Fokker Dr.I triplane of 1917. The Wrights are clearly exceptional, while no original Dr.I survives anywhere today.

By June 1940, the collection had been given notice to quit its premises at Brooklands to make way for vital war work. A dispersal plan was underway, but an air raid on 6th September at the airfield badly damaged at least two Blériots and a pair of Sopwith Baby floatplanes. Nash called the latter 'Schneiders', but he may have been using a generic phrase, not attempting the 'up' their provenance. The fuselage, mainplanes and a float from the bomb-damaged 'Schneiders' (8214 and 8215 supplied to the Italian government in July 1916 to act as patterns for production by Macchi) formed the basis of the complete Baby, called *The Jabberwock*, now at Yeovilton. Of the types listed earlier, none of them were mentioned again in post-war writings, so the assumption is they were also destroyed by enemy action or accident.

The impressive Sopwith Baby 'N2078' 'The Jabberwock' after completion of its restoration at the Royal Naval Aircraft Yard at Fleetlands, Hampshire, in 1970. This was based on salvaged elements of two Nash Collection 'Schneiders' bomb damaged at Brooklands in 1940. *Fleet Air Arm Museum*

By 1951 the Nash hoard was to be found lodging at RAF Hendon. Richard Nash was by then acutely aware that they needed a properly constituted home. The Science Museum had been approached about taking them on, but apparently declined. In December 1953, Nash sold them to the Royal Aeronautical Society, probably the only organisation with the 'clout' to get something done at the time. He insisted that the label 'Nash Collection' be used to refer to them and that none of them were ever to be flown.

Nine largely complete airframes were handed to the RAeS. Seven of them were shown off at their 'Garden Party' at Wisley in 1956 and by 1959 they were housed within the BEA Engineering complex at London Airport, Heathrow, where a largely uncoordinated restoration programme was initiated under the aegis of the Historic Aircraft Maintenance Group. In March 1963 the formative RAF Museum took on the Nash airframes on loan, moving them to Henlow. The Ministry of Defence bought them from the RAeS in March 1992 to ensure their permanence with the RAF Museum. Finally, in September 2004 the MoD gifted the airframes to the RAF Museum, thereby cutting through the problem that had existed preventing Hendon from applying for lottery money or similar grants, as it did not own its exhibits.

A 'squadron' of Bleriots

Dick Nash eventually owned no less than *five* Blériot monoplanes. Three (Type XIs 54 and 164 and Type XXVII 433) were presented to him at Le Havre, France, around 1935-1936 by pre-war display and racing pilot and garage proprietor Monsieur Molon. This gentleman had attended the pioneering 'Aviation Contest' at Doncaster, Yorkshire, in October 1909, very probably in one of the Type XIs that were brought by ship up the Thames, off-loaded and taken by truck driven by Dick Nash to Brooklands. Today, 164 'flies' inside the 'Milestones of Flight' hall at Hendon.

Nash's unique Type XXVII was built in 1911 by Société Blériot Aéronautique at Suresnes, near Paris. By August 1914 it was in store at Le Havre and remained so until it was transported to Brooklands. No.433 was returned to airworthiness but suffered a crash at Brooklands with Dick at the controls on 15th June 1936. It was repaired to static condition and it may well have been this incident that effected Nash's change of mind that rare aircraft should be flown only if a similar type was also in existence. With 433 in the care of the nascent RAF Museum, it was restored at Lyneham, Wiltshire, 1963 to 1964 and underwent further attention in the workshops at Cardington, Bedfordshire, from the late 1970s. It is now on show inside the Grahame-White Factory building at Hendon.

Believed to be at Honington, Suffolk, a line-up in May 1955: left to right: almost certainly Blériot X No.164, Sopwith Camel F6314, the Imperial War Museum's Bristol F.2b Fighter E2581 and a Hurricane.

The Blériot XXVII at Biggin Hill in May 1969.

There were two other Type XIs (Nos.5 and 16) with the former having been found in the north of England, according to Mr Nash. Both of these were wrecked by the Luftwaffe in the raid on Brooklands of 6th September 1940. Parts of one, believed to be No.16, are held by the RAF Museum at its 'deep store' at Stafford. Richard Nash wrote in 1950 that No.5 had been rebuilt using original Société Blériot Aéronautique drawings "for film purposes". It was given a rudder and short-span wings as employed by Louis Blériot for his famous cross-Channel flight of 25th July 1909. He is thought to have contracted this work to Dart Aircraft of Dunstable, Bedfordshire, under the guidance of that company's designer, Alfred Richard Weyl.

A Blériot (or parts thereof, perhaps of more than one) was retained by Dick at his home in Weybridge in 1953. This was very likely No.54 from the Le Havre cache and its fate is unknown.

Combined Avros

The military identity of the Avro 504K today displayed in Manchester's Museum of Science and Industry is unknown. Assembled from parts, it was registered as G-ABAA to G & H Aviation of Stag Lane in September 1930. By May 1936 it was operated by Williams and Co from Stanley Park and Squires Gate aerodromes, Blackpool. Dick acquired it in 1938 and it was ferried to Brooklands. Restored by Avro to flying condition as 'H2311' it was flown at the 1950 SBAC display at Farnborough. (H2311 was believed to be the Avro 504 in which King George VI learned to fly at the Royal Air Force College, Cranwell, in 1918.) In 1955 it was used in the filming of *Reach for the Sky* and it moved to Henlow to join the RAF Museum by 1968. It moved to Manchester, on loan, in February 1989. There it was returned to civil status, the work being completed in June 1991.

Avro 504K H2311 during a formal occasion at Andover in 1926 or 1927. This was the identity chosen for the 1950 restoration of the machine now on show at Manchester. *Peter Green collection*

Work in hand in Manchester during 1989 on the restoration of the Nash Collection Avro 504K G-ABAA. *Ken Ellis*

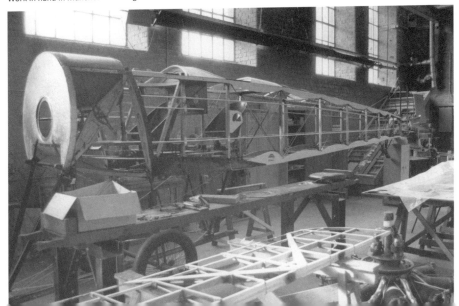

Believed taken at Abingdon in the early 1960s, the fuselage of Avro 504K G-EBJE ready for its challenging, hybrid, restoration. *MAP*

The other Nash Avro 504 graces the repositioned Grahame-White Factory building at the RAF Museum, Hendon. This was created from parts acquired by Mr Nash from a store near Shoreham, Sussex. The fuselage came from 504K G-EBJE, a machine reluctant to reveal its military past. It was used for joyriding by Southern Counties Aviation from January 1926 and then by none other than Frederick George Miles in the guise of his company, Southern Aircraft Ltd, from August 1926, both flying concerns from Shoreham. It was withdrawn from used by September 1934 and stored alongside the dismantled and damaged prototype Avro 548A G-EBKN. The wings from this machine were part of the cache that Dick Nash took over and these were fitted to the fuselage of Hendon's E449. This serial number has been confirmed as the identity of the wings – built by Harland and Wolff at Belfast in early 1918 – and was adopted as the overall 'label' for the completed restoration. The 548A was essentially a 504K re-engined with an 80hp (60kW) Renault and first appeared in April 1925. F G Miles bought the machine in 1929 and sold it on to Graham Head who flew it from Shoreham until it was damaged in a forced landing away from the aerodrome on 17th July 1930.

The first of four Avro 548As, G-EBKN, during acceptance trials at Martlesham Heath, Suffolk, in 1925. The wings of this machine were used in the restoration of the example now on show at Hendon. *MAP*

Ken Waller's Caudron in the static park at Hendon in June 1936. Behind is a Bristol F.2b Fighter and behind that the Sopwith Triplane now on display at Hendon. *Roy Spurgeon*

Exotic Biplanes

The RAF Museum's Caudron G.3, displayed at Hendon within the Grahame-White Factory hall in the colours of the RNAS Flying School at Vendôme in 1917, has unconfirmed origins. It very likely was built in 1916 by Caudron at its factory at Issy-le-Moulineaux, near Paris, or *possibly* the British Caudron Company at Cricklewood. By July 1921 it was in Belgium and registered as O-BELA with Société d'Enterprises Générales Aéronautique at Gosselies, reportedly having served with the Belgian Air Force. (The Belgian Air Force used the type from mid-1918 all the way through to 1928. Some aircraft were transferred to a civil-run school at Gosselies in the 1920s.)

The restoration shop at Henlow, Beds, in October 1968 with the Caudron in the foreground. *Peter Green collection*

In 1929 it became OO-ELA and by April 1930 was with the Club des Aviateurs de Belgique (Belgian Aero Club) at Brussels and registered to Jean Leduc and flown by him. Jean offered the Caudron to Ken Waller, chief flying instructor at Brooklands Aviation and well-known long-distance record-breaking pilot, who had earlier expressed interest in it. Ken ferried it from Brussels to Ostend to Lympne, arriving at Brooklands on 20th May 1936. The following month, it attended the opening of Shoreham Airport and was displayed at the Hendon Air Pageant. The British registration G-AETA was reserved for the Caudron, but never taken up. Ken is reported to have found the hangarage fees too much for him and turned to his neighbour at Brooklands, Dick Nash, who doubtless had been looking enviously at it ever since it arrived! It joined the ranks of the 'Horseless Carriages' and post-war moved to the custody of RAeS and then to the RAF Museum, initially going to Stradishall for some restoration, travelling to Henlow in 1966 and to Hendon in 1972.

The superb Farman biplane has been the most reclusive of the former Nash Collection. Built perhaps as early as 1913 at Buc by Henri and Maurice Alain Farman it is claimed to be the prototype F.40, although it is also referred to as an F.141. It is believed to have been kept as a 'works machine' and is said to have made at least four flights from Buc to Hendon during World War One with Maurice Farman piloting. Post-war, it continued to be a favourite of Maurice and was flown extensively by him, attending air events up to about 1933. It was registered as F-HMFI – an early example of a 'personalised' registration? In 1936 it was acquired by Dick Nash, by which time it had a total flying time of 1,040 hours. With the paddock number '3', the Farman was displayed at the 1936 or 1937 Hendon Air Pageant. When it joined the RAF Museum it travelled to Benson in the early 1960s where restoration was started, it is now at the Sir Michael Beetham Conservation Centre at Cosford.

The Farman in skeletal form at Benson, Oxfordshire, in September 1966.

Great War Adversaries

Three of the Nash Collection are iconic fighters from the Great War – Sopwith Camel, Fokker D.VII and Royal Aircraft SE.5a – the first two are on show within Hendon's 'Milestones of Flight' gallery, the latter is in the Grahame-White Factory building. The Nash Boulton and Paul-built Sopwith F1 Camel F6314 is a case in point. In April 1923 former RFC Camel pilot and motoring writer Grenville Manton of Tring, Herts, bought a Camel from Air Disposal Company stocks. He offered it up for sale and moved to North Wales and it is next recorded in Hornchurch, Essex, in 1935 owned by D C Mason. Dick Nash acquired what was almost certainly this example on 16th April 1936 and it was taxied at the Hendon Air Pageant of June 1936. By April 1950 the Camel was at RAF Colerne, Wiltshire (see Chapter 6) and from there to the RAeS and Heathrow, where engine runs taking place in October 1963.

Magnificent in its wholly authentic lozenge camouflage, Hendon's Fokker D.VII is a superb example of what can be achieved with unstinting restorative skills and research. This has not always been so! Mr Nash acquired it in Versailles in May 1938 and brought it to Brooklands. Dick said that it had been built in January 1918 and it had been used by Jagdstaffel 71 at Ostend, was abandoned there and ended up in France for film purposes. It possibly served with the Belgian Air Force and by 1931 was one of a trio put on the Belgian civil register and flown as a tourer or joyrider. The airframe *may* be a composite of at least two of these D.VIIs.

The Nash Fokker D.VII at Farnborough in July 1950. *MAP*

With skull-and-crossbones and a white and red colour scheme, it was shown statically at the 1950 Farnborough display. Beyond this it was restored at Heathrow under the aegis of the RAeS and this time appeared in another likely Jasta 71 scheme, this time all red. By then it was wearing the serial 8417/18 and this is believed to be the airframe's 'majority' identity. That being so, it was built in 1918 by Ostdeutsche Albatros Werke at Schneidermühl in Pomerania, now within Poland. After a period on display at the RAF Museum at Hendon, the D.VII moved to the workshops at Cardington where it was painstakingly returned to its accurate, wartime status.

Three former Savage Skywriting Royal Aircraft Factory SE.5as survive: G-EBIA at Old Warden, G-EBIB at the Science Museum and G-EBIC at Hendon, and all have a complex past. By the nature of the work they undertook with the aerial advertising company, overhauls saw wings and other items exchanged as needed to keep the fleet going. The Hendon example was registered to Major John 'Jack' Clifford Savage at Hendon in September 1923 and was withdrawn from use by September 1930, eventually joining Richard Nash's collection. Built by Wolseley Motors as F938 at Adderley Park, Birmingham, in 1918, it is known to have been with 84 Squadron, serving in Germany, in July 1919. By 1949 it was with 39 Maintenance Unit at Colerne and prepared for an appearance at the 1950 SBAC display at Farnborough. The lads at Colerne painted it up as 'B4563', a BE.2 serial! By 1959 the SE.5 was at Heathrow having a refurbish care of the RAeS and by 1968 was in store at Henlow waiting its turn to go on show at Hendon which was achieved in 1972.

Savage Skywriting's SE.5a G-EBIC at Lympne, Kent, in the late 1920s. Note how the exhaust has been extended down the fuselage and join with the port side example under the modified rudder. *MAP*

Nash Collection and the International Horseless Carriage Corporation

Type	Identity	Built	Arrived	Background / *current status, or fate*
Antoinette monoplane	–	1910	c 1935	assumed destroyed during World War Two
Avro 504K *	'E449'	1918	c 1936	9205M, composite of G-EBJE and Avro 548A G-EBKN, both ex Shoreham. *RAF Museum, Hendon*
Avro 504K	G-ABAA	c 1917	1938	ex 9244M, 'H2311', G & H Aviation. *Manchester Museum of Science and Industry,on loan*
Blériot XI	No.5	1909	c 1935	ex 'north of England'. *Damaged at Brooklands in air raid, 6th Sep 1940*
Bleriot XI	No.16	1909	c 1935	*damaged at Brooklands in air raid, 6th Sep 1940*
Blériot XI	No.54	1909	1936	ex Le Havre. Thought retained by Dick Nash in 1953 at Weybridge. *Fate unknown*
Blériot XI	No.164	1910	1936	ex 9209M, Le Havre. *RAF Museum, Hendon*
Blériot XXVII	No.433	1911	1936	ex 9202M, Le Havre. *RAF Museum, Hendon*
Caudron G.3	'3066'	1912	c 1937	ex 9203M, Ken Waller, G-AETA, Belgium, OO-ELA, O-BELA. *RAF Museum, Hendon*
Deperdussin	–	1911	c 1935	*assumed destroyed during World War Two*
Fokker E.III (?)	?	1916	c 1935	*assumed destroyed during World War Two*
Fokker D.VII *	8417/18	1918	1938	ex 9207M, Versailles, Belgium, Germany. *RAF Museum, Hendon*
Fokker Dr.I	?	1917	c 1935	*assumed destroyed during World War Two*
Royal Aircraft Factory SE.5a	F938	1918	c 1935	ex 9208M, Savage Skywriting, RAE 84 Sqn, RFC. *RAF Museum, Hendon*
Farman F.41	F-HMFI	1913	1936	ex Maurice Farman. *RAF Museum, Cosford, stored*
Sopwith F1 Camel *	F6314	1918	16 Apr 1936	ex 9206M, 'H508', Hornchurch, Wales, Tring, Waddon. *RAF Museum, Hendon*
Sopwith Baby	8214	1916	c 1935	damaged at Brooklands in air raid, 6th Sep 1940. *Used in composite reconstruction 'N2078' at Fleet Air Arm Museum, Yeovilton*
Sopwith Baby	8214	1916	c 1935	damaged at Brooklands in air raid 6th Sep 1940. *Used in composite reconstruction 'N2078' at Fleet Air Arm Museum, Yeovilton*
Wright glider	–	1903	c 1935	*assumed destroyed during World War Two*
Wright biplane	–	1908	c 1935	*assumed destroyed during World War Two*

Notes: * – Illustrated in the colour sections. Other than the Bleriot XI retained by Mr Nash at Weybridge, all of the airframes that survived the war went to Hendon, then Heathrow and via a variety of RAF stations until the RAF Museum at Hendon was established. Here is a good place to thank the Royal Air Force Museum, particularly the meticulous Andrew Simpson, for the excellent exhibit history documents that are constantly revised and up-dated. The author has made copious reference to these and continues to be astonished at their depth and scope. These are available from the RAF Museum website – **www.rafmuseum.org** – a superb service that many other museums would do well to emulate!

CHAPTER 2

Leicestershire Academy
Department of Aeronautical Engineering, Loughborough
1936 to 1961

Plans for the Leicestershire town of Loughborough to have its own aerodrome stemmed from 1933 but took some time to come to fruition. In May 1936, the corporation acquired land at Derby Road and Loughborough College expressed an interest in basing its thriving Department of Aeronautical Engineering there. At that point the college was using the former Premier Dance Hall on Ashby Road to house its huge collection of aero engines, some airframes and large amounts of training aids and machine tools.

Taking the initiative with the project, the college commissioned extensive plans that were revealed in November 1938. Construction was not complete when World War Two broke out but from 1940, the department was able to take up occupation and the former dance hall was largely vacated. A 21-year lease on the airfield was granted to the college and from October 1942 courses were being run for Fleet Air Arm officers. During the war, Airwork refurbished and converted Douglas Bostons and Havocs and Brush-built de Havilland Dominies, produced in the nearby Falcon Works, were flight tested at the new airfield.

Above: A lesson taking place amid the instructional airframes in the former Premier Dance Hall. To the left is the Bullpup, to the right the HST.10. *Roy Bonser collection via P Geary*

The post-war airframe hangar, with the Wellington XVI to the left. In front of the hangar are the Martlet, the two Hurricanes (one just inside) and the Spitfire. *Roy Bonser collection*

War work

When the war finished, the Airwork hangar was taken over by the college. The Grumman Martlet and Hawker Hurricanes, the main instructional airframes at the time, were transferred from what was known as the Boulton Paul hangar which then became the aero engine shop. Many other sections and components which had passed through over the years also made the short journey. With more space available other airframes were gradually acquired, including a Supermarine Spitfire, a Boston and a Vickers Wellington.

Loughborough College's Boston is thought to have served with the USAAF and the French Air Force, or to have been ordered by the latter but not delivered by the time of the Blitzkrieg. It carried the name *Shoo Shoo Baby* and the individual names by each of the crew positions – all adding considerable credence to its USAAF credentials. It serves as a great example of how to acquire an airframe for minimal outlay and this was explained in Roy Bonser's seminal book *Aviation in Leicestershire and Rutland*. In 1945 Airwork had several Bostons which had been declared Category E – fit for scrap only. Aeronautical Department staff, aware of the situation, persuaded the person responsible that it was highly unlikely that anyone could tell exactly *how many* aircraft constituted a scrap heap. One dark night, a flat tin of 50 Players cigarettes changed hands and a Boston was towed over to join the other airframes in the instructional hangar. There it remained until it was finally scrapped shortly before the department left for its new facility. It was another example of so near, yet so far for the UK's aviation heritage.

> *Opposite page top:* Airframes in the former Premier Dance Hall. Left to right: Baffin, Atlas and Bullpup. *Roy Bonser collection*
>
> *Opposite page bottom:* An image from a college brochure, showing the main hangar and some of the aero engines. The line up of aircraft, from the left, is: Shark, Sea Hurricane, Martlet, Hurricane IV. *Roy Bonser collection*

Tutors and pupils perched on top of the Boston 'Shoo Shoo Baby', acquired for the cost of a tin of cigarettes! *Roy Bonser collection*

Following de-requisition in 1947, the airfield saw little use and when the college's lease finally expired in 1961 it was closed. The department cleared its hangar, and in so doing disposed of the bulk of the contents including the four World War Two fighters, which all found homes either with historic collections or in the museums. The faculty took up residence in new buildings on the main campus.

A look through the table of airframes used by the college during its days at the airfield shows an intensity of types that today are extinct. Several would be candidates for our *Ones That Got Away* feature: the Armstrong Whitworth Atlas, a two-seat general purpose military biplane, being a case in point. Its fuselage was eventually converted into a gantry for servicing the lights in the hangar roofs. There were no less than *three* Blackburn types, including a pioneering prototype. Two were large naval torpedo biplanes, the Baffin (of 1932) and the Shark (1933), and either would today grace the Fleet Air Arm Museum, or add much-needed Blackburn 'flavour' to a collection. Extensive research has failed to pin down serial numbers for several Loughborough inmates.

The other was the Blackburn HST.10 – high speed transport – a ground-breaking 12-seat twin-engined, retractable undercarriage, airliner. Its development was delayed as the Brough plant was increasingly committed to military contracts, it was a private venture and cash was trickled to it, and in 1935 its talented designer, F Duncanson, was killed in a road accident. Rolled out in July 1936 it never flew. Taking up valuable space at the Humberside factory, it was snapped up by the college in early 1939. It is believed that when everything else moved from the former dance hall to the airfield, the HST.10 stayed where it was and was scrapped there in 1946. Several sources note that the rudder was kept and moved to the Loughborough campus – should we be looking in the dorms?

The Bristol Bullpup was a development of the famed Bulldog biplane fighter. The prototype appeared in April 1938 and served at Filton on development work until 1935, joining the college thereafter. The Fairey S9/30 was a biplane that first flew on 22nd February 1934 and could be considered as a 'stepping stone' to the Swordfish.

The twin-engined Gloster AS.31 cartographic survey biplane was originated by de Havilland (as the DH.67) but work on the Hercules airliner and the incredibly successful Moth 'family' meant that final design and construction was handed on to Gloster in November 1928. The Loughborough machine was the second of two, both of which appeared in 1929. It was retired on 17th September 1936 moving to Leicestershire the following year.

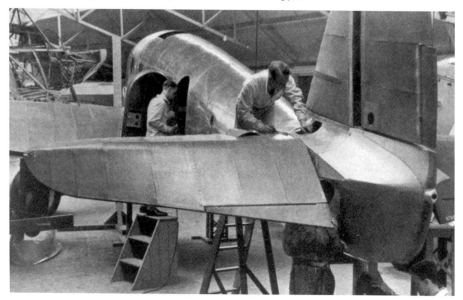

Students at work on the HST.10 inside the Premier Dance Hall. To the left is the extreme forward section of the Fairey S9/30 and to the right the Baffin. *Roy Bonser collection*

The engineless Atlas (left) and the Gloster Survey. *Loughborough Echo via Roy Bonser collection*

But *the* treasure that got away was another from the Fairey stable. On 6th February 1932 at Cranwell, a single-engined monoplane took over three-quarters of a mile to get airborne. The Lincolnshire airfield was purposefully the point of departure as its lush green flying field offered the longest runways in the country at the time. The two-seater needed the space; its laden weight was 17,500lb (7,938kg) in excess of the maximum weight of a Handley Page Heyford heavy bomber of the same era. The bulk of this uplift was fuel – sufficient to fly to South West Africa non-stop. And it made it, smashing a world endurance record in the process – 57 hours and 25 minutes and 5,410 miles (8,706km) later Fairey Long Range Monoplane K1991 landed near Walvis Bay. The pilot was Sqn Ldr O R Gayford DFC and it was navigated by Flt Lt G E Nicholetts AFC.

After a triumphant tour of Africa, K1991 was issued briefly to the Royal Aircraft Establishment at Farnborough, Hampshire, before it was transferred to the RAF technical school at Halton, Bucks, on 19th March 1933. Its use as an instructional airframe came to an end in November 1935 and the magnificent machine was handed on to Loughborough. It has already been noted that the HST.10 presented space problems for the college. How did it cope with the Long Range Monoplane's 82ft 0in (24.9m) wingspan? Did *all* of it come from Farnborough? Whatever, this was a sad end for an incredible piece of global aviation achievement.

Perhaps the greatest treasure to have slipped the net from the Loughborough airframes, Long Range Monoplane K1991.
Fairey

While these treasures slipped the net, Loughborough was an incredible pump-primer for the UK's aviation heritage. A large number of engines and components moved on to the RAF Museum, among others. The unique Grumman Martlet gravitated to the Fleet Air Arm Museum and the Hurricane IV joined what was called the Birmingham Museum of Science and Industry in 1961, but these days goes by the name of the Millennium Discovery Centre.

The Sea Hurricane and the Spitfire V moved by road to the Shuttleworth Collection at Old Warden in 1961 and went initially on static display. Both were recruited for use in the 1969 film *Battle of Britain*, although the Hurricane remained in the 'wings' and was not a 'star'. One 27th June 1975 the Spitfire was returned to the air at Duxford for Shuttleworth and has delighted crowds at Old Warden ever since. Duxford was also the venue for the debut post-restoration flight of Z7105 on 16th September 1995 – the first time a *Sea* Hurricane had returned to the skies. All of this was down to an incredible volunteer restoration team and the foresight of Loughborough College.

The college hangar with the Martlet in the foreground. Behind is the Hart Trainer still in the markings of its last unit, 12 Flying Training School at Grantham. *Jim Oates, via Roy Bonser collection*

The Spitfire V and the Martlet out on the airfield. Behind are visiting Tiger Moths from Nottingham University Air Squadron. *Jim Oates, via Roy Bonser collection*

Continuing story

With the move from the airfield to the main site, our story for *Lost Aviation Collections* really comes to an end. However, it would be a sin not to mention its later instructional airframes. Having disposed of many relics from an earlier age, more modern replacements were sought. Space was limited and accommodation could only be found for two airframes.

The first of these, an early Hunting Jet Provost, came on extended loan from the Shuttleworth Trust in April 1961. The Hunter F.4, acquired from Hawker Siddeley, arrived on 9th January 1962. By 1983 the fuselage frame of a Payne Knight Twister homebuilt biplane (either G-APXZ or G-ARGJ) was also inside the instructional hall. This is now with a private owner in North Yorkshire.

The jet duo became long-serving residents catering to the needs of students for over a quarter of a century. Further reductions in space allocated for 'hands-on' teaching brought about the disposal of the Hunter and the 'JP'. Today, the Jet Provost flies in military markings as 'XD693' with Kennet Aviation at North Weald in Essex. The Hunter was sold to Jet Heritage (Chapter 23) in October 1989 and was flying again in January 1994. Tragically, it was involved in a fatal accident at Dunsfold, Surrey, on 5th June 1998.

With another reorganisation – the faculty eventually became the Department of Aeronautical and Automotive Engineering of Loughborough *University*– there was space for only one airframe. Arriving in January 1991 was SEPECAT Jaguar GR.1 XX765 supplied on loan from British Aerospace at Warton, Lancashire. This was a one-off test-bed for Active Control Technology, or 'fly-by-wire'. The Jaguar was retained until an even more exotic machine arrived in June 1996. Also coming from Warton, this was the British Aerospace EAP, ZF534, a twin-engined single-seater used as a technology demonstrator to pave the way for the four-nation Eurofighter Typhoon. In 2010 it was announced that the EAP was to move to the RAF Museum at Cosford, Shropshire and this was imminent as the book went to press.

The new aeronautical department hangar building in 1979 showing the Jet Provost; the wing of the Hunter is in the foreground. *Roy Bonser*

Perhaps the last Loughborough airframe, the BAe EAP, illustrated on its first flight, 8th August 1986. *British Aerospace*

Loughborough College Department of Aeronautical Engineering

Type	Identity	Built	Arrived	Background / *current status*, or fate
Armstrong Whitworth Atlas	?	c 1927	?	? *Fuselage used as a gantry*
Blackburn Baffin	?	c 1934	?	? *Scrapped*
Blackburn Shark	?	c 1935	?	? *Thought returned to Fleet Air Arm circa 1945*
Blackburn HST.10	B-9	1936	early 1939	See text. *Scrapped in 1946*
Bristol Bullpup	J9051	1938	c 1935	See text. *Scrapped*
Douglas Boston	?	1941	1945	Or A-20 Havoc – see text. *Scrapped*
Fairey Long Range Monoplane	K1991	1932	c 1938	See text. *Scrapped*
Fairey S9/30	S1706	1934	c 1936	See text. *Scrapped*
Gloster AS.31 Survey	K2602	1929	c Mar 1937	See text. *Scrapped*
Grumman Martlet I	AL246	1940	c 1945	ex 768 and 802 Sqns. *Fleet Air Arm Museum, Yeovilton*
Hawker Hart Trainer	K6469	1936	c 1943	ex instructional 2045M, 12 and 1 Flg Tng Schs, 43 Sqn. *Scrapped circa 1946/1947*
Hawker Sea Hurricane Ib *	Z7015	1941	Nov 1943	ex Yeovilton, 759, and 880 Sqns. *Airworthy as G-BKTH with the Shuttleworth Collection, Old Warden*
Hawker Hurricane IV	KX829	1943	20 Feb 1946	ex 631 Sqn, 1606 Flt, 137 Sqn. *Millennium Discovery Centre, Birmingham*
Supermarine Spitfire Vc *	AR501	1942	21 Mar 1946	Central Gunnery School, 61 Oper Tng Unit, 1 Tactical Exercise Unit, 58 OTU, 422, 312, 504, 310 Sqns. *Airworthy as G-AWII with the Shuttleworth Collection, Old Warden*
Vickers Wellington XVI	R3237	1940	1945	ex 5 Ferry Pilots' Pool, Mk.Ic, 1429 Flt. *Scrapped*
British Aerospace EAP	ZF534	1986	Jun 1996	ex BAE Warton. See main text
Hawker Hunter F.4	XE677	1955	9 Jan 1962	ex HSA Dunsfold, 229 Oper Conv Unit, 111, 93 and 4 Sqns. See Chapter 23. *Registered G-HHUN, destroyed in fatal crash 5 Jun 1998.*
Hunting Jet Provost T.1	G-AOBU	1955	Apr 1961	ex Hunting, Luton, XM129, G-42-1. *Airworthy as 'XD693' with Kennet Aviation at North Weald, Essex*
Payne Knight Twister	?	c 1960	1983	see main text
SEPECAT Jaguar GR.1(mod)	XX765	1975	Jan 1991	ex Warton, BAe, Royal Aircraft Est, Aeroplane & Armament Exp Est, 226 Oper Conv Unit, 14 Sqn. *Royal Air Force Museum, Cosford*

Note: * – Illustrated in the colour sections.

ONES THAT GOT AWAY

Cierva C.9, 1930

Spaniard Juan de la Cierva was the first major advocate of practical rotary-wing flight, developing the Autogiro – a name he registered – featuring a main rotor that was unpowered, effectively a circular 'wing' above a conventional aircraft-like fuselage. Although the Autogiro quickly gave way to the helicopter from the late 1930s, the work of Cierva was seminal to the worldwide rotorcraft industry. Cierva set up a UK company on 24th March 1926 and commissioned a series of manufacturers to build types for him. At Hamble in Hampshire, Roy Chadwick and his team set about the lightweight C.9 under the Avro designation Type 576, for the Air Ministry. It utilised a fuselage very similar to the prototype Avro Avian sporting biplane, with a four-bladed main rotor, a substantial undercarriage and small wings to take some of the lift in forward flight. Bert Hinkler first flew the C.9, serial number J8931, at Hamble in September 1927 and it began trials with the Royal Aircraft Establishment at Farnborough, Hampshire, on 18th July 1928. Cierva himself flew J8931 at the RAE in late July 1928. It was returned to Hamble and was fitted with half-length, non-tapering rotors, and was ready in this form by early September. It was first flown at Farnborough in this guide on the 18th. In January 1930, its usefulness over, J8931 was gifted to the Science Museum. And there its history tapers out – what became of it? *KEC*

CHAPTER 3

Library of Flight
College of Aeronautics, Cranfield
1946 to 1982

As the Allies rolled their forces ever closer to the German border in 1944, it was possible to start to ponder on the peace that would eventually come. In aviation, it was clear that sweeping changes had been made in aerodynamics. Britain was acutely aware that it needed to stay with the impetus of this new creative wave or it would be forever in the shadow of the USA.

One way to help achieve this was to assimilate as quickly as possible the font of knowledge generated in Germany, where designers had pushed back the boundaries of design again and again. All of the Allies had their eyes on examples of German 'high tech' developments and there was a more-or-less structured share-out of 'booty'. For the USSR, things were more straightforward, what they occupied they seized, dismantled and returned to Soviet soil for assessment and exploitation. The race to absorb the huge mass of experience, knowledge and theory was on...

All this was necessarily a short-term matter where hardware, plans, calculations and extrapolations were digested, adopted, adapted or rejected. This would boost the armaments industry of the West for only a short period – such was the pace of the advances. What was needed was a longer view whereby houses of learning were established to introduce new thoughts at the 'grass roots' level so that future generations of designers and aeronautical engineers could benefit from new ideas and concepts.

In Britain, a method that appealed strongly to Clement Attlee's immediate post-war Labour government was to establish what would today be called 'centres of excellence'. One of these was the College of Aeronautics, created at Cranfield, Bedfordshire, in 1946. Not the least of the facilities handed on was a large part of the former RAF airfield, with hangars and a huge array of buildings. Two very influential supporters of the college were Sir Frederick Handley Page, head of the aircraft manufacturer named after him, and Sir Roy Fedden, aero engine maestro for Bristol and Rolls-Royce.

Above: A quarter of the Cranfield 'Library of Flight' hangar. Left to right, back row: Hawker P.1121, Avro Canada CF-100. Middle row: Me 163B, Sabre rear fuselage, Sea Hawk, Fairey Ultra Light Helicopter, TSR-2. Foreground, BP.111A. *Roy Bonser*

Most famous of Cranfield's fleet of test-beds, Lancaster I PA474, now with the Battle of Britain Memorial Flight. *College of Aeronautics*

The central location was a deciding factor, but one that also helped was the arrival in October 1945 of the Empire Test Pilots' School from Boscombe Down, Wiltshire. With ETPS co-located at the airfield, the test, trials and education flavour was firmly entrenched.

A wide range of post graduate courses was offered and research and development work for government agencies and industry was undertaken. The college operated its own aircraft, from Austers for air experience through to major test-beds – the most famous of which was Avro Lancaster I PA474 used for aerodynamic trials from March 1954 until 1963. It is now part of the Battle of Britain Memorial Flight based at Coningsby, Lincolnshire. (More on this 'Lanc' in Chapter 5.)

By the mid-1970s the name had changed to the Cranfield Institute of Technology to reflect the widening of its research and the syllabus and today, it has university status. Although aerospace occupies a smaller proportion of activities than in the heady days of the late 1940s and 1950s, Cranfield still 'buzzes' with projects that push the barriers further forward. The long-term vision of 1946 was certainly well-founded.

Operation MEDICO

Back to the last months of the war and the prospect of absorbing all that German data and experience. Under the codename Operation MEDICO, a search was undertaken from August 1945 to amass material for the as yet unnamed College of Aeronautics. Largest input came from the gutted Luftfahrt Akademie in Berlin – a similar body to what was planned for Britain. From the Akademie came tons of documents and books, calibration equipment, wind tunnels and a huge cache of aero engines.

Something in the order of 1,500 tons of material came to Cranfield under Operation MEDICO. The majority journied by sea and road but at least two of the Farnborough-based Royal Aircraft Establishment's (RAE) Transport Flight captured Junkers tri-motors were busy in and out of the Bedfordshire airfield from March to September 1946. In each case their point of origin within occupied Germany was Volkenrode – the former experimental establishment.

As well as a sectioned Ju 88 fuselage from the Akademie, the college received a Flettner Fl 282B Kolibri inter-meshing rotor helicopter; two Focke-Achgelis Fa 330A Bachstelze observation rotorkites; a Focke-Wulf Fw 190F-8/R15; a Junkers Ju 388L high altitude photo-recce aircraft; a Messerchmitt Me 163B Komet rocket-propelled fighter and a DFS 108-48 Grunau Baby IIB glider.

Of the former Luftwaffe machines, Ju 388L-1 500006 captured at Tarnewitz in May 1945 was of great interest, being the sixth example of this development of the Ju 88/Ju 188 line. Flown to Farnborough in September 1945, this airframe appeared at the famous German Aircraft Exhibition before moving on to Cranfield by 1948. The Fw 190 was also of interest, being a torpedo-fighter, captured at Travemünde in July 1945.

The Junkers Ju 388L that joined the Cranfield 'Library' – it was scrapped in the 1950s. *MAP*

Significant or odd... and no more

As equipment and courses were being assembled at Cranfield, government agencies gave the college consideration when it came to surplus hardware. The aircraft and aero engine industry also wanted to help and the number of instructional airframes grew. These machines – quite separate from the test and trials fleet – became known as the 'Library of Flight'. As well as whole airframes, fuselage sections, wing samples, major sub-assemblies and so on gravitated to Bedfordshire.

Oldest aircraft to 'serve' with the 'Library of Flight' was the prototype Percival Q.6, G-AEYE which made its first flight on September 14, 1937, at the hands of Edgar Percival. Withdrawn from use at Cambridge in May 1959 it moved on to Cranfield, but it had been scrapped by 1963. Well ahead of its time in 1937, it had far less to offer the aeronautical engineering students of the 1960s. (The sole surviving Q.6, G-AFFD, is currently being restored to flying condition at Seething in Norfolk.)

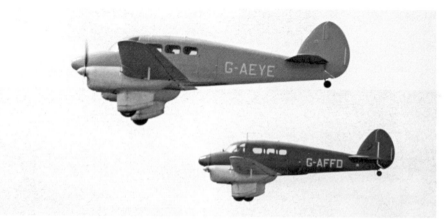

Publicity formation showing Cranfield's Percival Q.6 G-AEYE with the last survivor of the breed, G-AFFD. *Percival*

Another prototype that came the college's way was the third Avro Lincoln, PW932. It is thought to have arrived in the earliest days and lasted until the late 1950s. (On the trials fleet side, the college used Coventry-built B.2 RF342 from November 1962, replacing 'Lanc' PA474 as an aerodynamic test-bed. Retired on May 9, 1967, RF342 was ferried to the museum at Southend – see Chapter 7.

On 25th June 1947 Liberator VII EW611 was civil registered as G-AKAG for a one-off ferry flight to Cranfield for the 'Library of Flight'. In the foreground is the Me 163B. *KEC*

The third prototype Lincoln outside the college hangar. *Jeremy Baite*

The unflown Firth FH-1 twin-rotor helicopter. *Jeremy Baite*

During 1955 two radically different airframes – both flightless – arrived for the 'Library'. From Thame in Oxfordshire came the Firth FH-1 twin-rotor helicopter, powered by a *pair* of 145hp (108kW) Gipsy Major 10s, yet only seating a pilot and a passenger. Built in 1954 using the fuselage of the second prototype Planet Satellite pusher light aircraft, the FH-1 was not completed and passed on to the college, swelling its stock of rotary winged devices.

The other newcomer was a decidedly good-looking jet fighter which came from the Supermarine design centre at Hursley Park, Hampshire. This was the still-born Type 545, XA181, the ultimate development of the Swift lineage. Specification F.105D2 was issued in February 1952 for two supersonic versions of the Swift and the Type 545 used area-rule (or 'Coke-bottle') thinking on the fuselage, compound sweep on the wings and moved the intakes to the nose. Powered by a Rolls-Royce Avon RA.14, the first Type 545 would have had a speed of about Mach 1.3 and later versions could have gone about their business at around Mach 1.6-plus, toting radar in the redesigned nose. It was not to be, the project was cancelled in 1955. The substantially complete might-have-been moved to a new life at Cranfield. By 1967, only its wings survived which was a great pity as it would have made a great addition to Cosford's prototypes display.

Ultimate Swift development, the Supermarine 545. *MAP*

Pioneer rotorcraft

By the beginning of the 1960s, the airframes in the 'Library of Flight' were coming to the end of their useful lives. The technologies they were illustrating had been overtaken and other teaching methods and resources were available for students and researchers. So it was that covetous eyes focused upon the College of Aeronautics in the early 1960s... By then the 'museum movement' was gaining pace in the UK and the collection at Cranfield held many important and tempting treasures within. All of this meant that the instructional airframes found new keepers, with the last of the major items leaving by 1982.

As well as the airframes, the Cranfield campus had a wide range of components and sub-assemblies as teaching aids: a Hawker Typhoon (left) and Republic P-47 Thunderbolt rudder mounted for comparison. *Roy Bonser*

Five of the captured German airframes survived through into the 1960s and then into preservation. The Messerschmitt Me 163B-1A Komet rocket-powered point-defence fighter was acquired by the Museum of Flight at East Fortune and kindly refurbished for them by Marshall of Cambridge in 1976.

Three of the German survivors were rotorcraft, two being Focke-Achgelis Fa 330A-1 Bachstelze (Water Wagtail) single-seat submarine rotorkite reconnaissance platforms. One was acquired from Keil, the other almost certainly from the RAE, where a number of the little collapsible rotorkites, intended to have been towed behind surfaced U-Boats to act as much-extended 'crow's nest', had been gathered for tests. The former was returned to Germany in 1981, going to the Bückeburg helicopter museum, the other joining the Torbay Aircraft Museum (Chapter 11).

The other German rotorcraft survivor is a unique relic of World War Two and a very significant airframe. Flettner Fl 282b V20 Kolibri (Humming Bird), 280020, came to Cranfield from storage at Brize Norton, Oxfordshire, in 1946 and was the last of 20 prototypes, the first of which flew in 1941. The brainchild of Anton Flettner, the Fl 282 twin-rotor twin-seat observation and general duties helicopter was powered by a 160hp BMW-Bramo Sh 14A radial which drove two canted intermeshing rotors which did away with the need for a tail rotor.

Cranfield's Kolibri, carrying the four-letter identifier 'CJ+SN' was handed over to the British at Travemünde and was freighted to 6 Maintenance Unit at Brize Norton arriving in July 1945. It is of note that while this machine was of great technical interest, it was not flown or evaluated by the RAE – while the remarkably simple Fa 330 was. The V20 was delivered to the 'Library of Flight' on 1st August 1946. Exactly what state it was then in is unknown but certainly by the early 1960s it was an uncovered frame, engineless and with chopped-down rotors. To the great credit of the Midland Air Museum (MAM) at Coventry, the pioneering helicopter was recognised for what it was and preserved.

Post-war, three other rotorcraft of radically different ilk joined the college 'fleet'. In the early 1950s, a Sikorsky Hoverfly I was acquired and used as a rotor test-bed, being retired to the 'Library of Flight' by the early 1960s. Debate rages as to how much of which airframe went into this composite, but by the time it was acquired by the RAF Museum in 1967 it was refurbished as KK995 and today is displayed at Hendon.

Flettner Fl 282 helicopter with the Avro Canada CF-100 to the right. *Roy Bonser*

The incredible Fairey Rotodyne transport helicopter – elements of the main rotorhead and other items joined the 'Library of Flight'. *Fairey Aviation*

From the RAE at Thurleigh (Bedford) came the tip-jet driven Fairey Ultra-Light Helicopter G-APJJ which also gravitated to MAM. In 1965 large sections of the aborted Fairey Rotodyne compound transport helicopter arrived from White Waltham, Berkshire, these are now proudly part of what became the International Helicopter Museum at Weston-super-Mare. With a main rotor diameter of 90ft 0in (31.7m) and a length of 58ft 8in (17.88m) and powered by a pair of Napier Eland turboprops, this is another example of a type that really should have been preserved intact.

Warbirds

By 1948, the college had received a prototype Tempest II, LA607, from Hawker by 1948. It was the second Centaurus IV-engined example, making its first flight on 18th September 1943. In July 1966 it joined the Skyfame Collection (see Chapter 4) and moved to Duxford when the Imperial War Museum (IWM) provided a home for almost all of Skyfame in 1978 and 1979. In a surprise move in April 1983, Skyfame auctioned LA607 and it was acquired by well-known US collector Kermit Weeks, who moved it to Florida. Around the time that the Tempest arrived at Cranfield, a partially-sectioned Bristol Beaufighter nose section had also turned up, this gravitated to the RAF Museum.

Vought Corsair IV KD431 from 768 Squadron, Fleet Air Arm, arrived in November 1946 and another nautical type, Westland Wyvern TF.1 VR137 came from Yeovil in November 1950. The latter was an unflown Rolls-Royce Eagle-engined version of the Python turboprop-engined strike fighter and was destined to become a unique survivor of the breed. The Corsair was spotted by the short-lived Historic Aircraft Preservation Society (see Chapter 5) in May 1963 and moved to Yeovilton in Somerset. It and the Wyvern were taken on by the nascent Fleet Air Arm Museum.

Cranfield's Corsair was a founder member of the Fleet Air Arm Museum at Yeovilton. To the left is Grumman Martlet AL246 which came from Loughborough – see Chapter 2. *KEC*

Jet variety

The 1950s saw three fascinating jets join the 'Library of Flight'. First was the SARO SR.A/1 jet flying-boat fighter, fresh from its last public performance in which it landed on the Thames to become an attraction in the Festival of Britain, June 1951. While at Cranfield, one of the A/1's Metro-Vick Beryl 3,230lb st (14.36kN) turbojets was acquired by Donald Campbell for use in his jet-powered hydrofoil *Bluebird*, in which he met his death on Lake Coniston in 1967. On 16th October 1966, the A/1 made the road journey to Staverton to join Skyfame (again, see Chapter 4 for more).

The other two jets were lighter, both Turboméca Palas powered, and arrived in 1957. The Short Sherpa aero-isoclinic wing test-bed was first flown in October 1953 and was retired to Cranfield in April 1957. It moved to Bristol College of Advanced Technology in January 1964 and from there joined Skyfame in May 1966.

Somers-Kendal SK.1 G-AOBG had been designed as a midget jet racer by Hugh Kendal for well-known competition pilot Nat Somers. A wonderfully clean-looking machine, with Harrier-like undercarriage and a V-tail, it suffered a turbine failure in July 1957 and was retired to the 'Library. (Strictly speaking, as G-AOBG pre-dated the P.1127 by some four years, perhaps it should be said that the Harrier had an SK.1-like undercarriage!) The SK.1 s now with a private owner near Reading and may yet re-appear.

On 13th July 1975 a diminutive delta-winged jet left Cranfield by road, headed for MAM at Coventry Airport. This was Boulton Paul P.111A VT935 delta research platform, completed at Wolverhampton in 1950. The all-yellow delta, inevitably referred to as the 'Yellow Peril', came to the college at the end of its flying life at RAE Thurleigh in April 1959.

A rare jet fighter arrived from Zweibrücken in West Germany on 3rd October 1962, in the shape of Avro Canada CF-100 Canuck Mk 4B 18393. The all-weather 'Clunk' – Canadian rival to Gloster's Javelin all-weather fighter – had last served with the RCAF's 3 Wing in Germany and was presented as a gift to the college. With the mass exodus from the 'Library of Flight' in the mid-1970s, the CF-100 caught the eye of warbird operator Ormond Haydon-Baillie (Chapter 12) and under the civilian registration G-BCYK, it was ferried to Duxford on 29th March 29 1975.

Fifteen years after Hawker had presented Tempest LA607 the company passed on another airframe, this time the unflown, unfinished, controversial and cancelled Hawker P.1121 strike fighter. Sydney Camm had evolved a lovely-looking swept-wing jet fighter powered by a de Havilland PS.26 6 Gyron turbojet capable of 23,800lb st gulping its air through an under-fuselage scoop that the General Dynamics F-16 Fighting Falcon was to make de riguer in the 1980s. In the words of Derek Wood in his classic *Project Cancelled* (Jane's, 1986) "The P.1121 was to all intents and purposes the British Phantom", but it was not to be. Work on the prototype was stopped at Kingston in 1957 when it fell victim to the 1957 White Paper. Now the carcass is held in deep store for the RAF Museum.

The last major 'exhibit' to join the 'Library of Flight' needs no introduction and holds much in common with the P.1121, this being BAC TSR-2 XR222. The fourth prototype, it did not get to flight stage after the Healey axe fell on 6th April 1965. It moved from Weybridge to Cranfield in 1966 and then to the care of the IWM at Duxford in March 1978. The would-be strike fighter made a sad final addition to a 'Library' that had been central to the high hopes of the British aviation industry in the aftermath of World War Two. An unseen spin-off from the foundation of the College of Aeronautics was just how much of a conduit it was going to be allowing a bewildering number of rare types to eventually join museums.

Another view of part of Cranfield's amazing hangar. *Roy Bonser*

College of Aeronautics 'Library of Flight'

Type	Identity	Built	Arrived	Background / *current status*, or fate
Avro Lincoln I	PW932	1944	c 1946	Third prototype. *Scrapped by 1959*
Avro Canada Canuck Mk.4	18393	1955	3 Oct 1962	ex RCAF, 440, 419, 409 Sqns. Registered G-BCYK – see Chapter 12. *Imperial War Museum, Duxford*
BAC TSR-2 X0-4 *	XR222	1965	1966	ex Weybridge, unflown. *Imperial War Museum Duxford*
Boulton Paul P.111A *	VT935	1950	Apr 1959	ex RAE Bedford. *Midland War Museum, Coventry*
Bristol Beaufighter I nose	?	c 1941	1946?	? *Royal Air Force Museum, Hendon*
Canadair Sabre Mk.5	23219	1954	Feb 1960	ex RCAF, 439 and 414 Sqns. *Reduced to parts only by 1973*
Consolidated Liberator VII	G-AKAG	1944	Jun 1947	ex RAF EW611, no service, USAAF C-87 44-39219. *Scrapped in 1959, to a yard at Aylesbury, Bucks*
DFS Grunau Baby IIB	VN148	?	Jul 1947	ex Luftwaffe 'LN+ST'. *Thought under restoration in Wales*
Fairey Ultra-Light Helicopter	G-APJJ	1958	1959	ex White Waltham, RAE Bedford, FAA trials. *Midland Air Museum, Coventry*
Firth FH-1	G-ALXP	1954	1955	Prototype, unflown. *Scrapped by 1962*
Flettner Fl 282B V20 Kolibri	280020	1944	Aug 1946	ex Brize Norton, Travemünde, Luftwaffe 'CJ+SN'. *Midland Air Museum, Coventry*
Focke-Achgelis Fa 330A-1	100406	c 1943	1946	ex Keil, Germany. *Hubschrauber Museum, Germany*
Focke-Achgelis Fa 330A-1	100545	c 1943	1946	ex RAE Farnborough, Germany. See also Chapter 11. *Fleet Air Museum, Yeovilton*
Focke-Wulf Fw 190F-8/R15	AirMin 111	c 1944	1946	ex RAF Farnborough, Brize Norton, Travemünde, Luftwaffe. *Scrapped in the 1950s*
Hawker Tempest II	LA607	1943	circa 1948	ex Hawker, Langley. See also Chapter 4. *Fantasy of Flight, USA, registered N607LA*
Hawker Sea Hawk FB.5	WM994	1954	26 Apr 1974	ex Abroath, Hal Far Search and Rescue Flt, 806, 767 and 800 Sqns. Registered as G-SEAH – see Chapter 23. *Amjet, USA, registered as N994WM*
Hawker P.1121 fuselage	–	1958	1962	Unfinished prototype. *Royal Air Force Museum, Cosford*
Hiller UH-12B	G-ANOB	1958	1961	ex F-BGGZ, HB-XAI, I-ELAN, N8120H. *Stripped to rotor rig by 1964*
Junkers Ju 88	?	c 1942	1945	sectioned fuselage, ex Berlin, Luftwaffe. *Scrapped in the mid-1950s*
Junkers Ju 388L-1 V6	500006	1944	c 1948	ex Air Min 83, RAE Farnborough, Lübeck, Tarnewitz, Luftwaffe 'PE+IF'. *Scrapped in the mid-1950s*
Messerschmitt Me 163B-1	191659	c 1944	May 1947	ex Brize Norton, RAE Farnborough, Husum, Luftwaffe II/JG400. *National Museum of Flight Scotland, East Fortune*
Percival Q.6 *	G-AEYE	1937	1959	ex Cambridge, Southern Aircraft, RAF X9328, 2nd TAF Comm Flt, 6 AONS, Overseas A/c Del Unit, 24 Sqn, G-AEYE. *Scrapped, last noted May 1963*

Saunders-Roe SR.A/1	G-12-1	1947	1951	ex TG263. See also Chapter 4. _Solent Sky, Southampton_
Short Sherpa	G-36-1	1953	Apr 1957	ex G-14-1. See also Chapter 4. _Ulster Aviation Society, Northern Ireland_
Sikorsky Hoverfly I	KK995	1944	1949	ex Airborne Forces Experimental Est, AFEE, 43 OTU, USAAF 43-46558. _Royal Air Force Museum, Hendon_
Somers-Kendal SK.1 *	G-AOBG	1955	Jul 1957	Withdrawn Jul 1957, ex Woodley. _Privately owned, Reading_
Supermarine 545	XA181	1953	1955	Unflown prototype. _Reduced to wings only by 1967_
Supermarine Swift F.3	WK248	1954	10 Dec 1957	ex Fairey Av, Vickers, A&AEE. _Reduced to tail section by 1967_
Vickers Viking C.2	G-APAT	1947	1962	fuselage, ex Hurn, ex RAF VL232, King's Flight. _Scrapped by 1965_
Vought Corsair IV	KD431	1944	Nov 1946	ex 768 and 1835 Sqns, US Navy 14862. _Fleet Air Arm Museum, Yeovilton_
Westland Wyvern TF.1 *	VR137	1950	Nov 1950	Unflown prototype, ex Yeovil. _Fleet Air Arm Museum, Yeovilton_

Note: * – Illustrated in the colour sections.

CHAPTER 4

Founding Father
Short Sunderland Trust and the Skyfame Aircraft Museum
1961 to 1978

Skyfame's story begins in 1959 when members of Coastal Command and the wider public were involved in a campaign to bring one of the RAF's last operational Short Sunderland home to the UK. At Seletar in Singapore, 205 Squadron paid off the last two of these venerable flying-boats on 15th May 1959. The Ministry of Defence deemed that flying one home to Britain would be too expensive; besides with the RAF Museum no more than a pipedream, where would it go? The Sunderlands were quickly scrapped as they lay on the 'hard' at Seletar and that option was gone.

Part of the team trying to bring a Sunderland back was Peter F M Thomas. Thoughts turned to the Royal New Zealand Air Force and an appeal for £15,000 (that's £375,000 in present-day values) was launched. Sadly, they'd missed the boat (!) as the RNZAF machines had been retired several years before and restoring one to fly would have been prohibitive. Thankfully, the French Navy, the Aéronavale, had extended use of its last examples into 1960 – this gave the 'saviours' breathing space. ACM Sir Philip Joubert contacted Admiral Suquet and to everyone's joy, an example was gifted – airborne delivery included – to what was to become the Short Sunderland Trust. Eighteen months of hard slog had been vindicated.

The former flying-boat base at Pembroke Dock in south-west Wales had already been earmarked as the venue for the 'boat and a tract of land near a slipway secured. Pembroke Dock – 'PD' to those who were stationed there – was once a vast flying-boat base. The last operational RAF units operating from the slipways and waters of 'PD' were 201 and 230 Squadrons both flying Sunderland MR.5s and disbanded there side-by-side on 28th February 1957.

On 24th June 1961 Sunderland MR.5 ML824 arrived overhead, it had been flanked by a pair of St Mawgan-based Avro Shackleton MR.3s of 201 Squadron – one of the two units the flying-boat had served with during its time with the RAF. The following day, ML824 was formally presented to 78-year old Sir Oswald Short in his capacity of President of the Trust.

Above: Carrying 'stage make-up' to portray a well shot-up returnee, Mosquito TT.35 TA719 at Bovingdon during the filming of '633 Squadron' in 1963. *via Stuart Howe*

Escorted by a Shackleton MR.3 of 201 Squadron, Sunderland ML824 during its last flight, en route to Pembroke Dock, 24th June 1961. *Coastal Command*

Sunderland ML824 on its hard-standing at Pembroke Dock in 1968. *MAP*

THE LAST **SUNDERLAND**
FLYING BOAT

Preserved as a
Memorial by
The Short
Sunderland
Trust

OPPOSITE
THE
MARKET,
PEMBROKE
DOCK.

OPEN TO VISITORS . . .

Photo : Squibbs Studios

2-30 — 6-0 p.m. MONDAYS, WEDNESDAYS and FRIDAYS, 1st JUNE to 30th SEPTEMBER, inclusive. Admission to lower deck: 1s. 0d. ; Children 6d. Parties by special arrangement with the SECRETARY, PER ARDUA, FRESHWATER EAST, PEMBROKE

Hand-out for the Sunderland Trust's exhibition at Pembroke Dock. Black and white, it measured just under 5 by 4in (12.7 by 10.1cm).

Prior to the saving of ML824, the Ministry of Defence had deemed it uneconomic to return any of the final operational Sunderlands from Seletar in Singapore and they were hastily scrapped in the late 1950s.

As the survivor of the three Short brothers, founders of the oldest aircraft manufacturing concern in the world, Sir Oswald had a much more personal link with ML824 which had been built by his company at Sydenham, Belfast, and it joined 201 Squadron at Castle Archdale in November 1944 taking the codes 'NS-Z' (which it again wears today at Hendon). Beyond this came service with 330 Squadron at Sullom Voe and then storage at Wig Bay. In August 1950 ML824 was back at Sydenham being prepared for hand-over to the Aéronavale. On 28th October 1951 ML824 was delivered to Brest and served for nearly a decade, mostly out of Dakar, French West Africa, latterly with 50 Escadrille de Servitude.

By the late 1960s, visitor figures at 'PD' were on the decline and it was realised that it would be better if ML824 found a home with a larger organisation that could restore it and, hopefully, put it under cover. Negotiations with the RAF Museum bore fruit and the huge task of moving the 'boat was assessed. A large assault landing-craft took the fuselage on a voyage around Land's End and up the Thames where it was off-loaded and made the difficult road journey to Hendon in the early hours of 21st March 1971. It went on show at Hendon in 1976, initially outside, but from 1978 was installed in the Battle of Britain hall.

As a post-script to this part of the story, on 25th September 2009 the Pembroke Dock Flying-Boat Centre, administered by the Pembroke Dock Sunderland Trust and hosted by the Milford Haven Port Authority, was opened to the public. Attending was Wg Cdr Derek Martin OBE who flew 210 Squadron Sunderland I T9044 a short time before it was wrecked in a gale and sank at 'PD' on 21st November 1940. The Trust has located and recovered some parts, including a Bristol Pegasus, and is campaigning to salvage the rest.

First of the crusaders

Knowledge and experience gained in tracking down the Sunderland, and opening it up on a regular basis to the public, gave Peter Thomas the idea of establishing a museum devoted to aviation. A two year hunt for suitable airframes and a venue was begun. Up until this point, the Imperial War Museum and the Science Museum had significant airframes on show, but these were only a *part* of their remit. At Old Warden in Bedfordshire, the Shuttleworth Collection boasted a significant number of aircraft, some static most airworthy, but also had a large number of carriages, motorcycles and cars on its 'books'. Peter was convinced the time had come for a 'pure' aviation museum.

Now is a good time to review the 'batting order' of aviation heritage organisations in the UK during the 1960s. Museums with an aviation theme were thin on the ground, but there were several major 'players' in the pipeline and a flood to follow in the 1970s and 1980s. A series of organisations (often with the 'APS' suffix – Aircraft Preservation Society) were also striving to establish a collection of aircraft and, perhaps, a museum. (Take a look at the table opposite.)

Museums and Collections of the 1960s

From	Name, location	Notes
9 Jun 1921	Imperial War Museum, London	Royal opening, see below. Still going strong!
1920s	Science Museum, London	First airframe acquired 1913; still going strong!
1932	Shuttleworth Collection, Old Warden	Date first aircraft acquired; regular public opening from the 1950s and still going strong!
1958	Salisbury Hall, London Colney	Mosquito prototype W4050 brought on site Sep 1958; limited public viewing from early 1960s. Thrives today as the de Havilland Aircraft Heritage Centre
1961	Museum of Science and Industry, Birmingham	Founded in 1950, first airframe 1961. Closed down 1997, re-opened as Thinktank, 2001
1963	Skyfame Aircraft Museum, Staverton	See the text in this chapter
1964	Fleet Air Arm Museum, Yeovilton	Still going strong!
1965	Newark Air Museum, Newark	Opened generally to the public 14th Apr 1973 and still going strong!
1967	British Historic Aircraft Museum, Southend	BHAM collecting from 1967, failed to open doors. Became Historic Aircraft Museum – see Chapter 7
1969	Airborne Forces Museum, Aldershot	Open to the public March 1969, limited access prior to that. Today located within the IWM at Duxford
1969	Glasgow Museum of Transport	Opened 1964; first airframe arrived 1969. Last airframe on show 1997
–	Royal Air Force Museum 'outstations'	See Chapter 6
1956	Merseyside Society of Aviation Enthusiasts	Rescued Avro Avian 1960; became founder airframe of NAPS – see below. Last airframe (an Fa 330 gyrokite) moved on 1983
1962	Northern Aircraft Preservation Society	Renamed The Aeroplane Collection and still going strong!
1962	Solway Group of Aviation Enthusiasts	Rescued Hart Trainer K4972; became Solway Aviation Group and opened Solway Aviation Museum in mid-1980s
1963	Historic Aircraft Preservation Society	see Chapter 5
1967	Midland Aircraft Preservation Society	Opened the Midland Air Museum at Coventry Airport, 1977
1967	South Wales Historic Aircraft Preservation Society	See Chapter 8

Notes: Given here are museums with more than one airframe and substantial supporting material on show to the public. A handful of museums held a single 'token' aircraft with little in the way of related display items; eg the City of Bristol Art Gallery and Museum with a Bristol Boxkite replica from 1967 and the Royal Scottish Museum in Edinburgh with the original Pilcher Hawk from November 1963. (The Hawk had previously been on show at the RSM in Edinburgh from 1920 to 1939.)

Let's swerve 'off message' for a moment or two... King George V officially opened the Imperial War Museum on 9th June 1920. Harald Penrose in the third element, *The Adventuring Years*, of his fantastic quintet *British Aviation* quotes the following airframes as on display: Royal Aircraft Factory BE.2c*, RE.8*, Sopwith Camel*, Salamander, Triplane*, Nieuport Nighthawk, Parnall Panther, Bristol F.2b Fighter*, Short seaplane [Type 184]*, Norman-Thompson flying-boat, 'Friedrichshafen bomber' [G.III?], 'Roland' [LFG Roland D.II?], 'all-metal Junkers [CL.I?], 'reconnaissance LVG' [C.IV]*, 'Gotha bomber' [G.II, III, IV or V?]. The square brackets are mine. Those machines still around today are marked with an asterisk (*). As the Imperial War Museum thrives today, it does not come within the remit of this book – yet the tasty types mentioned above certainly count as 'Lost'.

Peter Thomas, a true pioneer of UK aviation museums. *Skyfame*

The name 'Skyfame' was settled upon quite early in the process and an appeal for a site was initiated at the same time as hunting down potential exhibits. In the spring of 1963 both of these quests began to bear fruit. The first exhibit, airworthy de Havilland Mosquito TT.35 TA719, was secured although it was needed on the set of the film *633 Squadron* at Bovingdon and it did not join the museum until David Ogilvy flew it in on 16th October. At the same time as TA719 joined up, the manager of Staverton, near Cheltenham, Glos, outlined a deal with a hangar and hard-standing that gave ease of public access and the 'sweet spot' of a collection on an operational airfield. The Skyfame Aircraft Museum came into being officially on 31st August 1963 and from the start had to be self-sustaining; it would have to meet its costs, including the salaries of its staff. A large and vibrant Supporters' Society was also established, with John Fairey as its chairman and Peter and Olive Swettenham looking after its many activities. From the earliest days, one of Skyfame's wardens was Tony Southern – see Chapter 22.

While awaiting the 'film star' Mosquito, the first aircraft to touch down at Staverton was the former London School of Flying Anson I G-AMDA. Skyfame's aim from the very beginning was to keep airworthy as many of its exhibits as possible and to stage regular flying displays. An original 'Flying Flea' from Southend and Guy Baker's Cierva C.30A autogiro arrived in late 1963. John Schooling was at the helm of Airspeed Oxford G-AHTW on 25th March 1964 when it arrived from Elstree. This was a well timed event as three days later the Skyfame Aircraft Museum was officially opened. (Hard on its heels was the Fleet Air Arm Museum at Yeovilton in Somerset, which opened its doors on a regular basis that summer.)

The Oxford was an acquisition very dear to the heart of Peter Thomas. His elder brother, Desmond Patrick, had won his 'wings' on the type while training to become a bomber pilot with 2 Service Flying Training School at Brize Norton, Oxfordshire. Flying a Wellington from Malta, Desmond was killed in action on 17th July 1941 – he was just 19. The museum was sub-titled the Desmond Commonwealth Flying Memorial in tribute to Desmond and to all of the British Commonwealth flyers of World War Two.

A selection of Skyfame guidebooks.

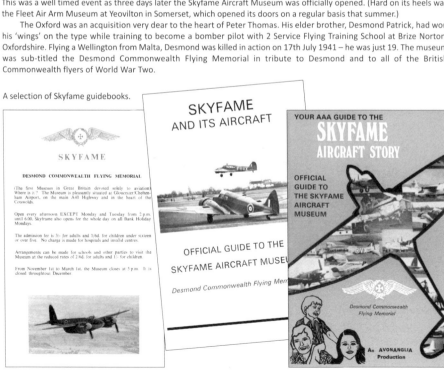

In 1964 the term 'warbird' was not in wide use, but in its first whole year Skyfame discovered the perils of operating such aircraft. Mosquito RS709 – known to all at the museum as 'George' – suffered a belly-landing on 27th July 1964, thankfully without injury to its crew. It never flew again. Amazingly, at that time a replacement was at hand, across at Bovingdon, TT.35 RS709 was taking part in the making of *Mosquito Squadron* and when its film role was over flew to Staverton on 24th September 1964. To help combat rising costs, it was sold in the USA and flew away to Booker, Bucks, in preparation for the challenging ferry flight. This machine came back across 'The Pond' in late 1981 to join Warbirds of Great Britain – see Chapter 13.

Varied fleet

Although it could not be flown, one of the most significant of the aircraft presented to Skyfame was the Avro-built Cierva C.30A G-ACUU which served with Air Service Training at Hamble on the Solent. It was impressed for radar calibration work with 1448 Flight at Halton, Bucks, in September 1940 as HM580. The unit was renamed 529 Squadron in June 1943 but in October that year HM580 suffered a major accident. It was rebuilt and entered storage at Kemble in November 1945. Acquired by the Cierva Autogiro Co in November 1946 it was registered as G-AIXE, but reverted to G-ACUU when its identity was re-discovered. It was based at Eastleigh, near Southampton, where it was used to familiarise Cierva's test pilots ready for the massive three-rotor Air Horse and the Skeeter rotorcraft that the company were developing. From 1950 it was flown at Elmdon by Guy Baker until its certificate of airworthiness expired in April 1960.

As recounted above, Anson I G-AMDA was the first aircraft to arrive by air at the new venture. Built in 1938, after a long and varied career, mostly as a 'taxi' for the ferry pilots of the Air Transport Auxiliary it was civilianised at Squires Gate, Blackpool, as G-AMDA in October 1953. It joined Derby Aviation at Burnaston in 1955 and was used for survey work. Peter Thomas acquired it from the London School of Flying at Elstree but a landing accident on 2nd November 1972 put paid to its flying days.

Cierva C.30A G-ACUU at Duxford after restoration to its wartime guise. *IWM*

Fresh from conversion by Fairey at Ringway, Firefly TT.1 SE-BRD prior to departure to Sweden in 1949. *Fairey Aviation*

Hatfield-built Oxford I G-AHTW was the last of its type to fly in the UK. Issued to the RAF as V3388 in November 1940 it saw no operational service, moving through a series of maintenance units and contractors until it was offered for disposal at 15 Maintenance Unit, at Wroughton in Wiltshire on 9th May 1946. It was acquired by Boulton Paul Aircraft for use as a 'hack' from their Pendeford, Wolverhampton, base and registered to them 29 days later. 'BP' used it until its certificate of airworthiness expired in December 1960 when it passed to the Wolverhampton Aero Club and it was from there that it was acquired by Skyfame.

Thanks to John Fairey, on 5th May 1964, Skyfame's sixth aircraft was also its most far-flung. Bright yellow Firefly I SE-BRD flew into Staverton from Gothenburg in Sweden, piloted by Tage Paller with engineer Kenneth Skold. It was registered as G-ASTL on 1st June and quickly given Fleet Air Arm colours and the name *Sir Richard Fairey* in honour of Richard's father, the founder of the famed aircraft manufacturing company. Built at Heaton Chapel and test flown from Ringway, it was issued to the Fleet Air Arm as Z2033 in April 1944, joining 731 Squadron at East Haven, Scotland in March 1945. It suffered a ground accident and found its way back to Fairey at Ringway in October 1945. In March 1949, reconditioned as a target-tug to TT.1 status, it was delivered to Svensk Flygstjanst AB for contract work with the Royal Swedish Air Force, until replaced by Douglas Skyraiders in the early 1960s.

On 24th September 1964 former Skyways Avro York G-AGNV was headed for Staverton on its – and the type's – last ever flight. For some of the way it was escorted by a pair of Handley Page Hastings transports of 24 Squadron from Colerne in Wiltshire. No.24 had flown the three-tailed, four-engined transport from 1943 to 1951 when it took on Hastings. Four years later, thanks to the generosity of Bill Betteridge, John Fairey and Peter Swettenham a 24 Squadron Hastings joined Skyfame. First joining the RAF in October 1948, TG528 was thrown straight into the Berlin Airlift and flew with 47 Squadron from Schleswigland. Like many of the breed, TG528 had a long and varied history, last serving with 24 Squadron from July 1967. Offered for sale straight out of service the transport flew into Staverton on January 24, 1968.

Saunders-Roe SR.A/1 TG263 afloat on the River Medina in front of the famous Columbine hangar at East Cowes, Isle of Wight, July 1947. Like the Sherpa and the Tempest, it came to Skyfame from Cranfield.

The fuselage of Short Sherpa G-36-1 inside the Skyfame hangar. Behind is the nose of Halifax PN323. Leaning against the wall is the only part of the Sherpa's wing to make the journey from Cranfield; while the fuselage is preserved in Northern Ireland, the wing is no longer extant.

Uneven struggle

By the mid-1970s, Skyfame's airworthy inmates had all ended their flying days and joined the rest of the collection as static exhibits. It was becoming clear that the cold winds of the economy were biting hard. The 1976 edition of the official guidebook, *The Skyfame Aircraft Story*, contained a telling paragraph: "Skyfame's problems will be familiar to many other small independent activities. Started with modest funds while aircraft was a crusade rather than a popular activity, it has had to keep pace with soaring costs and meeting increasing competition without any support from official sources. Despite the headaches and worries, the survival of Skyfame is due to the refusal to admit defeat, not only by the directors but also by the band of dedicated supporters whose help and assistance has been an outstanding feature of the whole venture. Their spirit is both an inspiration and a criticism of the lack of official interest in the early years when too many valuable aircraft were allowed to disappear." The piece ended with a poem: "Thank God for the enthusiasts / Whose enterprise alone / Told red tape-strangled bureaucrats / It *can* and *will* be done."

Despite this determination, Skyfame closed the hangar doors for the last time on 2nd January 1978. Negotiations with the Imperial War Museum at Duxford resulted in the biggest rescue operation ever staged in the UK. Work started on the mass departure on 25th January with the first whole airframe – the Sycamore – leaving on 5th February. A brilliantly co-ordinated to-ing and fro-ing of articulated trucks made for a very smooth operation. By 1980 most of the airframes were assembled and on show at Duxford.

Sycamore III G-ALSX flying along the River Severn in 1951. *Bristol*

At first the airframes were on loan to the Imperial War Museum with arrangement allowing for their phased acquisition. On 14th April 1983, auctioneers Christie's sold the Hawker Tempest on behalf of Skyfame at a huge sale staged at Duxford. The prototype fighter was acquired by well-known US collector and pilot Kermit Weeks for £85,000. By 1987 the remainder of the Skyfame collection that had re-located to Duxford was wholly owned the Imperial War Museum.

After the closure of the museum Peter Thomas and his wife Gwladys, who had worked tirelessly alongside him at Staverton, retired to Scotland. On 18th May 2005 Peter died, he had been a pioneer of the UK aviation preservation movement and an inspiration to many.

Tempest II LA607 on the flight line at Staverton during a Skyfame flying day.

Short Sunderland Trust and the Skyfame Aircraft Museum

Type	Identity	Built	Arrived	Background / current status, or fate
Short Sunderland MR.5	ML824	1944	24 Jun 1961	ex Aéronavale, RAF 330 and 201 Sqns. *RAF Museum, Hendon*
Airspeed Oxford I *	G-AHTW	1940	25 Mar 1964	ex Elstree, Boulton Paul, RAF V3388, no service. *Imperial War Museum, Duxford*
Auster AOP.9	XR267	1965	Oct 1974	ex Bristol, Congresbury, Army Air Corps/RAF, St Athan, no service. See Chapter 22. *Airworthy, Hucknall, Notts as G-BJXR*
Avro Anson I *	G-AMDA	1938	Jul 1963	ex London Sch of Flg – Elstree, Derby Av, Squires Gate, RAF N4877, Watchfield Stn Flt, 3 Ferry Pool, 3 Ferry Pilots Pool. *Imperial War Museum, Duxford*
Avro York C.1 *	G-AGNV	1944	9 Oct 1964	ex Skyways, BOAC, RAF TS798, no service. *Royal Air Force Museum, Cosford*
Bristol Sycamore III	G-48/1	1951	Jul 1969	on loan, ex G-ALSX, Tanganika VR-TBS, G-ALSX. *The Helicopter Museum, Weston-super-Mare*
Chilton DW.1A	G-AFGI	1939	1968	on loan, see also Chapter 6. *Airworthy, Reading-based owner*

Type	Identity	Built	Arrived	Background / *current status, or fate*
Cierva (Avro) C.30A	G-ACUU	1934	c Sep 1963	ex Elmdon, Cierva Autogiro Co, Southampton, G-AIXE, RAF HM580, 529 Sqn, 1448 Flt, G-ACUU Air Service Tng, Hamble. *Imperial War Museum, Duxford*
De Havilland Mosquito TT.35	TA719	1945	Jul 1963	G-ASKC, ex Shawbury, *633 Squadron*, RAF TA719 3/4 Civilian Anti-Aircraft Co-op Unit, 4 CAACU. *Imperial War Museum, Duxford*
De Havilland Mosquito TT.35 *	RS709	1945	24 Sep 1964	G-ASKA, ex *Mosquito Squadron*, Bovingdon, *633 Squadron*, RAF 3/4 Civilian Anti-Aircraft Co-op Unit, 236 Op Conv Unit. To USA as N9797 Dec 1971, to Warbirds of GB as G-MOSI Nov 1979. See also Chapter 13. *National Museum of the USAF, Dayton, Ohio, as 'NS519'*
De Havilland Vampire T.11	WZ515	1953	19 Mar 1973	ex Hawker Siddeley, Woodford, Hawarden, St Athan, 4 Flg Tng Sch, 8 FTS, 56, 253 and 16 Sqns. *Solway Aviation Museum, Carlisle*
DH Sea Venom FAW.22	WM571	1954	30 Apr 1969	ex Yeovilton, Fleet Air Arm, Air Director School, 831 and 891 Sqns. *Solent Sky, Southampton, stored*
Fairey Firefly TT.1	SE-BRD	1944	5 May 1964	G-ASTL, ex Svensk Flygstjanst AB, Gothenburg, Fleet Air Arm Z2033, 731 Sqn. *Fleet Air Arm Museum, Yeovilton*
Handley Page Halifax A.VII	PN323	1944	30 Oct 1965	cockpit, ex Radlett, RAF PN323, Handley Page. *Imperial War Museum, South Lambeth, London*
Handley Page Hastings C.1A *	TG528	1947	24 Jan 1968	ex RAF 24 Sqn, 24-36 Sqn pool, 242 Operational Conv Unit, 53-99 Sqn pool, 47 Sqn. *Imperial War Museum, Duxford*
Hawker Tempest II	LA607	1943	2 Sep 1966	ex Cranfield – see also Chapter 3. *Fantasy of Flight, USA, registered N607LA*
Mignet HM.14 'Flying Flea'	G-ADXS	1935	c Sep 1963	on loan, ex Southend. See also Chapters 7 and 19. *Real Aeroplane Co, Breighton, Yorks*
Mignet HM.14 'Flying Flea'	'G-ADRG'	1974	1975	built at Staverton. See Chapter 22. *Stondon Transport Museum, Lower Stondon, Beds*
Miles Magister I *	G-AFBS	1939	16 Oct 1965	ex Bristol, G-AKKU, RAF BB661, 10 Flg Instructors Sch, .8 Elementary Flg Tng Sch, G-AFBS. *Imperial War Museum, Duxford*
Percival Proctor III	G-ALCK	1944	23 Feb 1966	Tamworth, Woolsington, RAF LZ766, HQ Bomber Comm, 21 Elementary Flg Tng Sch. *Imperial War Museum, Duxford*
Saunders-Roe SR.A/1 *	G-12-1	1947	16 Oct 1966	ex Cranfield, TG263. See also Chapter 3. *Solent Sky, Southampton*
Short Sherpa	G-36-1	1953	May 1966	ex Cranfield, G-14-1. See also Chapter 3. *Ulster Aviation Society, Northern Ireland.*

Note: * – Illustrated in the colour sections.

CHAPTER 5

High Ambitions
Historic Aircraft Preservation Society and Reflectaire
1963 to 1972

Captained by Wg Cdr John Hampshire RAAF, Avro Lancaster VII G-ASXX touched down at Biggin Hill, Kent, on 13th May 1965. Twenty-three days and 12,000 miles (19,311km) previously the crew had embarked on an epic ferry flight, starting off from Mascot, New South Wales, Australia. The word was hardly in common usage in 1965, but the UK's largest privately-owned 'warbird' had arrived in the UK. There were high hopes for *Double-X-ray*; sadly, it was to fly just 14 times with its new owners, shutting down for what transpired to be the last time on 26th June 1970.

Fast forward a quarter of century to East Kirkby airfield in Lincolnshire and, despite the odds, all four engines of that very same 'Lanc' burst into life again. By then owned by Fred and Harold Panton and known to one and all as *Just Jane*, G-ASXX has been the centre-piece of the Lincolnshire Aviation Heritage Centre since 1988. Since then, *Jane* has regularly delighted countless visitors by taxying on the former Lancaster base and has taken a growing number of people for a never-to-be-forgotten taxi ride. For some time now, the team at East Kirkby has been looking into returning G-ASXX to airworthiness and major steps have been made towards that end.

As *Just Jane* is the flagship of the LAHC at East Kirkby, so it was that, as G-ASXX, it was the standard bearer for the Historic Aircraft Preservation Society. Formed in 1965, the origins of HAPS go back two more years to the setting up of Air-Britain's Air Relics Research Group. This band of enthusiasts was researching historic aircraft, particularly those that could be considered 'at risk' and in need of finding a caring home. For a variety of sound reasons, Air-Britain did not want to own airframes, but several of the members of ARRG were very keen to do so – hence the creation of HAPS.

Above: En route to the UK, Lancaster G-ASXX stopped over at Butterworth in Malaya. It was given an escort by Royal Australian Air Force EE Canberra B.21 A84-307 and RAF Handley Page Victor K.1A XH591. *RAF FEAF*

Opposite page: Seafire FR.47 VP441 alongside a Hawker Sea Hawk on the flight line at an airshow at Culdrose in 1967. The propeller was an adapted from one originally fitted to a Shackleton. *Roy Bonser*

Exhibit hunting

Boldly wishing to act as a *national* preservation centre, HAPS teams roamed far and wide to locate and ideally acquire deserving airframes. Membership was limited to just 25 initially, but with the arrival of the Lancaster, this was widened to bring in more funds. The County Flying Club at Biggin Hill was happy to allow use of the clubroom as a base, but in essence members were widely scattered across the UK. Several airframes were brought to 'The Hill' while others were found homes directly from where they had been found. As such it is difficult to list these under the HAPS 'banner' and the table gives those that can be considered as central to its being.

There was *another* source of confusion relating to just what constituted the HAPS 'fleet'. For a while, the Lancaster shared its ramp at Biggin Hill with Hawker Sea Fury FB.11 WJ288, this and fellow WJ244 had been delivered for the nascent British Historic Aircraft Museum – BHAM. (Both had come from the Hawker Siddeley store at Dunsfold, Surrey; WJ244 arriving at the 'Hill' in 1964 and WJ288 on 2nd September 1966. The former was to become the all-red G-FURY – see Chapter 18.) Also destined for BHAM was North American Mitchell N9089Z which was parked up at Biggin Hill after use as a camera-ship (and brief on-screen appearance) in the film *633 Squadron*. BHAM also had *national* dreams and had 'feelers' out for potential exhibits in a similar manner to the search that HAPS was carrying out. To outsiders, it was an easy mistake to see HAPS and BHAM as one and the same. The latter organisation de-camped to Southend, Essex, in 1966 and 1967 – see Chapter 7 for more.

To return to HAPS, G-ASXX was registered on 22nd October 1964 to Malcolm Dudley Norwood 'Bill' Fisher and William Russell Snadden. Bill was co-founder and chairman, an aviation insurance broker and later ran a company specialising in the acquisition and sale of types such as Austers and Chipmunks, among others. Russ was the man behind the epic 19-year restoration of Messerschmitt Bf 109G-2 *Black Six*. UK civil registered as G-USTV this first flew on 17th March 1991 and delighted airshow audiences until a force-landing just beyond the eastern Duxford perimeter on 12th October 1997 put paid to its flying days. This magnificent machine is now in the 'Milestones of Flight' hall at the RAF Museum, Hendon, and Russ is restoring a 1944 Bücker Bestmann in Scotland.

Several types were 'discovered' by HAPS, or were peripheral to its operation. Two aircraft displayed at the Fleet Air Arm Museum at Yeovilton, moved to Somerset through intervention by members. Vought Corsair IV KD431 went directly from Cranfield (see Chapter 3) to the soon-to-be-opened collection in May 1963. Long derelict at Thame airfield, Oxfordshire, Russ Snadden shelled out £25 to a Shefford, Beds, scrapyard for the hulk of Supermarine Walrus I G-AIZG in June 1963. (That £25 in present-day values would be more like £500 – hardly an 'impulse buy'!) This went to Yeovilton, via a comprehensive restoration at HMS *Condor*, the Air Engineering School at Arbroath in Scotland. The Walrus almost certainly owes its survival to Russ.

Kent-based Roger Barham acquired Percival Proctor IV G-AOAR and returned it to military guise as NP181 at Biggin Hill. Its fate is not confirmed, but it is believed to have been scrapped in the 1970s. Damaged Aeronca 100 G-AEVS was tracked down at Shoreham in Sussex and it was planned to bring it to the Kent airfield for restoration and possible use as a 'hack' for members, but this was not carried out. Today, affectionately known as *Jeeves* from its registration, it flies with the Real Aeroplane Company at Breighton in Yorkshire.

Australian connections led to the purchase (for £200) of former Royal Australian Navy Fairey Firefly TT.5 VX388. On 8th July 1966 this was bought by Bill Fisher where it was stored at Camden, New South Wales. Plans announced in 1967 said that if £5,000 could be raised, the Firefly was to be ferried back to the UK in much the same manner as the Lancaster. This venture came to nought and the Firefly is today part of the Camden Museum of Aviation.

Fellow travellers

As well as the Lancaster, three other airframes stayed with HAPS all the way through to its final guise as Reflectaire Ltd. The first of these was Supermarine Seafire FR.47 VP441 which had been with an Air Training Corps unit since the mid-1950s at Saltash, Cornwall. Saved from almost certain oblivion, it was moved on loan directly to Culdrose on 24th January 1964 for restoration and display at the Cornish naval base. The loan was called in under Reflectaire and VP441 was delivered to Lavenham, Suffolk, on 20th July 1969. It was not re-assembled as it was shortly to make the journey to Hullavington, Wiltshire, and ended up at Squires Gate, Lancs, by August 1970.

The Seafire among the uncut scrub at Squires Gate in 1972. *MAP*

There is much that could be written about Percival Mew Gull G-AEXF, most of it intertwined with that exceptional pilot, Alex Henshaw. Hatfield was the venue for the 1938 King's Cup air race and Alex and the Mew Gull sizzled across the finishing line at 236.25mph to take the prestigious trophy. That was just to keep his hand in until he took off from Gravesend in Kent for his famous out-and-back record to South Africa on 5th February 1939. Cramped into the tiny cockpit, with fuel tanks moulded almost all around him, Alex returned to his point of departure a staggering 106 hours, 16 minutes later.

Sold in France in the summer of 1939, it survived the Nazi occupation of France to return for a renewed racing career in 1950. While practicing for the Tees-side air races on 7th August 1965 *X-ray-Fox* suffered engine failure and Ernie Crabtree carried out a force-landing near Catterick, Yorkshire. The pilot was OK, but G-AEXF far less so. In 1966 Ernie presented the damaged machine to HAPS and it was taken to Personal Plane Services at Booker in Buckinghamshire, for repair. It is unlikely that any work was undertaken and the hulk of Henshaw's wooden-hulled miracle turned up at Blackpool Airport – more later.

The beautiful Mew Gull G-AEXF in its 1937 configuration. *MAP*

Splattered with oil and dog tired, Alaex Henshaw is lifted from the cramped cockpit of Mew Gull G-AEXF at Gravesend on 9th February 1939 at the end of his incredible Cape 'dash'. *Peter Green collection*

Many letters were sent around the globe enquiring about potential additions to the collection. One of these, to the Italian Air Force (ItAF) soliciting information on Canadair-built former RAF North American Sabres came up with a surprising result. The Italian authorities declared that HAPS could have one! Documentation declared that the machine involved would be 19477 and it was this that was UK civil registered on 24th March 1966 as G-ATBF to Bill Fisher and Bernard Robin Clarkson. In the now established fashion, it was hopefully planned to fly the Sabre to Biggin and there were apparently desires that it could even be used to break some flying records. This plot does not seem to have got through to the Italians, who dismantled MM19477 in readiness for the road journey to Kent.

When the desire to have a complete Sabre was expressed, the ItAF substituted another, MM19607, and *Bravo-Fox's* documentation was amended on 3rd March 1967. Surrounded by increasing costs, HAPS dropped the idea of flying the 'new' G-ATBF home and this example was *also* dismantled, arriving by road at Biggin Hill in 1967. The received Sabre was first flown at Cartierville, Quebec, on 18th March 1953 and delivered to the Aeroplane & Armament Experimental Establishment at Boscombe Down, Wiltshire, on 22nd July 22 as Sabre F.4 XB733. It left A&AEE service on 4th March 1955 and on 25th August 1956 joined the ItAF, serving with 4ª and 2ª Aerobrigata, respectively. After Biggin Hill, the Sabre ended up at Blackpool via Lavenham and Hullavington, in Luftwaffe colours.

Sabre 19607 in dismantled state at Lavenham after the move from Biggin Hill. *Jonathan Garroway*

Despite its provenance as a former RAF Sabre F.4, a crude Luftwaffe paint scheme was applied to Sabre G-ATBF at Blackpool. *Miles Burroughs*

Flagship

Lancaster NX611 started life at Austin Motors, Longbridge, as a Mk.III but was completed as its first Mk.VII. It was issued to the RAF on 16th April 1945 and spent much of its time in store. On 31st May 1951, NX611 was taken on charge by Avro at Woodford, for conversion for the French Aéronavale using Western Union financing. Work complete, the 'Lanc', now with the serial number WU15, was delivered to France on 6th April 1952. The third unit to use WU15 was Flottille 25F at Lann-Bihoué, Brittany. In 1958, 25F converted to Lockheed P2V-7 Neptunes. By 1962 WU15 was being refurbished at Le Bourget, Paris, and given a tropical all-white colour scheme.

In its new colours, No.15 was ferried to Escadrille de Servitude 9S at Tontouta, New Caledonia. In 1964 the last three of these veterans were retired in favour of Douglas C-54 Skymasters. By this time WU15 had about 2,200 hours 'on the clock'. HAPS had been campaigning to take on one of these survivors and pleas were answered when No.15 was delivered to Bankstown, New South Wales, in August 1964, ready to collect.

The destination of Biggin Hill had come about largely because of the addresses of several of the HAPS leading lights. When approached about the possibility of a Lancaster coming from Australia, the operators of Biggin Hill offered free ramp space providing it could 'star' at the 1965 'Air Fair'. Some of the airfield management also had hopes that a museum could be established at the famous Battle of Britain station and contributions from HAPS would be very welcome.

Close-up of the nose of G-ASXX at Biggin Hill in May 1965. Major sponsors were Hawker Siddeley (aka Avro), fuel came from Shell and Surfers Paradise of Queensland. *Stuart Howe*

After the euphoria of the arrival, hard work followed to get *Double-X-ray* ready for UK certification. This took much time and a lot of expense and it was not until 6th May 1967 that it was air-tested. For this and all the other flights the captain was gifted pilot Sqn Ldr Neil Williams – more of him in Chapters 10 and 13.

Another Lancaster flew in the UK during 1965 – just the once. This was Mk.I PA474 which on August 18th was ferried from Henlow, Beds, where it had been in the RAF Museum's 'pending tray', to Waddington, near Lincoln. (PA474 had served as an aerodynamics test-bed for the College of Aeronautics at Cranfield, Beds – see Chapter 3.) Work was completed on PA474 on 7th November 1967 when it was test flown, ready for its first season on the airshow 'circuit' the following year. As related, NX611 had finally got back into the air at Biggin Hill on 6th May that year. So, adding to the worries of HAPS was the availability of the RAF 'Lanc' at appreciably less cost to event organisers. Flown from Waddington until 20th November 1973 when PA474 moved to Coltishall, Norfolk, to join the Battle of Britain Memorial Flight. Today, PA474 is still with BBMF and based at Coningsby, just seven miles from *Just Jane's* home at East Kirkby. For more on PA474's Waddington days, turn to Chapter 10.

Wilderness years

HAPS became a not-for-profit company limited by guarantee in February 1967. While this made sure that the major players were not exposed to potentially massive financial liability, it also meant that control could be wrested by a well-organised faction securing a majority of votes. This is exactly what happened in 1968. Members were persuaded to transfer the assets to Reflectaire Ltd with paid employees and ostensibly run on a commercial footing. You could call this democracy in action or a short, sharp lesson in asset maximisation – aka capitalism. At this point most HAPS grandees parted company with the new creation.

They were not alone. The operators of Biggin Hill felt that a for-profit set-up could not bask in free ramp fees. Besides, the owners of the airfield had ruled out the museum proposal and the local appeal of the bomber was palling. Lancaster G-ASXX, along with the Mew Gull, Sabre and Seafire and the increasing piles of artefacts that had been donated, all had to move on. By the middle of 1969 the Reflectaire Preservation Group had come into being, hopefully to engage volunteers to work alongside the full-time engineering staff.

On 30th March 1969, the Lancaster left Biggin Hill for Lavenham in Suffolk, a former wartime USAAF Consolidated B-24 Liberator base offering somewhat basic accommodation. A change of landowner brought about another migration. 'Feelers' were put out for the next venue in what was becoming a hand-to-mouth management exercise. The CO at Hullavington, Wiltshire, offered a hangar as a temporary home and Neil Williams was again in command when G-ASXX flew there on 7th February 1970. This was to be a very short stay. In the naïve belief that a visitor centre could be opened *within* an operational RAF station, the public were invited – at a fee – to come and inspect the bomber and perhaps buy some souvenirs! Quickly a directive explaining that this was unacceptable was issued and Reflectaire and its airframes were on the move again.

An offer from the management at Blackpool's Squires Gate Airport was seized upon. Flight No.14, and G-ASXX's last, was staged on 26th June 1970. The choice of venue had a lot to do with expediency and desperation, but Blackpool also seemed to offer advantages. Closeness to the seaside and holiday resorts is a strategy adopted by several organisations studied in this book: the Southend-based Historic Aircraft Museum (Chapter 7), Devon's Torbay Aircraft Museum (Chapter 11), the Humberside APS's brief sojourn close to the promenade at Cleethorpes (Chapter 15) and the Island Aeroplane Collection (Chapter 27) at Sandown on the Isle of Wight. It should be stressed that any comparison of the above bodies and Reflectaire extends only to the 'Location, Location, Location' adage and not a qualitative one regarding the 'visitor experience'.

During its overhaul at Biggin Hill 1965 to 1967, G-ASXX adopted camouflage and the fortunate codes of 218 Squadron, spelling out 'HA-P'. It is illustrated at Lavenham.

Precious few 'punters' left the beaches and Golden Mile and all of its attractions, despite a few publicity stunts. A trek to the airport seemed to offer little and the 'museum' established at Squires Gate was pitiful. Airline passengers coming and going were equally not diverted by the sight of a few motley aeroplanes. If the 'Lanc' could fly, that would bring in the crowds and revenue. Occasionally an engine, or two, would be run to provide a taste of the possible, but this was not a crowd-puller. The collection was entering a spiral dive.

I visited Reflectaire in 1971, travelling up from Liverpool on a Ribble bus, and was appalled at what I saw. Overgrown blast pens, flat tyres on the Lancaster, the Seafire in poor state and, worst of all, the centre section and cockpit area of the smashed Mew Gull was sitting in a huge pool of water. A quick paddle revealed that there was water sloshing within the wing ribs and the fuselage. I paid the extra to go through the Lancaster's interior and was shocked to find a couple of kids draping themselves within, one of whom was studiously picking at the covering on the radio station seat. I was asked to sign a petition to prevent the 'museum' being 'evicted' from the airport. This steadfastly refused to do. When I enquired if there was anyone remotely older than the children that seemed to inhabit the site and I was told "Not today…"

It was therefore not a revelation when Blackpool Airport served a notice to quit on Reflectaire on 5th November that year. The company was wound up by liquidators Bernard Phillips & Co of New Cavendish Street, London W1. The company's Percy Phillips FCCA FCIS noted in November 1971 that the airframe assets available were: "Lancaster, Seafire, Sabre, Percival Mewgul [sic], a Slingsby glider. Also the following extremely valuable aircraft are on loan to the Fleet Air Arm Museum, Yeoverton [sic], Somerset." He added: "I would prefer to sell the lot as a whole, and offers in the region of £30,000 are anticipated." The status of the Corsair and Walrus were settled separately, thankfully staying at Yeovilton. The Seafire was acquired by the first of a series of American owners and exported to the USA, taking on the civil registration N47SF. On 14th April 2004 at Breckenridge, Texas, this one-of-a-kind variant was flown following extensive restoration. The parlous state of the Mew Gull was defended because it had been the victim of a vandal attack, but even if that was so it did not excuse it being left in a pool of water. Like the Seafire, the Mew Gull was also rebuilt and it took to the air again on 16th April 1978. Today it flies from the Real Aeroplane Company's aerodrome at Breighton, Yorks. During its illustrious career, G-AEXF was much rebuilt and repaired, but the near miraculous transformation it required post-Reflectaire produced a superb replica with necessarily minimal salvage from the Cape 'dash' record-breaker.

With hopes of a single, quick sale dashed, piecemeal disposal of the remainder of Reflectaire's chattels, in the form of an auction, was staged on 29th April 1972 through Henry Spencer & Sons of Retford, Notts. Of the 60-odd lots, five were airframes: Lot 43 was described in the catalogue as "A Glider (in need of restoration)" which very probably was Tutor BGA.475; Lot 48 was "A number of fuselage frames for a Hawker Hurricane" and two Hurricane pilot seats; Lot 54 was a fuselage frame from an Auster 6. The Sabre (Lot 62) was acquired by Lord Lilford's land agent, Thomas Bracewell, for £380 to become a plaything for his sons Giles (7) and Roger (11) at his farm at Much Hoole, Lancs. When they grew tired of it, the jet was entered in the Christie's auction at Duxford on 13th August 1984, travelling there (and back) on a flat-bed trailer. It reached £1,100, below its reserve and remained unsold. There was no trace of the Sabre at Much Hoole in 1987.

Sabre G-ATBF dismantled in a barn at Much Hoole, August 1983. *Alan Curry*

The liquidators had placed a reserve of £16,500 on Lot 63, Lancaster G-ASXX. The highest bid received by auctioneer Rupert Spencer, was £9,500 from Gordon Briggs, an Accrington-based scrap dealer. Among the 300 or so attending was Thomas Bracewell's boss, Lord Lilford, and he settled post-sale for a reported £12,500 (£200,000 in present-day values) and set about evaluating his options. All the while the bomber was still out in the elements at the airport and incurring ramp fees. Realising that it would cost a fortune to return to airworthiness, he came to the conclusion that the noblest thing to do was to put it into the care of the RAF. It was arranged to display it on the gate at Scampton, Lincs, for an initial ten-year loan. (In November 1970, Scampton's previous 'gate guardian' the famous Lancaster I R5868 *S-for-Sugar*, veteran of 137 'ops', left by road for Bicester, Oxfordshire, for refurbishing prior to going on show at the RAF Museum at Hendon in 1972.)

On 2nd August 1973 a Handley Page Hastings T.5 of the Scampton-based Strike Command Bombing School arrived at Squires Gate. It was carrying the station CO, Gp Capt Richard Lockyer, along with the vanguard of an RAF team who were to dismantle the Lancaster and take it by road to its new home. Lord Lilford was in attendance for the official hand-over ceremony.

We need to cut a long story short at this point and note that on 10th August 1974 a superbly restored NX611 was officially unveiled on the gate at Scampton. On 1st September 1983 there was another function to mark a change of hands, this time Fred and Harold Panton received the aircraft from Lord Lilford, having reached an agreement to purchase it. It was resolved to allow NX611 to adorn the entrance at Scampton for another five years, while things were prepared at East Kirkby. During May 1988 the bomber was dismantled and trucked to its new home to begin a wonderful transformation.

'Just Jane' in full glory at East Kirkby in August 2010. *Ken Ellis*

Historic Aircraft Preservation Society and the Reflectaire

Type	Identity	Built	Arrived	Background / *current status*, or fate
Avro Lancaster VII *	NX611	1945	13 May 1965	G-ASXX, ex Australia, Aéronavale WU15, RAF NX611, St Athan, Llandow. *Taxies at the Lincolnshire Aviation Heritage Centre, East Kirkby*
NAA (Canadair) Sabre IV *	MM19607	1953	1967	G-ATBF, ex Italian Air Force, RAF F.4 XB733, A&AEE, RCAF 19607. *Last known stored at Much Hoole, Lancs, Aug 1983*
Percival Mew Gull	G-AEXF	1936	1966	ex ZS-AHM. *Airworthy at Breighton, Yorks*
Supermarine Seafire FR.47	VP441	1947	24 Jan 1964	ex Saltash, RNEC Manadon, 804 Sqn. *Airworthy as N47SF in Texas*

Note: * – Illustrated in the colour sections.

CHAPTER 6

RAF Museum 'Out-Stations'
Stepping Stones to Hendon

Her Majesty Queen Elizabeth II opened the Royal Air Force Museum at Hendon on 15th November 1972. Tracing its flying origins to 1909 the former airfield site has been developed ever since with the latest project, the multi-million pound Battle of Britain 'Beacon' is currently at the fund-raising stage. Visitors in the 1970s were rightly impressed with the large number of iconic machines on display, all within the wonderfully conserved yet modernised 'Belfast truss' World War One-era hangars. Few of them would have appreciated that there were at least *as many again* aircraft that could have gone on display. This amazing accumulation, which has gone on to spawn in the 'second' RAF Museum at Cosford, Shropshire, and form the bulk of the contents of the Museum of Science and Industry in Manchester all came about through incredible efforts to 'stock-pile' during the 1960s.

Prior to that, the amassing of aircraft and artefacts to tell the story of the Royal Air Force fell largely to the Air Historical Branch of the Ministry of Defence and to interventions by the Commanding Officers and others at the then many RAF stations, squadrons and technical schools. The AHB was charged with the accumulation of documentation on all aspects of the RAF, a font of material handed down from operational units or collated in other ways. During World War Two, it was clear that some aircraft were of national, if not global, significance and something should be done to identify and, hopefully, preserve them. Many of those 'tagged' survive today and form the backbone of the RAF Museum, but others slipped the net for a variety of reasons. After 1945, many so-called 'AHB collection' aircraft were stored, often taking on a gypsy-like existence. Among the RAF stations used as repositories were: Biggin Hill, Cranwell, Fulbeck, Gaydon, Henlow, Stanmore Park, Swinderby, Tern Hill, Topcliffe and Wroughton. Other than the lucky few who wrote and asked if they could take a look around, these places were decidedly *not* for public inspection, except on the occasional open day.

Above: A sortie over the Isle of Wight in 1949 by the first UK all-swept wing (including the tailplanes) jet – Supermarine 510. Later modified to Type 517 status, VV106 was displayed at Colerne and St Athan. *Vickers-Armstrongs*

As well as the AHB 'policy' many airfields and technical schools had 'historic' airframes and some personnel recognised this, holding on to them for longer than normal procedure would have permitted. Much of this was 'ad hoc' and in many cases, downright covert! By the late 1950s, the need to establish a national tribute to the exploits and heritage of the RAF was beginning to crystallise. Aware of the accumulations across the Force, a 'round-robin' letter from the Air Ministry in October 1959 called upon all RAF Stations and units to search for records, photographs, engines, equipment and airframes. In the reply from RAF Colerne in Wiltshire was mention of two German aircraft (He 162 and Me 163), two Spitfires (Mk.II P7350 and Mk.XVI RW388) plus a Meteor F.4 (VT229).

From these four 'founder members', Flt Lt R W Osborne started in 1964 to gather aircraft, including the Hawker P.1052 and Supermarine 517 'one-offs' from Cardington. At Colerne there was never an established post of 'curator' or 'manager', nor was there a single man-hour officially sanctioned for this activity. In time it was arranged that the role of officer-in-charge of the 'museum' became a secondary duty of the CO of the Hercules Component Repair Flight. Everything was volunteer labour and this was the same at all of what became known as 'out-stations' of the RAF Museum. Trevor Hope of the Supply Squadron, for example, always took a day's unpaid leave prior to an open day to dust down the aircraft.

Initially conceived as opening up on the 50th anniversary of the RAF – 1st April 1968 – the massive effort required to create the RAF Museum slipped through into the 1970s. Henlow in Bedfordshire became the hub of the operation but four major 'out-stations' emerged, Colerne, Finningley and St Athan all now no longer RAF bases. At first, these three were open only on special occasions, mostly the 'At Home' days staged to mark the anniversary of the Battle of Britain in September each year. Each, particularly Colerne, expanded their operations to allow for greater public access. The other was Cosford and in 1979 the trustees of the RAF Museum accepted management of the collection there and it has since blossomed into a nationally important venue in its own right.

Museum in the making

Colerne, west of Chippenham, had a background that made it ideal for its eventual, unintended, role as a museum. On 1st January 1940 an Aircraft Storage Unit, 39 Maintenance Unit, was established and part of the airfield functioned in this manner until October 1953. Meanwhile, from 4th May 1948 a Special Installation Flight, 49 MU, was set up, providing pre-delivery and modification facilities for a wide range of types. This task, mostly concerning 'black boxes', continued until 49 MU was wound up on 1st March 1962, but avionics work remained a forte of the base through to its eventual demise.

Among the flying units post-war was 238 Operational Conversion Unit which trained night-fighter crews from 1952 to 1957 on Bristol Brigands and later Gloster Meteors. On charge as 'X' of 238 OCU from 9th May 1955 until January 1958 (by which time the unit was at North Luffenham in Rutland) was Meteor NF.14 WS838. In February 1972 this machine was appropriately retired to the museum at Colerne.

From 1957 to 1968 the airfield was home to Handley Page Hastings of Transport Command – see Chapter 4 for a 'side-effect' of this. From April 1967 another airlifter, the Lockheed Hercules, became a common sight with Colerne becoming the type's engineering base. But huge 'Herks' could not use most of the hangars scattered around the perimeter, so they were left temptingly empty. With the blessing of a string of OCs zealots on the base filled the spaces with historic aircraft.

From 1945 onwards, Colerne often was home to historic types and two of the earliest were from the store of captured aircraft at nearby 6 MU Brize Norton, Oxfordshire. (Heinkel He 162 120227 and Messerschmitt Me 163 191904, both stayed on station until such time as they were absorbed by the museum.) Others appeared as part of a brief turnaround for preparation for display and or other special purpose, for example Fieseler Fi 156C-7 Storch 475081 was issued to 49 MU in mid-1956 but had moved on by that October. No.49 MU was allocated Meteor F.4 VT229 for ground instructional purposes as 7151M on 27th July 1954 and after that it 'lingered' as a museum airframe. In August 1956 bright yellow Auster WE600 arrived at 49 MU for a four-month 'special fit' in readiness for its time with the British Antarctic expedition. It was back – this time as a museum piece – in late 1964.

'Founder member' Me 163B-1 191904 at Colerne in 1957 with an operational Hastings behind. *Peter Green collection*

But *the* founder member of the collection was Battle of Britain veteran Spitfire II P7350 that today is the 'star' of the Coningsby-based Battle of Britain Memorial Flight. In July 1948 salvage merchants John Dale and Sons Ltd purchased P7350 among many others that were lying at 39 MU. Bill Page, the company's general manager recognised the Mk.II's worth and offered it back. Museum curator Flt Lt John Frapwell, writing in *Air Clues* for February 1974 noted that Bill: "must go down as a very far-sighted man, and, perhaps unwittingly, one of the first aeronautical archaeologists, for he offered Spitfire P7350 to Colerne for preservation as it seemed a shame to destroy them all. There was considerable objection from the Ministry on the grounds, presumably, that the aircraft had been bought for scrap and scrapped it should be."

Battle of Britain Memorial Flight's 'Baby Spitfire', Mk.II P7350, showing the Folland Gnat T.1s of the 'Red Arrows' the way to an airshow, circa 1976.

Much-loved venue

The table charts the incredible variety of aircraft that constituted the Colerne museum as such. The reader should note that some machines issued to the three 'out-stations' dealt with in this chapter were on site for a comparatively short time. While every effort has been made to make the tables exhaustive, there will be some that have escaped the net. Over to the ever-poised *W&R* readers to fill in any gaps!

As the collection at Colerne grew, visitors to the annual open day spread the word that here was something to behold. It was not until 1964 that it was opened on an occasional basis in addition to the 'At Home' days. By 1971 Cpl David Johnson was in charge and beyond that came Flt Lt John Frapwell, who was probably the most responsible for the incredible expansion and its increasingly good name. By 1973 it was open Sundays at six-weekly intervals during the summer months – a staggering 150,000 people made the trek that year.

The incredible assembly on the front cover and featured again in the *Story of a Photograph* later was a bitter-sweet moment for the collection. Sadly, the occasion for this intensive game of aeronautical chess taken on 19th June 1975 was the impending closure of RAF Colerne and the removal of the exhibits to what Hendon was by then calling 'Regional Museums'. As part of the wind-down, the Ministry of Defence took the then unusual (or perhaps this was even the first) step of staging an auction. Going under the hammer on 2nd March 1976 were Anson TX226, Javelin XH892, Meteor VT229 and Provost XF690. Colerne closed as an RAF station on 31st May that year. Today, it is a major Army base and, thankfully, the runways are still used by the Grob Tutors of Bristol University Air Squadron and 3 Air Experience Flight.

Flt John Frapwell and his team were naturally gutted at the closure; they had put vast numbers of off-duty man-hours into the running of this exceptional collection. As with all servicemen faced with cuts and the axe, the team took it all stoically. Each and every one of them could bask in a job very well done.

Mosquito TT.35 TJ138 during its time with 5 CAACU, mid-1950s.

Designed to evaluate the concept of a pilot flying in the prone position, Meteor F.8 WK935 during flight test from Bitteswell, 1954. *Armstong Whitworth*

Hastings C.1 TG536 at Colerne in 1974.

Dragonfly HR.3 WG725 inside one of the storage hangars at Colerne. It wore a non-standard camouflage scheme.

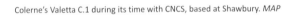

Colerne's Valetta C.1 during its time with CNCS, based at Shawbury. *MAP*

The Story of a Photograph

During the summer of 1975 there were a lot of visitors to Colerne as word got out that the very friendly and informal collection was in its last season. Those making the pilgrimage were presented with a six-page hand-out run off on an ink duplicator and stapled in the corner explaining how the V-shaped formation came about. Entitled *The Story of a Photograph*, the introduction read as follows:

"The photograph of all 35 aircraft comprising the RAF Colerne Aircraft Museum was taken between 12:20 and 12:40pm on Thursday, 19th June 1975. The design and layout of the aircraft was controlled by Flt Lt John Frapwell, movement of the aircraft was supervised by Chief Tech Geoff Richardson and the photograph was taken by station photographers Senior Aircraftsmen [SAC] Trevor Olner and Ronald Phillips using a Rolleiflex with a Tessar 1:3.5 lens.

"The task of moving so many old aircraft, many without brakes or proper towing bars, was a long and daunting job. The Simon's Lift gantry from which the photograph was taken was not available until the morning so that the aircraft could be only approximately located... It was necessary to go up in the lift several times to note which aircraft needed to move so that they did not obscure others.

"On the morning of the 19th there was quite a strong breeze with created a problem for the lightweight Blériot; it was wheeled out from the hangar by six airmen and one SAC. [The latter], Peter Elston, is actually in the photograph hanging on grimly to stop the Blériot blowing away. Another airman is holding down the 'Flying Flea'.

"Because RAF Colerne is to close in 1976 the Museum aircraft are being moved by road to other RAF Regional Museums at St Athan, Cardiff, Cosford, Wolverhampton and Finningley, Yorks. Just eight weeks after this photo was taken the first aircraft, the Spitfire 24, was moved away and one of the best Aircraft Museums in the country began its demise."

The aircraft in the Colerne 'V-Formation' have been numbered and their fates or present-day status are as follows:

1   Handley Page Hastings C.1 TG536 went to the fire school at Catterick, Yorks, and perished by 1989. The wings went to the Yorkshire Air Museum's Halifax recreation, *Friday the 13th*.
2   Douglas Dakota IV 'KG374' reverted to its correct identity KN645 and is displayed within the National 'Cold War' Exhibition at the RAF Museum, Cosford, Shropshire.
3   Gloster Javelin FAW.9 XH892 is displayed at the Norfolk and Suffolk Aviation Museum, Flixton, Suffolk.
4   De Havilland Mosquito TT.35 TJ138 is at the RAF Museum, Hendon, London.
5   A tight group of airframes in between the Hastings, Liberator and Dakota: Heinkel He 162A 120227 (fuselage only, under restoration) now at the RAF Museum, Hendon; Westland Dragonfly HR.3 WG725 at the Australian Museum of Flight, Nowra, New South Wales; Bensen B-8 G-ASPX was destroyed in fatal crash in Wales, 16th November 1989; Mignet HM.14 Pou du Ciel ('Flying Flea') G-AEEH at the RAF Museum, Cosford; and Chilton DW.1 G-AFGI is airworthy with a Reading-based owner.
6   De Havilland Vampire T.11 XD542 is with a private owner near Beverley, Yorks.
7   Hawker Hunter F.2 WN907, the cockpit is with the Robertsbridge Aviation Centre, Robertsbridge, Sussex.
8   Gloster Meteor F.4 VT229 is stored at Fantasy of Flight, Polk City, Florida, USA.
9   Consolidated Liberator VI KN751 at the RAF Museum, Hendon.
10   Vickers Valetta C.1 WD159 was taken to the training area at Ewyas Harold, Hereford, blown up in December 1977 during an SAS training exercise.
11   English Electric Canberra B.2 WJ676, the cockpit is with a private owner at South Shields, Tyne and Wear.
12   English Electric Canberra B(I).8 WT346 with the Royal New Zealand Air Force Museum at Wigram.
13   Avro Anson C.19/2 TX226 kept as a source of spares for the Air Atlantique Classic Flight at Coventry, Warwickshire.
14   Supermarine 517 VV106 stored at the Fleet Air Arm Museum, Yeovilton, Somerset.
15   Gloster Meteor NF.14 WS838 on loan to the Midland Air Museum, Coventry.
16   Hawker Sea Fury FB.11 VR930, with the Fleet Air Arm Historic Flight, Yeovilton.
17   Messerschmitt Me 163B 191904 at the Luftwaffen Museum, Berlin, Germany.
18   Hawker Hunter F.3 WB188 on loan at the Tangmere Military Aviation Museum, Sussex.
19   Supermarine Spitfire F.24 PK683 at Solent Sky, Southampton, Hampshire.
20   Gloster Meteor F.8 WK935 prone-pilot conversion, is displayed at the RAF Museum, Cosford.
21   English Electric Lightning T.5 XM967 went to the fire dump at Kemble, Glos, and expired by 1980
22   Consolidated PBY-6A Catalina L-866 displayed at the RAF Museum, Cosford.
23   De Havilland Vampire FB.6 J-1172 is at RAF Museum's 'deep store' at Stafford, Staffs.
24   Avro Shackleton T.4 nose WG511 (trailer mounted, rear on and just discernible) kept at Coventry, Warwickshire.
25   Supermarine Spitfire V BL614 displayed at the RAF Museum, Hendon.
26   De Havilland Vampire F.3 VT812, on show at the RAF Museum, Hendon.
27   Hawker P.1052 VX272 stored at the Fleet Air Arm Museum, Yeovilton.
28   Percival Provost T.1 XF690 airworthy as G-MOOS with a Somerset-based owner.
29   Blériot XI G-AVXV believed airworthy in France as F-AZIN.
30   Handley Page HP.115 XP841 within the 'Leading Edge' hall at the Fleet Air Arm Museum, Yeovilton.

RAF Colerne Aircraft Museum

Type	Identity	Built	Arrived	Background / *current status, or fate*
Auster C4 'Antarctic'	WE600	1951	c Oct 1964	ex Bicester 7602M, Trans-Antarctic Expedition, 663 Sqn (as T.7). Moved on to Finningley, see later. *RAF Museum, Cosford*
Avro Anson C.19/2	TX226	1946	1964	ex 7865M. Shawbury, Flg Tng Command Comm Flt, Jurby, 187 Sqn, Hemswell and Coningsby Stn Flts, Central Bomber Est. *Held by Air Atlantique Classic Flight as a source of spares at Coventry, Warks*
Avro Shackleton T.4	WG511	1952	c 1972	cockpit, ex Bicester, St Mawgan, Maritime Op Tng Unit, Kinloss Wing, MOTU, 120 and 42 Sqns. *Private owner, Coventry, Warks*
Avro 707C	WZ744	1953	1966	ex 7869M, Royal Aircraft Est – Thurleigh. Moved on to Finningley, see later. *RAF Museum, Cosford*
Bensen B.8	G-ASPX	1969	c 1972	On loan from the Goldsmith Trust. Moved on to St Athan, see later. *Destroyed in fatal crash 16 Nov 1989*
Blériot XI	G-AVXV	1910	c 1970	ex Ampsin, Belgium. (On loan from the Goldsmith Trust.) Moved on to St Athan, see later. *Believed airworthy in France as F-AZIN*
Chilton DW.1	G-AFGI	1938	c 1972	ex Staverton. See also Chapter 4. *Airworthy, Reading owner*
Consolidated PBY-6A Catalina *	L-866	1945	29 May 1974	ex 8466M, Danish AF, US Navy 63993. *RAF Museum, Cosford*
Consolidated Liberator VI *	KN751	1945	11 Jul 1974	ex Indian AF HE807, RAF KN751, 99 Sqn. *RAF Museum, Hendon*
De Havilland Tiger Moth	NL985	1944	c 1971	ex Cwmfelinfach 7105M, 9 Fg Tng Sch, 2 Grading Sch, London Univ Air Sqn, Queens Univ Air Sqn, 11 and 5 Reserve Fg Schs, Birmingham Univ Air Sqn, 16 and 14 Elementary Fg Tng Schs. See also Chapter 17. *Moved on to Finningley, see later. Salisbury owner, registered as G-BWIK and believed under restoration*
De Havilland Mosquito TT.35	TJ138	1945	c 1964	ex Bicester, Shawbury, 7607M, 5 Civilian Anti-Aircraft Co-op Unit, 98 Sqn. Moved on to Finningley, see later. *RAF Museum, Hendon*
De Havilland Vampire F.3	VT812	1947	1964	ex 7200M, Cardington, 602, 601, 614 and 32 Sqns. *RAF Museum, Hendon*
De Havilland Vampire FB.6	J-1172	1952	29 Jul 1974	ex 8487M, Dubendorf, Swiss AF. *RAF Museum, Stafford, stored*
De Havilland Vampire T.11	XD542	1953	1964	ex Melksham 7604M, Fighter Weapons Sch, Central Gunnery Sch. *Privately owned at Beverley, Yorks*
Douglas Dakota IV	'KG374'	1944	1 May 1974	ex Air Forces North, SHAPE, Malta, BAFO Comm Flts, 2nd Tac AF Comm Sqn, USAAF 44-77003. *RAF Museum, Cosford, as KN645*
English Electric Canberra B.2	WJ676	1954	1963	ex Melksham 7796M, 245, 35, 50 Sqns. *Privately owned cockpit section at South Shields, Tyneside*

Type	Identity	Built	Arrived	Background / current status, or fate
English Electric Canberra B(I).8	WT346	1956	17 Jun 1962	ex 8197M, 16, 3, 14, 88 Sqns, Aeroplane &Armament Exp Est, 88 Sqn. *Royal New Zealand Air Force, Wigram, NZ*
English Electric Lightning T.5	XM967	1962	9 Jan 1975	ex 8433M, T.5 prototype. *Perished on the fire dump at Kemble, Glos, by 1980*
Gloster Meteor F.4	VT229	1948	1964	ex 49 MU 7151M, 209 Advanced Fg Sch, 207 AFS, 616 Sqn. *Fantasy of Flight, Florida, USA, in store*
Gloster Meteor F.8(mod)	WK935	1954	c 1964	ex 7869M, Royal Aircraft Est. Moved on to St Athan, see later. *RAF Museum, Cosford*
Gloster Meteor NF.14 *	WS838	1954	Feb 1972	ex Royal Aircraft Est – Thurleigh, Royal Radar Est, 64 Sqn, 238 Op Conv Unit. *On loan to the Midland Air Museum, Coventry*
Gloster Javelin FAW.4	XA634	1956	c 1964	ex Melksham 7641M, Gloster. *Displayed at RAF Leeming, Yorks*
Gloster Javelin FAW.9R	XH892	1958	c 1964	ex 7982M, Shawbury, 29, 64, 23 Sqns. *Norfolk and Suffolk Aviation Museum, Flixton*
Handley Page Hastings C.1	TG536	1948	Jan 1974	ex Strike Cmd Bombing Sch, Bomber Cmd Bombing Sch, 242 Op Conv Unit, 48 Sqn, 242 OCU, Lyneham, Dishforth and Topcliffe pools. *Destroyed at RAF Catterick, Yorks, fire school, by 1989*
Handley Page HP.115 *	XP841	1960	1 Feb 1974	ex Royal Aircraft Est – Thurleigh. Moved on to St Athan, see later. *Fleet Air Arm Museum, Yeovilton*
Hawker Hurricane II	LF686	1944	1965	ex Hullavington, Bridgnorth 5270M, 41 Op Tng Unit. *National Air and Space Museum, Udvar Hazy Center, Dulles, USA*
Hawker Sea Fury FB.11	VR930	1948	15 Jan 1965	ex HSA Dunsfold, Fleet Requirements Unit, Lossiemouth, Anthorn, 801 Sqn, Anthorn, 802 Sqn. *Royal Navy Historic Flight, Yeovilton*
Hawker P.1052	VX272	1948	1964	ex Cardington, Halton 7174M. Moved on to St Athan, see later. *Fleet Air Arm Museum, Yeovilton, stored*
Hawker Hunter F.2	WN907	1954	1964	ex Melksham 7416M, 257 Sqn. Moved on to St Athan, see later. *Cockpit with the Robertsbridge Aviation Centre, Sussex*
Hawker Hunter F.3	WB188	1951	c 1965	ex Melksham, Halton 7154M. Moved on to St Athan, see later. *On loan from the RAF Museum to the Tangmere Military Aviation Museum, Sussex*
Heinkel He 162A-2	120227	120227	by 1961	ex Leconfield, Farnborough VN679, Air Min 65, Leck, Luftwaffe. Moved on to St Athan, see later. *RAF Museum, Hendon*
Messerschmitt Me 163B-1	191904	1944	c 1949	ex Brize Norton, Royal Aircraft Est – Farnborough Air Min 219, Husum, Luftwaffe. Moved on to St Athan, see later. *Luftwaffen Museum, Berlin, Germany*
Mignet HM.14 'Flying Flea'	G-AEEH	1936	1975	ex Bath, Whitchurch. Moved on to St Athan, see later. *RAF Museum, Cosford*

Type	Identity	Built	Arrived	Background / *current status, or fate*
Percival Provost T.1	XF690	1955	Nov 1968	ex 8041M, Shawbury, Civilian Air Traffic Control Sch,Central Nav and Control Sch, 64 Group Comm Flt, Queens Univ Air Sqn. *Airworthy as G-MOOS, Somerset owner*
Stampe (SNCAN) SV-4B	G-AWIW	1947	1971	ex Rothmans team, F-BDCC. See also Chapter 7. *Privately owned, stored at Cosford*
Supermarine Spitfire II	P7350	1940	Jul 1944	ex G-AWIJ, *Battle of Britain*, Colerne, 57 Op Tng Unit, Central Gunnery School, 64, 616, 603, 266 Sqns. *Airworthy with the Battle of Britain Memorial Flight, Coningsby*
Supermarine Spitfire V	BL614	1942	Oct 1972	ex Wattisham, Credenhill 4354M, 118, 64, 222, 242, 611 Sqns. Moved on to St Athan, see later. *RAF Museum, Hendon*
Supermarine Spitfire XVI	RW388	1945	Jan 1952	ex Fighter Cmd Control & Reporting Sch, 612 and 667 Sqns. *Potteries Museum and Art Gallery, Stoke-on-Trent*
Supermarine Spitfire F.24	PK683	1946	Nov 1972	ex Changi 7150M, Singapore Aux AF. *Solent Sky, Southampton*
Supermarine 517 *	VV106	1948	1964	ex Cardington, Halton 7174M. Moved on to St Athan, see later. *Fleet Air Arm Museum, Yeovilton, stored*
Supermarine Swift FR.5	WK281	1956	c 1962	7712M, ex Northolt, 79. *RAF Museum, on loan to Tangmere Military Aviation Museum, Tangmere*
Vickers Valetta C.1	WD159	1950	2 Sep 1964	ex Civilian Air Traffic Controller Sch, Central Nav and Control Sch, 233 Sqn, Ferry Support Sqn, 52 Sqn. *Blown up in an exercise at Ewyas Harold, Hereford, Dec 1977*
Westland Dragonfly HR.3	WG725	1951	1966	ex Weeton 7703M, Royal Aircraft Est. *Museum of Flight, Nowra, Australia*

Note: * – Illustrated in the colour sections.

ONES THAT GOT AWAY

Westland Whirlwind, 1947

Although only 116 examples of the Westland Whirlwind were built, the type has always evoked considerable interest. Harald Penrose flew the prototype, L6844, from Boscombe Down, Wiltshire, for the first time on 11th October 1938. It was not until 7th December 1940 that the sleek, twin Rolls-Royce Peregrine powered fighter entered operational service, with 263 Squadron. Orders were dramatically cut back and the last example came off the Yeovil, Somerset, production line in December 1941. Only one other unit, 137 Squadron, flew the Whirlwind in combat, from September 1941 to June 1943. In late 1944, Westland acquired P7048, once flown by 137 Squadron, and brought it back to Yeovil, placing it on the civil register as G-AGOI on 29th March 1945. It was painted in a grey overall colour scheme and was flown as part of the manufacturer's unofficial 'historic flight' until it was dismantled at Yeovil in May 1947; the last of its breed. *Westland*

Finningley, Yorkshire
1966 to 1979

When Finningley closed on 31st March 1996 it was a sad day for aviation in the area around Doncaster and for the RAF in particular. It was a case of another RAF station destined for use by light industry, or a housing estate, or regular car boot sales – either way, a waste of fine runway. In a remarkable reversal of fortunes, the former flying training base was transformed and in April 2005 opened up as Doncaster-Sheffield Robin Hood Airport.

In 1966 the main runway at Finningley didn't handle Boeing 737s, it was pounded by Avro Vulcans of 230 Operational Conversion Unit. In the calm of the early evening of 11th September that year, the runway gave way to V-Bombers and allowed a frail biplane to make a series of 'hops'. This was a faithful replica of the Wright Flyer of 1903 built by a team led by Wg Cdr T M Fennell of the Finningley Vintage Aircraft Club. The replica was a major attraction at that year's 'At Home' open day and airshow, held every September to mark the Battle of Britain. About the same time the station was offered Meteor F.8 WL168 and this was accepted by the CO, Gp Capt J A G Jackson CBE. With the Flyer replica and the Meteor, a decision was made to develop a collection. During the lifetime of the RAF Finningley Station Museum the airframes were available for close inspection every September, or by prior appointment. Initially, Wg Cdr J P Bullock, the Officer Commanding the Engineering Wing, located the exhibits. As with Colerne and St Athan, the whole thing was run entirely as a spare-time venture.

When Finningley was chosen as the venue for the Royal Review of the RAF to mark the Queen's Silver Jubilee, the collection of historic aircraft became a victim of collateral damage. There was to be a huge static display, not to mention a massive flypast, in front of invited guests on 29th July 1977 and the following day the public were to be allowed in to witness a similar junket. Attendance figures vary, but 150,000 is as good a figure as any for the 30th.

All the hangars would be needed and so the museum airframes were dispersed, never to return. The bulk moved to Swinderby, Lincs, with others going to Cosford, Shropshire. As will be seen from the table, some faced the axe. The Newark Air Museum elected to acquire the Shackleton MR.3/3 and it was dismantled and removed to be painstakingly put back together again. Today, the public can tour inside WR977 and many visitors are gobsmacked to discover that this huge maritime patroller did not fly in but arrived in sections, by road. Appropriately, the last exhibit to leave Finningley was also the one that inspired the start of the collection, the Wright Flyer travelled to Cardington, Bedfordshire, in 1979.

Above: No matter what was in the visiting static each year for Finningley's 'At Home' airshow, the station museum's Beverley C.1 XL149 dominated the skyline.

In a bizarre twist of fate, Avro 707A WZ736 was saved from the fire dump at Colerne (illustrated there April 1967) and restored by the Finningley collection. *Roy Bonser*

Messerschmitt Me 262A-2a 112372 at the 1975 Finningley 'At Home'.

Boulton Paul Defiant N1671 at the RAF50th anniversary celebrations at Abingdon, June 1968. It moved to Finningley the following month. *Roy Bonser*

The 'Claybourn' Flying Flea inside the museum hangar at Finningley, 1969. *Roy Bonser*

The remains of Argosy C.1 XN819 on the fire dump at Finningley, September 1983. Note that the cockpit has been removed, it was converted into a procedure trainer and is now a 'working' exhibit at the Newark Air Museum. *Roger Richards*

RAF Finningley Station Museum

Type	Identity	Built	Arrived	Background / *current status, or fate*
Armstrong Whitworth Argosy C.1	XN819	1962	Jul 1972	8205M, ex 114, 267 and 105 Sqns. To the fire dump by 1977. *Cockpit at Newark Air Museum, Newark*
Auster C4 'Antarctic'	WE600	1951	c 1976	ex Colerne, Bicester 7602M, Trans-Antarctic Expedition, 663 Sqn (as T.7). *RAF Museum, Cosford*
Avro Shackleton MR.3/3	WR977	1957	Nov 1971	8186M, ex 203, 42, 206, 203, 42, 201, 206, 201, 220 Sqns. *Newark Air Museum, Newark*
Avro 707A	WZ736	1953	c 1967	ex Colerne fire dump, Royal Aircraft Est – Thurleigh, Aeroplane & Armament Exp Est. *RAF Museum, loan to Museum of Science and Industry, Manchester*
Avro 707C *	WZ744	1953	c 1966	ex Colerne, 7869M, Royal Aircraft Est – Thurleigh. *RAF Museum, Cosford*
Avro Vulcan B.1	XH498	1958	Oct 1967	7993M, ex Waddington Wing, 50 and 617 Sqns. *Scrapped 1970*
Blackburn Beverley C.1	XL149	1957	Mar 1970	7988M, ex 30 Sqn, 242 Op Conv Unit. *Broken up Mar 1978, Cockpit at Aeroventure, Doncaster*
Boulton Paul Defiant I	N1671	1940	23 Jul 1968	ex Abingdon, St Athan, Fulbeck, Stanmore Park, Cardiff, Hullavington, 285, 307 Sqns. *RAF Museum, under restoration by the Medway Aircraft Pres Soc, Rochester*
De Havilland Tiger Moth	NL985	1944	c 1976	ex Colerne, Cwmfelinfach 7105M, 9 Fg Tng Sch, 2 Grading Sch, London Univ Air Sqn, Queens Univ Air Sqn, 11 and 5 Reserve Fg Schs, Birmingham Univ Air Sqn, 16 and 14 Elementary Flg Tng Schs. See also Chapter 17. *Salisbury owner, registered as G-BWIK and believed under restoration*
De Havilland Mosquito TT.35	TJ138	1945	1975	ex Colerne, Bicester, Shawbury, 7607M, 5 Civilian Anti-Aircraft Co-op Unit, 98 Sqn *RAF Museum, Hendon*
De Havilland Vampire T.11	XD506	1954	Sep 1967	7983M, ex CATCS, CNCS, 5 F;g Tng Sch, 206 Advanced Flg Sch. *Jet Age Museum, Staverton, stored*
Fairey Delta 2	WG777	1956	1967	7986M, ex Royal Aircraft Est – Thurleigh. *RAF Museum Cosford*
Gloster Meteor F.8	WL168	1954	1969	ex St Athan, Heywood 7750M, Sylt, 604, 111. *Yorkshire Air Museum, Elvington*
Gloster Javelin FAW.4	XA549	1954	c 1967	ex Swanton Morley 7717M. *Scrapped 1976*
Handley Page Hastings C.1a	TG605	1949	5 Sep 1967	7987M, ex 24-36 Sqns pool, 114, 24 Sqns, 53-99 Sqns pool, Lyneham Wing, 24 Sqn, Topcliffe and Dishforth Wings. *Scrapped on site*
Hawker Hunter F.4	XF309	1956	c 1966	ex St Athan 7771M, 229 Op Conv Unit, 112 Sqn. *To Hawker Siddeley May 1973 as G-9-420 to the Kenyan Air Force as Mk.80 805 Dec 1974*
Hunting Jet Provost T.1	XD674	1955	1972	ex 71 MU Bicester 7570M. *RAF Museum Cosford*
Messerschmitt Me 262A-2a	112372	1945	c 1966	ex Gaydon, Cranwell, Farnborough, VK893, Air Min 51, Luftwaffe. *RAF Museum, Hendon*

Type	Identity	Built	Arrived	Background / current status, or fate
Mignet HM.14 'Flying Flea'	G-AEKR	1936	1960	ex Doncaster, on loan. *Replica at Doncaster Museum and Art Gallery.* See Note [1] below
Percival Proctor III	Z7197	1940	c 1966	ex G-AKZN, RAF Air Service Training, 18 Elementary Flg Tng Sch, 1 Radio Sch, 2 Signals Sch. *RAF Museum, Stafford, 'deep store'*
Percival Provost T.1 *	XF545	1955	Jun 1967	7957M, Shawbury, 6 and 2 Flg Tng Schs. *Private owner, Reading area, stored*
Short SB.5 *	WG768	1952	1968	ex Empire Test Pilots School, Royal Aircraft Est – Thurleigh, RAE – Farnborough, Aeroplane & Armament Exp Est, RAE – Thurleigh, A&AEE. *RAF Museum, Cosford*
Supermarine Spitfire XVI	TE184	1945	c 1968	ex Henlow, Royton 6850M, Newcastle upon Tyne, Central Gunnery Sch, 607 Sqn, 226 Op Conv Unit, 203 Advanced Flg Sch. *Airworthy as G-MXVI, London-based owner*
Supermarine Swift FR.5 *	WK281	1956	Mar 1967	ex Colerne 7712M, Northolt, 79. *RAF Museum, on loan to Tangmere Military Aviation Museum, Tangmere*
Wright Flyer 1903 replica	–	1966	11 Sep 1966	Built at Finningley. *Yorkshire Air Museum, Elvington*

Note: * – Illustrated in the colour sections. [1] Original destroyed in a hangar fire at Finningley, 5th September 1970. Replica using some original metal components built at RAF Oakington, Cambs, as replacement.

St Athan, Wales
1964 to 1989

Like the Colerne collection, the gathering of historic airframes at St Athan came into being by happenstance. The massive storage and maintenance base near Barry on the South Wales coast served in the role of out-station for the growing RAF Museum for longer than the two other major locations that we have studied. Like its Wiltshire counterpart, the airfield had all the facilities necessary to support restoration and conservation. No.4 School of Technical Training was formed there on 1st September 1938, initially taking vast numbers of trainees in all forms of engineering and other aircrew tasks. The SoTT was officially disbanded in late 1977, but elements remained well into the 1990s. Alongside the SoTT, 19 Maintenance Unit was formed on 7th February 1939 as an Aircraft Storage Unit, later taking on the wider role of an Aircraft Supply and Servicing Depot, until it was disbanded in December 1963. Later in 1939 an extensive Aircraft, Engine and Motor Transport Repair Depot, 32 MU, came into being, running until being wound down in November 1968. Today the airfield is run by the Ministry of Defence under the grand title of Defence Support Group – Large Aircraft Business Unit working on types such as the RAF's Vickers VC-10 tanker fleet.

Putting an exact date on when St Athan became a 'collection' is not an easy task. As with Colerne, aircraft were issued for the technicians, instructors and engineers to prepare for an exhibition or special occasion. The SoTT had a range of instructional airframes at any time and some of these, when no longer suitable for training purposes, were held at the station as 'historic' (eg Provost T.1 WV499 was issued to 4 SoTT in 1964, joining the Historic Aircraft Collection seven years later). By 1964 – in common with many RAF stations – St Athan was holding an 'At Home' open day and airshow every September and the occasion was taken to display some of the 'older' airframes held by the base. By then, there was an extensive workshop facility regularly, if not continually, restoring for the RAF Museum-to-be. When the Historic Aircraft Collection (HAC) opened up on a more regular basis, it was also possible to inspect work-in-hand and this was one of the joys of making the trek to South Wales.

Indigenous exhibit

As will be seen from the table listing St Athan's 'museum' airframes, there was an incredible throughput over 25 years. The earliest museum inmate was not an RAF machine at all, it was none other than the first aircraft to be built and flown in Wales. This was Charles Horace Watkin's CHW monoplane *Robin Goch* (robin redbreast). This was designed and built by Charles, with a little help from his friends, at Maendy near Cardiff from 1907 until at least 1909. Fitted with a 40hp three-cylinder also designed by Charles, it was claimed to have 'hopped' in 1909 and made a cross-country flight the following year. It was flown extensively until 1916 when it was put into store.

Above: Awaiting the public at a mid-1980s 'At Home' day at St Athan, the Messerschmitt Me 410 and Kawasaki Ki 100.

The owner/designer/pilot offered it on loan to RAF St Athan in 1959 and to the eternal credit of the OC of the time this very significant monoplane was taken 'on board'. Long after the rest of the HAC had been dispersed, *Robin Goch* was kept on. In January 1998 the importance of this aircraft was at last recognised by Wales, going on show in the National Museum and Gallery of Wales. This bestowed status was not to last, the CHW moving to the Collection Centre at Nantgarw, a large object store for the principality's museums. In 2007 the Watkins moved to Sawnsea, far from its birthplace and relevance, and it 'flies' within the National Waterfront Centre.

Museum workshop

As explained, St Athan had a major role in restoring and rebuilding airframes destined for Hendon. One of these was Bristol Beaufighter TF.X RD253 that had been gifted to the UK by the Technical Institute of Lisbon, Portugal, in 1965. Across at 71 Maintenance Unit at Bicester in Oxfordshire, an engineless Beaufighter was being prepared for donation to the National Aeronautical Collection at Rockliffe, Ontario, in exchange for the Fairchild-built Bolingbroke IVT that is now in the Battle of Britain Hall at Hendon. For this project, elements of RD253 were employed but in 1967 its turn came and it was issued to the workshop at St Athan. Flt Lt Len Woodgate was put in charge of this and work was so well advanced that the 'Beau' – with one engine fitted – appeared at the 'At Home' display that year.

On 19th September 1940 Canadian Fg Off 'Willie' Wilcox of 98 Squadron was tasked to fly Fairey Battle I L5343 from its base at Kaldadarnes, Iceland, to Akureyri on the island's north coast. The Battles provided rudimentary coastal patrol, but in this case, he was to deliver a propeller needed for a grounded aircraft, thousands of cigarettes for the troops stationed there and one Lt Col H Davies, who wished to inspect the nicotine-craving soldiers. As so often on Iceland, the weather was to change prospects dramatically, and 'Willie' was compelled to perform a passable force-landing on a beach not far from his intended destination. Pilot, passenger, propeller and cigarettes eventually made it through to Akureyri. The Battle lay where it fell.

In 1972 personnel from RAF Leeming took part in an epic recovery of the remains of L5343. Part of the team was Len Woodgate and he was to supervise its initial restoration back at the Yorkshire base. In 1980, Len was posted back to St Athan and he took charge – in his 'spare' time – of the HAC. The Battle project had been put into store at Henlow, Bedfordshire, and Len decided once again to take it under his wing and it moved to Wales in 1981. The completed restoration was rolled out 6th March 1990 going on to display at Hendon. Len had to leave his pet project in 1983, becoming the curator of the Aerospace Museum (as it was then known) at Cosford.

Axis powers outpost

Ask most people that visited St Athan during its days as an out-station and they will wax lyrical about the captured enemy aircraft. By 1977 the Welsh airfield could boast the largest assemblage of Luftwaffe types on view to the public. Not only could the public get close to these amazing types at each open day, the policy of restoring engines to function whenever it was possible meant that audiences could be treated to the spectacle of a ground-run. In September 1984 the audience stood transfixed while the 14-cylinder air-cooled two-row radial BMW 801D-2 methanol-water boosted to 2,100hp of the Focke-Wulf Fw 190F roared into life! Two years later, a select few got to hear a noise unlikely to be experienced again. This time it was the turn of another 14-cylinder air-cooled two-row radial to burst into action – the Army Type $ (Mitsubishi Ha-33) of 1,500hp on the front of the Kawasaki Ki-100. Incredible!

By then the Axis collection was a shadow of its former self because of the good job well done in the workshops at St Athan and elsewhere. On 28th November 1978 the Battle of Britain Hall at Hendon was opened, presenting its visitors with icons from both sides of the decisive 1940 aerial conflict amid great atmosphere and detail, but necessarily inert.

By the mid-1980s, the HAC was available on the first Sunday of each month as well as for the September 'At Home' display. This step had come about because of the increasing number of parties who wished to make the pilgrimage and it was deemed easier to open up more regularly to help meet the demand.

About this time the two 'regionals', Cosford and St Athan, decided that it would be better for visitors if a level of specialisation could be introduced. There followed a period where lorries plied the roads between the two RAF stations, exchanging exhibits. Broadly, Cosford took on the prototypes and experimentals, while St Athan became *the* centre, outside of Hendon, for Axis aircraft.

However the end came in 1989, service requirements dictating that the space and facilities that had been the HAC were better employed in other ways. Cosford took on the bulk of the airframes, with some going to Hendon. Following in the mould of the wind-down of Colerne, Phillips were brought in to 'hammer' surplus machines. This took place at the auctioneer's Cardiff office on 21st September 1989 and the following were offered: Auster XR243, Canberra WD935, Provost WV499, Skeeter XN341, Swallow XS650 Vampire FB.5 WL505 and Vulcan XM602. The latter was sold to a London property dealer for £33,000 – that would be around £132,000 in present day values. It seems the scheme was to relocate it and turn it into an attraction, but the costs involved defeated the scheme. It lingered on the airfield until it was cut up in October 1992; the cockpit section being saved.

RAF St Athan Historic Aircraft Collection

Type	Identity	Built	Arrived	Background / *current status, or fate*
Auster C4 'Antarctic'	WE600	1951	c 1979	ex ex Swinderby, Finningley, Colerne, Bicester 7602M, Trans-Antarctic Expedition, 663 Sqn (as T.7). *RAF Museum, Cosford*
Auster AOP.9	XR243	1962	Mar 1976	ex Quedgely 8057M, St Athan, Middle Wallop. *Auctioned 21 Sep 1989, no details*
Avro 504K replica	'H1968'	1968	c 1970	ex Halton. *Yorkshire Air Museum, Elvington*
Avro Vulcan B.2	XM602	1964	1984	8771M, ex 101 Sqn, Waddington Wing, 35 Sqn, 230 Oper Conv Unit, Wadd Wing, Cottesmore Wing, 12 Sqn *Scrapped on site Oct 1992, nose with Museum of Science and Industry, Manchester*
Bensen B.8	G-ASPX	1969	1976	On loan from the Goldsmith Trust, ex Croydon. *Destroyed in fatal crash 16 Nov 1989*
Blériot XI	G-AVXV	1910	1976	ex Colerne, Ampsin, Belgium. (On loan from the Goldsmith Trust.) *Believed airworthy in France as F-AZIN*
Boulton Paul Defiant I	N1671	1940	Dec 1967	ex Fulbeck, Stanmore Park, Cardiff, Hullavington, 285, 307 Sqns. *RAF Museum, under restoration by the Medway Aircraft Pres Soc, Rochester*
Bristol Scout replica	'A1742'	1962	1976	ex Colerne, Weeton. *On loan to Shuttleworth Collection, Old Warden*
Bristol Beaufighter TF.X	RD253	1944	1967	7931M, ex Portuguese Air Force BF-13, RAF, no service. *RAF Museum, Hendon*
De Havilland Mosquito TT.35	TJ138	1945	Nov 1986	ex Swinderby, Finningley, Colerne, Bicester, Shawbury, 7607M, 5 Civilian Anti-Aircraft Co-op Unit, 98 Sqn *RAF Museum, Hendon*
De Havilland Vampire FB.9	WL505	1951	1969	ex Ely 7705M, 19 Sqn, RAF College, 73 Sqn. *Stored as G-FBIX at Bournemouth, Dorset*
English Electric Canberra B.2	WD935	1951	Mar 1975	8440M, ex Wroughton, 360 and 97 Sqns, RAAF A84-1, Vickers Red Dean missile trials. *Scrapped on site Nov 1989, nose at Aeroventure, Doncaster*
Fairey Battle I	L5343	1940	1981	ex Henlow, Leeming, Iceland, 98 and 266 Sqns. *RAF Museum, Hendon*
Fiat CR.42 Falco	MM5701	1940	1968	ex Biggin Hill, Fulbeck, Wroughton, Stanmore Park, Air Fighting Dev Unit, Royal Aircraft Est, BT474, Italian Air Force. *RAF Museum, Hendon*
Fieseler Fi 156C-7	475081	1944	June 1973	ex Coltishall, Bircham Newton, 7362M, Fulbeck, Royal Aircraft Est VP546, Air Min 101. *RAF Museum, Cosford*
Focke-Wulf Fw 190A-8/U1 *	584219	1944	1970	ex Gaydon, Henlow, Fulbeck, Wroughton, Stanmore Park, Wroughton, Brize Norton, Air Min 29, Farnborough, Karup, Luftwaffe. *RAF Museum, Cosford*
Gloster F9/40 Meteor *	DG202/G	1943	c 1962	ex Yatesbury, Locking 5758M, prototype. *RAF Museum, Cosford*

Type	Identity	Built	Arrived	Background / current status, or fate
Gloster Meteor IV Special	EE549	1946	c 1966	ex Innsworth 7008M, Fulbeck, Cranwell, Central Fighter Est, Fighter Command Comm Sqn, RAF High Speed Flt. EE549 *returned* to St Athan by Sep 1981, from Abingdon and Hendon. *RAF Museum, on loan to Tangmere Military Aviation Museum*
Gloster Meteor T.7/8	WA634	1949	1964	ex Martin-Baker. *RAF Cosford*
Gloster Meteor F.8(mod)	WK935	1954	6, Oct 1975	ex Colerne 7869M, Royal Aircraft Est. *RAF Museum, Cosford*
Gloster Meteor F.8	WL168	1954	1969	ex Swinderby, Finningley, St Athan, Heywood 7750M, Sylt, 604, 111. *Yorkshire Air Museum, Elvington*
Gloster Meteor NF.14	WS843	1954	Mar 1967	ex Henlow 7937M, St Athan, Kemble, 1 Air Nav Sch, 228 Oper Conv Unit. *RAF Cosford*
Handley Page HP.115	XP841	1960	1976	ex Colerne, Royal Aircraft Est – Thurleigh. *Fleet Air Arm Museum, Yeovilton*
Hawker Hart Trainer	K4972	1935	c 1969	ex 1546 Sqn ATC, Carlisle, Wigton 1764M, 2 Flg Tng Sch. *RAF Museum, Hendon*
Hawker P.1052	VX272	1948	1975	ex Colerne, Cardington, Halton 7174M. *Fleet Air Arm Museum, Yeovilton, stored*
Hawker Hunter F.2	WN907	1954	20 Oct 1975	ex Colerne, Melksham 7416M, 257 Sqn *Cockpit with the Robertsbridge Aviation Centre, Sussex*
Hawker Hunter F.3	WB188	1951	1975	ex Colerne, Melksham, Halton 7154M. *On loan from the RAF Museum to the Tangmere Military Aviation Museum, Sussex*
Heinkel He 111H-23	701152	1944	Sep 1969	ex Henlow, Biggin Hill, Fulbeck, Stanmore Park, Royal Aircraft Est, 56th Fighter Group USAAF, Luftwaffe. *RAF Museum, Henlow*
Heinkel He 162A-2	120227	120227	1975	ex Colerne, Leconfield, Farnborough VN679, Air Min 65, Leck, Luftwaffe. *RAF Museum, Hendon*
Hunting Jet Provost T.1	XD674	1955	c 1979	ex Swinderby, Finningley, 71 MU Bicester 7570M. *RAF Museum Cosford*
Junkers Ju 87D-3 *	494083	1944	Aug 1960	ex Biggin Hill, Fulbeck, Wroughton, Stanmore Parke, Eggebek, Luftwaffe. *RAF Museum, Hendon*
Junkers Ju 88R-1	360043	1943	Aug 1973	ex Biggin Hill, Fulbeck, Wroughton, Stanmore Park, Central Fighter Est PJ876, 1426 Enemy Aircraft Flt, Royal Aircraft Est, Luftwaffe. *RAF Museum, Hendon*
Kawasaki Ki-100-1b *	16336	1945	Nov 1985	Cosford, Henlow, Biggin Hill, Fulbeck, Wroughton, Stanmore Park, Sealand, Japanese Air Force. *RAF Museum, Hendon*
Messerschmitt Bf 109E-4/B	4101	1940	1969	ex Henlow, Biggin Hill, Fulbeck, Wroughton, Stanmore Park, DG200, 1426 Enemy Aircraft Flt, Aeroplane & Armament Exp Est, de Havilland, Rolls-Royce Hucknall, Royal Aircraft Est, Luftwaffe. *RAF Museum, Hendon*
Messerschmitt Bf 110G-4/R6	730301	1944	Aug 1973	ex Biggin Hill, Stanmore Park, Royal Aircraft Est, Air Min 34, Karup, Luftwaffe. *RAF Museum, Hendon*

Type	Identity	Built	Arrived	Background / *current status, or fate*
Messerschmitt Me 163B-1	191904	1944	1976	ex Colerne, Brize Norton, Royal Aircraft Est – Farnborough Air Min 219, Husum, Luftwaffe. *Luftwaffen Museum, Berlin, Germany*
Messerschmitt Me 410A-1/U2	420430	1944	1984	ex Cosford, Fulbeck, Wroughton, Stanmore Park, Brize Norton, Farnborough, Air Min 72, Vaerlose, Luftwaffe. *RAF Museum, Cosford*
Mignet HM.14 'Flying Flea'	G-AEEH	1936	1975	ex Colerne, Bath, Whitchurch. *RAF Museum, Cosford*
Mitsubishi Ki-46 III *Dinah*	5439	1945	1968	ex Biggin Hill, Fulbeck, Wroughton, Stanmore Park, Sealand, Allied Technical Air Int Unit – South East Asia, Japanese Air Force. *RAF Museum, Cosford*
Percival Proctor III	Z7197	1940	c 1979	ex Swinderby, Finningley, G-AKZN, RAF Air Service Training, 18 Elementary Flg Tng Sch, 1 Radio Sch, 2 Signals Sch. *RAF Museum, Stafford, 'deep store'*
Percival Provost T.1	WV499	1953	1971	ex Weeton 7698M, 6 Flg Tng Sch. *Registered as G-BZRF, private owner, stored Weston Zoyland, Somerset*
Royal Aircraft Factory BE.2 rep	'6232'	1962	c 1969	ex Halton. *Yorkshire Air Museum, Elvington*
Saunders-Roe Skeeter AOP.12	XN341	1960	Dec 1971	ex 4 Sch of Tech Tng 8022M, 3 Royal Tank Regt, 651 Sqn. *Stondon Transport Museum, Lower Stondon, Beds*
Slingsby Swallow TX.1	XS650	1964	1984	8801M, ex Central Glding Sch. *Auctioned 21 Sep 1989 and airworthy by 1992*
Sopwith Camel replica	'D3419'	1962	c 1969	ex Colerne. *Montrose Air Station Heritage Centre, Montrose*
Supermarine Spitfire V	BL614	1942	1976	ex Colerne, Wattisham, Credenhill 4354M, 118, 64, 222, 242, 611 Sqns. *RAF Museum, Hendon*
Supermarine Spitfire IX	MK356	1944	1969	ex Henlow, Bicester 5690M, Hawkinge, Halton, 84 Group Supp Unit, 443 Sqn. *Airworthy with Battle of Britain Memorial Flt, Coningsby*
Supermarine 517	VV106	1948	1975	ex Colerne, Cardington, Halton 7174M. *Fleet Air Arm Museum, Yeovilton, stored*
Supermarine Swift FR.5	WK281	1956	c 1979	ex Swinderby, Finningley, Colerne 7712M, Northolt, 79. *RAF Museum, on loan to Tangmere Military Aviation Museum, Tangmere*
Watkins CHW	–	1909	1959	on loan from C H Watkins, Cardiff. *National Waterfront Museum, Swansea*
Westland Whirlwind HCC.12	XR486	1964	1981	8727M, ex 32 Sqn, Queen's Flt, 32 Sqn, QF. *Became G-RWWW. The Helicopter Museum, Weston-super-Mare*

Note: * – Illustrated in the colour sections.

Rolls-Royce test pilot Harvey Heyworth flying Messerscmitt Bf 109E DG200 on a sortie out of Hucknall, Notts, in February 1941. Harvey was too tall to fly with the canopy hood down, so had it removed! This aircraft was part of the Historic Aircraft Collection and is now at Hendon. *MAP*

Publicity hand-out for the St Athan collection.

St Athan's Historic Aircraft Collection was renowned for getting the engines running on several of its exhibits – see the colour section. This policy extended to the many powerplants held – a Gnome rotary delighting audiences in 1986. *RAF St Athan*

The Fiat CR-42 'arrived' in the UK following a forced-landing at Orfordness, Suffolk, on 11th November 1940. It was salvaged and evaluated at Farnborough.

The bright red Watkins 'Robin Goch' at St Athan in February 1974.

The Fairey Battle in the workshop hangar at St Athan, March 1985. *RAF St Athan*

The team from RAF Leeming that recovered the Battle from its resting place in Iceland during 1973. Standing, fifth from the left is Flt Lt Len Woodgate, the expedition leader. *via Len Woodgate*

A major restoration project at St Athan was Bristol Beaufighter TF.X RD253 (left). Alongside is the engineless RD867 which was sent to Canada in 1969 in an exchange for the Bolingbroke that is now on show at Hendon. *RAF St Athan*

Martin-Baker's ejection seat test-bed Meteor T.7/8 WA634 during a ground-level firing. The aircraft was basically a T.7 two-seater, but fitted with a tail under from an F.8. *Martin-Baker*

CHAPTER 7

Private Sector
British Historic Aircraft Museum and the
Historic Aircraft Museum
1967 to 1983

There are two phases to the story of the museum at Southend Airport. The two ventures shared some airframes in common, but in their capabilities and aspirations they could not have been more different.

In Chapter 5 the British Historic Aviation Museum was mentioned as having its origins at Biggin Hill. Wanstead-based Anthony John 'Tony' Osborne had gathered two Hawker Sea Furies and a North American Mitchell at the Kent airfield. Also at Biggin was the Historic Aircraft Preservation Society, the concern that had brought former French Navy Avro Lancaster G-ASXX to the UK from Australia. Both of these bodies entertained hopes of a collection of national status on the former Battle of Britain fighter station.

It seems that there was no love lost between them. This showed itself in the January 1967 issue of *Spitfire*, the journal of the BHAM's supporter 'wing'. A piece by-lined 'Director General' (that was Tony Osborne's title) stated: "Due to the lack of co-operation between the management of Biggin Hill aerodrome and our museum, it is with deep regret that I have to inform our members and friends that an alternative site is being sought for the museum. The situation has been aggravated by the attitude of [name with-held – KE] and the HAPS who are not willing to co-operate in any way with the establishing of this, the first NATIONAL museum." [The capitals are those of the *Spitfire*.]

"SPITFIRE"
The Journal of the
British Historic Aircraft Museum

SEPTEMBER 1967

Above: Ekco's bulbous-nosed Avro XIX radar test-bed and the Blackburn Beverley in HAM's generously-sized aircraft park, September 1972. *Stuart Howe*
Right: The September 1967 issue of 'Spitfire', the journal of the BHAM.

Southend choice

By May 1967 Tony Osborne was in a position to announce that the BHAM was negotiating with the airport authorities at Southend for a 6-acre site. Mr Osborne had certainly pulled out all the stops in his search for exhibits. First to arrive were the 'founders' from Biggin Hill: Sea Fury WJ244 and the Mitchell in 1966 with the other Sea Fury following in May 1967. Aerial deliveries commenced on March 14, 1967 when Avro Anson C.19 G-AVHU, registered eleven days earlier to Mrs Lesley Anne Osborne, touched down from Shawbury. Five days after the Anson, it was the turn of Percival Proctor IV G-AOBW.

Then came real 'heavy metal' in the shape of the former Cranfield and Napier aerodynamic test-bed Avro Lincoln B.2 G-APRJ which arrived on 9th May. It had been registered to AJO in his capacity of 'Trustee of the Assets of the British Historic Aircraft Museum'. Built at Baginton, Coventry, as RF342 it was taken on RAF charge in June 1945. Destined for the Telecommunications Flying Unit, it went there via Airwork at Langley in November 1948. During its days with the TFU at Defford, it was fitted with the nose, from the pilot's windscreen forward, of Lancaster I TW911. (From March 1946 TW911 served with Armstrong Siddeley as a test-bed and was dismantled at Bitteswell in 1952.) After radar and avionics trials work, RF342 joined Napier at Luton for icing trails in January 1959 and became G-APRJ, later G-29-1. In November 1952 it moved to Cranfield for further test work by the College of Aeronautics. As related in Chapter 3, this machine replaced Lancaster PA474 at the College of Aeronautics, Cranfield, Beds – PA474 now of course flies with the Battle of Britain Memorial Flight. Beyond Southend, this machine went on to a complex life – more of this in Chapters 13 and 25.

The Lincoln in September 1959, during its days with Napier. On its spine is an airfoil section and in front of that a rig that would spray water on to the leading edge for icing trials. *D Napier & Sons*

Appeals had been made to governments far and wide for presentations to the new museum. The Swedes responded with a SAAB J29, which in 1951 was the first swept-wing jet fighter type to enter service in Europe,. This was gifted to the UK in a ceremony at the RAF College, Cranwell, before it flew on to Southend on 13th June. Another machine *alleged* to have been donated by a government to the museum and/or Great Britain was Noorduyn-built Harvard IIb which flew with the Swiss Air Force as U-322. This was G-AXCR registered to Mrs Osborne on 27th March 1969 but was exported to West Germany and *Charlie-Romeo* was cancelled on 1st September 1969, becoming D-FHGK in its new home.

Mr Osborne also ran Target Towing Aircraft Ltd (TTA), a company specialising in the acquisition and operation of former military types. On 8th November 1968 half-a-dozen former RAF Shawbury-based Central Air Traffic Control School Percival Provost T.1s were registered to TTA as G-AWTB to 'G. They were all cancelled as sold in West Germany – the same destination as the Harvard – via an owner with a Coventry address on 24th March 1969. TTA then took delivery of former Rolls-Royce test-bed Gloster Meteor NF.14 G-ASLW on 4th July 1969. This machine ditched in the Atlantic off Cape Verde on 6th November 1969; the pilot ejected and was picked up by a passing ship. Another NF.14, WS804, formerly with the Royal Aircraft Establishment, Thurleigh, was registered to TTA as G-AXNE on 28th August 1969. It was abandoned following a forced landing at Bissau in Portuguese Guinea, Africa, on or about the 21st September. This intriguing story is told in painstaking detail by Mike Draper in Chapter 11, 'The Meteor Job', of his exceptional book *Shadows: Airlift and Airwar in Biafra and Nigeria 1967 to 1970* (Hikoki, Aldershot, 1999). Various problems including investigations in April 1970 into the export of the Meteors meant that Tony Osborne's dream of establishing the BHAM at Southend was dashed. On the eastern perimeter, the airframes started to languish and, in the airport office, to run up ramp fees.

Renaissance

The airport authorities were as patient as they could be, but historic aircraft quickly become eyesores when unattended and the grass grows long. There would come a time when they would have to be sold off, or more likely scrapped. In need of much care and attention they may have been, nevertheless this collection still represented a 'instant' museum. A consortium was formed to try again as part of a development involving massive investment on the western boundary, not far from the threshold of Runway 06. Today, the buildings still survive, surrounded by other structures, but in those days the site offered views of activities at the airport. Budge Brothers Ltd of Romford and Canterbury Management Co Ltd of Basildon created a huge, glass-walled display hall, reception area, shop and cafetaria, workshop space and offices. Also in the complex was the Airport Hotel, including the 'Zero Six' disco, the de Havilland banqueting suite and the Concorde restaurant. As noted in Chapter 4, Skyfame was the UK's first 'pure' aviation museum; here was a wider interpretation that did not put all the eggs in one basket, the aviation heritage content was *part* of a broader package.

The HAM building in July 1972, shortly after it was opened.

Historic Aircraft Museum (Southend) Ltd in Aviation Way was inaugurated with a grand opening ceremony on 27th May 1972 and air display. TV and radio personality and aviation enthusiast Keith Fordyce was the commentator – see Chapter 11 for his own museum venture. The first curator was John Widdall and he was followed by W H 'Bill' Gent. Leslie Hunt, based at Leigh-on-Sea and author of the incredible worldwide survey of aviation heritage, *Vintage Aircraft*, took up the role of honorary historical adviser. Bill Gent, who also became chairman of the volunteer organisation, the Historic Aircraft Society, had been a keen supporter in the BHAM days and had helped to run the BHAM Association.

HAM's first souvenir booklet and the very popular publicity hand-out that included instructions so that it could be folded into a high-performing paper dart, complete with roundels on the wings!

Ringing the changes

The surviving BHAM airframes were put through a restoration and spruce-up programme in 1971 while the building phase moved on apace. More exhibits were sourced and as a major alteration to the skyline, Blackburn Beverley C.1 XB261 flew in from Boscombe Down, Wiltshire, on 6th October. This huge airlifter first took to the air at Brough on Humberside on 5th July 1955 and served all of its life with the Aeroplane & Armament Experimental Establishment as a general load-shifter and on air-drop tests.

In the space of a decade HAM received two avionics test-beds of very different eras and formats. Built at Yeadon, Leeds, in mid-1945 as a civil version of the Anson, Avro XIX G-AGPG was used by the manufacturer until it joined to Skyways Coach Air at Lympne, Kent, in July 1961. In October 1967 it replaced Anson I G-ALIH with Ekco Electronics as a bulbous-nosed radar test-bed at Southend. *Papa-Golf* was withdrawn from use in 1971 and the following year went on display at the HAM, for a reported £300. Delivered to Elstree on 15th January 1960, Piaggio P.166 G-APWY quickly passed to the McAlpine Group at Luton. The Marconi Company acquired it in May 1967 to act as a flying laboratory and general transport; for the former role the lower rear fuselage was modified to allow the fitment of test equipment. Retired in early 1981, *Whisky-Yankee* was presented on loan to the HAM, arriving there on 18th February. With the closure, G-APWY made one last flight, to the Science Museum's out-station at Wroughton on 1st June 1983 to become a member of its somewhat reclusive collection.

Marconi's Piaggio P.166 visiting Southend in July 1973.

Acquiring a 'Heinkel' from the 1969 film *Battle of Britain* was a gifted move. Southend's G-AWHB was one of two CASA-built Heinkel He 111H-16s with Rolls-Royce Merlin 500-20-2s flown from Tablada, Spain, for the UK end of the filming. Designated 2-111B by CASA it was issued to the Spanish Air Force as B2I-57 on 3rd December 1951. *Hotel-Bravo* was ferried Tablada–Jersey–Duxford on 21st May 1968 and when all was 'in the can' was stored at West Malling in Kent. In March 1972 it moved to Southend to become a 'star' item at the opening of HAM. Auctioned on 10th May 1983 it fetched £26,000 going to the still-born London War Museum – for that story, see Chapter 24.

'Battle of Britain' CASA 2-111 G-AWHB in late 1968, at the end of filming.

Gifted by the Belgian government, F-84F Thunderstreak FU-6 during its official hand-over, November 1973.

Management at HAM quickly adopted the concept of hangarage 'arrangements' for owners of airworthy, or other interesting, aircraft. As other venues have discovered since, this can lead to sudden removals of exhibits, but does give variety. Located on the edge of the airport, a taxiway allowed movements to and from the museum. Taking advantage of this was Tony Haig-Thomas, who based his extensive 'squadron' of de Havilland Moth types with HAM. Over the years, Tony has operated a variety of types, including Grumman TBM-3R Avenger G-BTDP, which he based at North Weald, Essex, from January 1989 until it was sold in Switzerland in 2006. Today, he is an aviation trustee at the Shuttleworth Collection and flies Piper L-18C G-BLPE. The winter of 1981-1982 brought a small 'invasion' as the replica aircraft from Thorpe Park in Surrey sheltered from the climate – see Chapter 14.

Several Stampe biplanes 'lodged' with HAM, including G-AXYW, which flew with the famous Rothmans team.

During an intensive time in November 1973, warbird operator Ormond Haydon-Baillie had three of his treasures flown from Canada to Southend: Silver Star CF-IHB (Canadian version of the Lockheed T-33 'T-Bird') on the 9th, Sea Fury FB.11 CF-CHB on the 24th and Silver Star CF-EHB on the 30th. His plan was to operate his growing warbird 'stable' from HAM. En route to Harwich docks at that point was a large consignment of Fairchild-built Bolingbroke IVT airframes and engines for a planned restoration to put a Blenheim back into UK skies. The following year, Ormond moved to Duxford – more of this in Chapters 12 and 16.

Ormond Haydon-Baillie's Silver Star 'Black Knight' in the HAM's display hall, April 1974.

Sea Fury CF-CHB outside the HAM after its epic transatlantic ferry flight, November 1973.

Another era

As 1982 ended, visitor figures at HAM were not a source of joy. Since November 1973 Queens Moat Houses plc had run the museum-hotel-entertainment complex under a management contract and subsequently purchased the entire site. The company took the decision that the museum building could be more profitably employed in another way. Besides this the struggle to keep the airframes on external display in good condition was a major headache. In the preface to the sale catalogue, this was explained: "Queens Moat Houses have regretfully decided that in the best interests of all concerned it would be more advantageous to sell the exhibits individually to those who have not only the means but the enthusiasm to care for these unique machines". Auction house Phillips was called in and a sale of the aircraft and extensive support material was held on 10th May 1983 with former RAF Beverley navigator Jeremy Collins overseeing proceedings. Eighteen of the exhibits were put under the hammer; Widgeon G-ANLW, on loan to HAM from Southend operator Helicopter Hire, was offered on behalf of its owners and six other light aircraft were also put into the sale. (See the table for the museum aircraft in the auction.) Aircraft and artefacts that had been on loan were dispersed back to their owners.

The prospects of someone buying the Beverley were not good, but Ian Huddlestone became the owner of all 79,234lbs, 38ft 9in high and 162ft span of it, for £3,200. (That would be around £13,000 in present-day values.) Ian came to an arrangement with the hotel and leisure complex so that the giant served as an awesome 'gate guard' for the HAM building that had been transformed into 'Roller City'. The inevitable happened in early May 1989 and XB261 was scrapped on site. The sheer bulk of the Beverley and time constraints mitigated against a re-location and rescue. The Duxford Aviation Society succeeded in acquiring the cockpit section and today it is on show at the Newark Air Museum.

Proof that there is nothing new under the sun occurred 27 years later. On 20th July 2010 a huge crane delicately positioned two former Royal Australian Air Force Hawker Siddeley HS.748-2s in the grounds of the Skylark Aviation Hotel at Southend. Both of the twin-turboprops had been in storage since 2005. Formerly the Essex County Hotel, the Skylark is located on Aviation Way on the westerly perimeter of Southend Airport. That's just a bit further along the road from where aviation heritage and property development combined in another era.

Historic Aircraft Museum

Type	Identity	Built	Arrived	Background / *current status, or fate*
Auster J/1N Alpha	G-AJUO	1947	c 1974	on loan. *Damaged beyond repair in Essex, 2 Jan 1976*
Avro Anson C.19	TX211	1946	14 Mar 1967	G-AVHU, ex Shawbury, 12 Group Comm Flt, Sch of Land-Air Warfare, 31 Sqn, Sch of Photography, 3 Group Comm Flt. *Scrapped on site, Jul 1972*
Avro XIX Series 2	G-AGPG	1945	c 1972	ex Pye, Ekco, Avro. # £2,800. *Stored Hooton Park, Cheshire*
Avro Lincoln B.2 *	RF342	1946	9 May 1967	ex Cranfield, G-APRJ / G-36-3, Napier G-29-1, G-APRJ, RF342, Telecommunications Flg Unit, Defford. # £8,500. See also Chapters 13 and 25. *Majority with Australian National Aviation Museum, stored. Nose at Flying Heritage, Seattle, USA*
Blackburn Beverley C.1 *	XB261	1955	6 Oct 1971	ex Boscombe Down. # £3,200 *Scrapped on site May 1989. Cockpit with Newark Air Museum*
De Havilland Moth	G-ATBL	1933	c 1973	on loan, ex Swiss HB-ABA and CH-353. *Somerset owner, airworthy*
De Havilland Puss Moth	G-AEOA	1931	c 1975	on loan, ex Booker, RAF ES921, 5 Group Comm Flt, 1660 Conv Unit, 5 Gp CF, Air Transport Aux. *Essex-based owner*
De Havilland Tiger Moth	G-ANPE	1940	c 1981	on loan, ex France F-BHAT, G-ANPE, RAF T7397, 19 Res Flg Sch, 18 Elementary Flg Tng Sch. *Hampshire owner, airworthy*
De Havilland Tiger Moth	G-APMM	1942	c 1972	ex RAF DE419, 21 Elementary Flg Tng Sch. *Sold in Sweden Mar 1990*
De Havilland Tiger Moth	DE208	1942	c 1972	G-AGYU, on loan. *Worksop owner, airworthy*
De Havilland Fox Moth	G-ACEJ	1933	c 1972	on loan, ex Giro Aviation, Scottish Motor Traction Co. *Northamptonshire owner, airworthy*
De Havilland Dragon *	G-ACIT	1933	Jun 1971	on loan, ex Beagle – Rearsby, Blackpool, BEA Scottish, Highland Airways. # £28,000. *Science Museum, Wroughton*
De Havilland Leopard Moth	G-ACLL	1934	c 1977	on loan, ex RAF AW165, Airborne Forces Exp Est, 7 and 6 Anti-Aircraft Co-op Units, Ringway Stn Flt. *Isle of Man owner, stored*
De Havilland Hornet Moth	G-ADLY	1935	c 1972	on loan, ex RAF, W9388, 526 Sqn, 3 and 4 Coastal Patrol Flts, G-ADLY Lindsay Everard – *Leicestershire Foxhound II. Netherlands-based owner, airworthy*

Type	Identity	Built	Arrived	Background / *current status, or fate*
De Havilland Dragon Rapide	G-AIUL	1944	1972	remained dismantled, ex British Westpoint, RAF NR749, Kemble, 2 Radio School. *Stored at Chirk, Wales*
De Havilland Moth Minor	G-AFNG	1939	c 1972	on loan, ex RAF AW122, Empire Air Armament Est, Wyton and Binbrook Stn Flts, G-AFNG. *Isle of Man owner, stored in Galway, Ireland*
De Havilland Vampire T.11	XD527	1954	c 1972	ex Aviation Traders, HSA, 8 Flg Tng Sch, RAF College, Central Flg Sch, 9 FTS. *Scrapped c 1977*
De Havilland Vampire T.11	XK625	1956	20 Mar 1973	ex Woodford, St Athan, 8 and 7 Flg Tng Schs. *Brenzett Aeronautical Museum Trust*
DH Australia Drover II	'VH-FDT'	1952	19 May 1967	ex Squires Gate, G-APXX, Australia VH-EAS. # £ 1,700. See also Chapters 9 and 13. *Stored, Booker, Bucks*
English Electric Lightning F.1	XG325	1959	c 1975	cockpit, on loan, Wattisham, Foulness, Aeroplane & Armament Exp Est. *No.1476 Sqn Air Training Corps, Rayleigh*
Fairchild Argus I	G-AJOZ	1942	c 1967	ex Sywell, RAF FK338, Kemble, Air Transport Aux, 2 Ferry Pool, USAAF 42-32142. *Yorkshire Air Museum, Elvington*
Fairchild PT-26 Cornell	N9606H	1942	c 1971	ex USA, RCAF FJ662, USAAF 42-15491. See also Chapter 19. *Under restoration as G-CEVL in Lincolnshire*
Fiat G.46-4 *	–	c 1949	1971	ex Shoreham, Northolt, Italian Air Force. # £3,400. *Under restoration in Norwich*
Fieseler Fi 156C-3 Storch	D-EKMU	1943	1972	ex D-EKMU, OE-ADR, Swedish AF Fv3812, Luftwaffe. # £24,000. See also Chapter 24. *Fantasy of Flight, USA*
Gloster Meteor T.7	VZ638	1949	12 Jan 1972	ex Kemble, College of Air Warfare, RAF College, 237 Op Conv Unit, 501 Sqn, Biggin Hill Stn Flt, Fighter Command Comm Sqn, 85, 54, 25 and 500s Sqns. # £6,500. See Chapter 23. *Registered as G-JETM, Gatwick Aviation Museum, Charlwood*
Gloster Javelin FAW.9	XH768	1957	c 1972	ex Cranwell 7929M, 29, 11 and 25 Sqns. # £1,000. *To West Germany Aug 1983*
Hawker Typhoon Ib	–	1941	21 Nov 1981	on loan, returned to owner circa 1982
Hawker Sea Fury FB.11	CF-CHB	1951	24 Nov 1973	on loan – see Chapter 12, ex Canada, Cold Lake, Australia, Royal Aus Navy 724 Sqn. *Registered as N895HW, Washington State, USA*
Hawker Sea Fury FB.11	WJ244	1952	c 1966	ex Biggin Hill, Dunsfold, Fleet Requirements Unit, 801 Sqn. *Became G-FURY, take up the story in Chapter 18.*
Hawker Sea Fury FB.11 *	WJ288	1949	6 May 1967	ex Biggin Hill, Dunsfold, Fleet Requirements Unit, 1833, 1832 and 804 Sqns. # £34,000. See also Chapter 13. *Was UK registered as G-SALY, USA, registered as N15S*
Hawker Sea Hawk FGA.6	XE489	1955	20 May 1967	ex Fleet Requirements Unit, 806 Sqn. # £6,500. Became G-JETH – see Chapter 23. *Majority sold in Netherlands Aug 1989*

Continued on page 99

Nash Collection: Avro 504K 'E449' at Abingdon, Oxfordshire, September 1967. *Roy Bonser*

Nash Collection: Fokker D.VII 8417/18 at Henlow, Beds, 1969.

Nash Collection: Sopwith Camel F6314 at Abingdon, Oxfordshire, June 1968. *Roy Bonser*

Loughborough College: Hawker Sea Hurricane I Z7015 at Old Warden, Beds, September 1963. *Roy Bonser*

Loughborough College: Supermarine Spitfire V AR501 at Old Warden, Beds, May 2004. *Ken Ellis*

Cranfield: BAC TSR-2 X0-4 XR222 at Cranfield, Beds, June 1974. *Roy Bonser*

Cranfield: Boulton Paul P.111A VT935 at Cranfield, Beds, May 1963. Background left to right: Tempest II, Supermarine 545, Sabre Mk.5, CF-100 Canuck, Me 163B-1 Komet. *Roy Bonser*

Cranfield: Percival Q.6 G-AEYE at Cranfield, Beds, May 1963. *Roy Bonser*

Cranfield: Somers-Kendal SK.1 G-AOBG at Cranfield, Beds, May 1963. *Roy Bonser*

Cranfield: Westland Wyvern TF.1 VR137 at Yeovilton, Somerset, 1967.

Skyfame: Airspeed Oxford I V3388 at Staverton, Glos, September 1965. *Roy Bonser*

Skyfame: Avro Anson I G-AMDA with the London School of Flying at Elstree, Herts, June 1962. *Roy Bonser*

Skyfame: Avro York C.1 'LV633' at Staverton, Glos, July 1968. *Roy Bonser*

Skyfame: de Havilland Mosquito TT.35 RS709 at Staverton, Glos, April 1967. *Roy Bonser*

Skyfame: Miles Magister I G-AFBS at Staverton, Glos, April 1967. *Roy Bonser*

Skyfame: Handley Page Hastings C.1A TG528 at Staverton, Glos, July 1968. *Roy Bonser*

Skyfame: Saunders-Roe SR.A.1 TG263 at Staverton, Glos, April 1967. *Roy Bonser*

Historic Aircraft Preservation Society: Avro Lancaster VII NX611 at Biggin Hill, Kent, May 1965. *Roy Bonser*

Historic Aircraft Preservation Society: Avro Lancaster VII NX611 at Biggin Hill, Kent, June 1967.

Historic Aircraft Preservation
Society: Canadair Sabre 19607 at
Biggin Hill, Kent, May 1968.

Colerne: Consolidated PBY-6A Catalina L-866 at Colerne, Wilts, June 1975.

Colerne: Consolidated Liberator VI HE807 / KN751 at Colerne, Wilts, July 1974.

Colerne: Mosquito TT.35 TJ138, 1966.

Colerne: Gloster Meteor NF.14 WS838 at Colerne, Wilts, June 1975.

Colour plate section 1

Colerne: Handley Page HP.115
XP841 at Farnborough, Hants,
September 1962. *Roy Bonser*

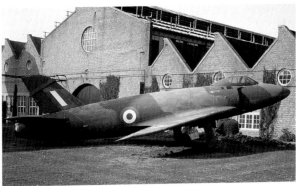

Colerne: Supermarine 510 VV106
at Cardington, Beds, April 1964.
Roy Bonser

Finningley: Avro 707C WZ744 at
Finningley, Yorks, September 1968.
Behind: Avro 707A WZ736 and
Hastings C.1A TG605. *Roy Bonser*

Finningley: Percival Provost T.1 7957M at Finningley, Yorks, September 1968. *Roy Bonser*

Finningley: Short SB.5 WG768 at Finningley, Yorks, September 1968. *Roy Bonser*

Finningley: Supermarine Swift FR.5 WK281 at Finningley, Yorks, September 1970.

St Athan: Focke-Wulf Fw 190F-8/U1 584219 at St Athan, Wales, September 1984. *Alan Curry*

St Athan: Junkers Ju 87D-3 494083
at Hendon, London, June 1975.

St Athan: Kawasaki Ki-100-1b 16336
at St Athan, Wales, September
1986. *Alan Curry*

Historic Aircraft Museum: Avro Lincoln B.2 RF342 at Southend, Essex, June 1970.

Historic Aircraft Museum: Blackburn Beverley C.1 XB261 at Southend, Essex, October 1971.

Historic Aircraft Museum: CASA 2-111B G-AWHB at Southend, Essex, June 1976.

Historic Aircraft Museum:
de Havilland Dragon I G-ACIT at
Sywell, Northants, April 1962.
Roy Bonser

Historic Aircraft Museum: Hawker
Sea Fury FB.11 WJ288 at Biggin
Hill, Kent, September 1966.

Historic Aircraft Museum: Fiat
G.46 at Southend, Essex,
September 1975.

Historic Aircraft Museum: North American TB-25J Mitchell 'HD368' at Southend, Essex, May 1977. Behind is Beverley C.1 XB261.

Historic Aircraft Museum: Percival Proctor IV G-ANZJ at Baginton, Warks, April 1966. *Roy Bonser*

Historic Aircraft Museum: SAAB J29F 29640 at Southend, Essex, March 1968.

Wales Aircraft Museum: North American F-100D Super Sabre '63000' at Cardiff Airport, Wales, June 1991.

Lasham: Airspeed Ambassador G-ALZO at Gatwick, Sussex, October 1966. *Roy Bonser*

Lasham: Avro York G-ANTK at Lasham, Hants, July 1965. *Roy Bonser*

Lasham: Gloster Meteor F.8 WH291 of 85 Squadron, May 1974. *Roy Bonser*

Strathallan: Avro Shackleton T.4 VP293 at Strathallan, Scotland, August 1977. Behind is Comet 2R XK655.

Strathallan: de Mosquito TT.35 RS712 at Strathallan, Scotland, July 1979. *Alan Curry*

Strathallan: Hawker Hurricane XII
'P3308' at Strathallan, Scotland,
July 1979. *Alan Curry*

Strathallan: Westland Lysander III
'V9441' at Strathallan, Scotland,
April 1985.

Strathallan: Reid and Sigrist Desford
VZ728 at Rochester, Kent, 1973.

Torbay: de Havilland Tiger Moth
G-ANSM at Sibson, Cambs, June
2009. *Ken Ellis*

Torbay: de Havilland Sea Venom
FAW.22 XG629 at Higher Blagdon,
Devon, June 1979.

Torbay: Westland Dragonfly HR.5 WN499 at Higher Blagdon, Devon, June 1979. *Ken Ellis*

Haydon-Baillie: Avro Canada CF-100 Canuck Mk.4B 18393 at Duxford, April 1975.

Haydon-Baillie: Canadair Silver Star Mk.3 G-OAHB at Duxford, October 1974.

Haydon-Baillie: Hawker Sea Fury FB.11 WH589 at Duxford, October 1974.

Haydon-Baillie: North American
P-51D Mustang I-BILL, 1977.

Warbirds of Great Britain: Boeing
B-17G Flying Fortress G-FORT at
Bitteswell, May 1987. *via Roy
Bonser*

Warbirds of Great Britain:
CASA 2-111B G-BDYA at
Blackbushe, September 1976.

Warbirds of Great Britain: CASA 352L G-BECL at Blackbushe, September 1976.

Warbirds of Great Britain: Hawker Sea Fury T.20S 'DW-A' at Blackbushe, September 1976.

Warbirds of Great Britain: North American P-51D Mustang G-PSID crossing the Lutterworth Road at Bitteswell, March 1987. *Roy Garner via Roy Bonser*

Thorpe Park: Fokker D.VII static replica at Chertsey, Surrey, May 1982.

Thorpe Park: Sopwith Camel 'C1701' and Fokker Dr.I '102/17' replicas at Chertsey, Surrey, May 1982.

Thorpe Park: Supermarine S.5 scale replica 'N220' at Chertsey, Surrey, May 1982.

British Aerial Museum: Auster AOP.9 XR241 at Middle Wallop, Hants, June 1982. *Roy Bonser*

British Aerial Museum: Beech 18 3TMs G-BKGL and G-BKGM at Duxford, Cambs, September 1982.

British Aerial Museum: Max Holste Broussard 92 at Duxford, Cambs, July 1983.

British Aerial Museum: Morane-Saulnier MS.502 Criquet 'FI+S' at Duxford, September 1981.

Vintage Aircraft Team: Sandy Topen with de Havilland Vampire T.11 WZ507 at Duxford, Cambs, 1981.

Vintage Aircraft Team: de Havilland Vampire FB.5 VZ304 in 'Aerodrome' colours as 'Z-77' at Duxford, Cambs, November 1982.

Vintage Aircraft Team: The 'cast' of 'The Aerodrome' at Duxford, Cambs, October 1982. Left to right: T-33s 'Z-86' and 'Z-47', Vampire T.11 'Z-52', Vampire FB.5 'Z-77' and Meteor NF.14 'Z-14'.

Vintage Aircraft Team: Lockheed T-33A '91007' at Duxford, Cambs, August 1985.

Spencer Flack: Hawker Sea Fury T.20S G-BCOW at Blackbushe, Hants, April 1976.

Spencer Flack: Hawker Sea Fury FB.11 G-FURY, July 1981.

Spencer Flack: Hawker Hunter F.51 G-HUNT, June 1980.

Spencer Flack: North American P-51D Mustang 511371 at North Weald, September 1988. *Ken Ellis*

Spencer Flack: Supermarine Spitfire FR.XIV G-FIRE, June 1981.

Loughborough Leicestershire: Avro Vulcan B.2 G-BLMC at East Midlands Airport, Leics, February 1985.
Peter Green

Patrick Lindsay: Fiat G.46 G-BBII at Rochester, Kent, August 1975.

Patrick Lindsay: Morane-Saulnier MS.230 G-AVEB at Booker, Bucks, September 1971.

Patrick Lindsay: Sopwith Triplane 'N5430' at Duxford, Cambs, May 1983.

Hunter One: Gloster Meteor TT.20 WM167 at Blackbushe, Hants, April 1976.

Hunter One: Hawker Hunter F.51 G-HUNT at Hurn, Dorset, September 1985. Behind is Hawk Sea Hawk FB.5 G-SEAH.

Hunter One: Hawker Hunter composite at Biggin Hill, Kent, July 1986. *Alan Curry*

Hunter One: Hawker Hunter T.7 G-BOOM at Biggin Hill, Kent, May 1983.

Hunter One: Supermarine Swift F.7 XF114 at Cranfield, Beds, June 1966. *Roy Bonser*

Whitehall Theatre: Hispano Buchón 'Yellow 14' at Duxford, Cambs, May 1982.

Charles Church: Pilatus P.2-06 'CC+43' at Old Warden, Beds, August 1996. *Sam Tyler*

Charles Church: Supermarine Spitfire V 'EE606' at Popham, July 1989. *Doug Hall*

Wessex: de Havilland Dragon Rapide G-ACZE at Woburn Abbey, 1988. *Sam Tyler*

Wessex: de Havilland Leopard Moth G-AIYS at Old Warden, Beds, June 1988. *Roy Bonser*

One That Got Away: Miles Marathon CF-NUH at Wymeswold, March 1963. *Roy Bonser*

One That Got Away: Aviation Traders Carvair G-AOFW at Southend, July 1978. *John Uncles*

One That Got Away: Boeing 707-436 G-APFJ at Cosford, Shropshire, April 1985. *Alan Curry*

ONES THAT GOT AWAY

Cierva Air Horse, 1958

On page 31, readers were left with a conundrum about the fate of a pioneer Cierva Autogiro – the C.9 of 1930. Post war, the Cierva Autogiro Company was based at Eastleigh, near Southampton, then and now famous as the birthplace of the Spitfire. By 1946, the design team had abandoned the 'free-wheeling' gyroplane concept and was convinced that a large capacity helicopter would find a ready military and civilian market. The outcome was the then world's largest rotorcraft, powered by a 1,620hp (1,208kW) Rolls-Royce Merlin driving *three* rotors on out-riggers. It could carry 24 passengers, or a jeep, or a crop-spraying rig. Two prototypes were ordered against Specification E19/46 with construction shared between Cierva and Cunliffe-Owen, the latter also located at Eastleigh. The first ungainly Air Horse, VZ724 (also allocated the civil registration G-ALCV – illustrated), flew at Eastleigh on December 8, 1948 but was involved in a fatal accident on 13th June 1950. By that time the under-capitalised company was struggling and no orders were on the horizon. On 22nd January 1951, Saunders-Roe bought out Cierva and took on its Skeeter light helicopter for production. The Cowes-based company wanted nothing to do with the Air Horse and so the second machine, WA555 (also G-ALCW), was put into store at a Ministry of Supply depot at Byley, near Middlewich in Cheshire. If this seems odd, it is possible that it was hoped to resurrect what was now an 'orphan' design. Its continued existence was speculated upon well into the 1960s. The very first edition of *Wrecks & Relics* laid this to rest; WA555 had been scrapped in March 1958.

One That Got Away: Miles Marathon, 1963

Miles Marathon IA CF-NUH lasted in open store at Wymeswold until it was scrapped in 1963. In 1964 G-AMHT was scrapped at Shoreham and the type became extinct in the UK. (JA6009 held on at Nagoya in Japan until the early 1970s.) CF-NUH had first plied the skies as VR-NAT of West African Airways from 1952. It returned to the UK in 1955 and became XJ831 with the Royal Aircraft Establishment at Farnborough. In 1958 Air Navigation and Trading at Squires Gate added it to the incredible list of types it had owned or operated. As G-AMHV it served them briefly, being retired in mid-1960. It then flew to Wymeswold for a Canadian customer, but it got no further than Leicestershire. *(See colour section.)*

ONES THAT GOT AWAY

One That Got Away: Boeing 707-436, 2006

When Rolls-Royce Conway powered Boeing 707 G-APFJ touched down at Cosford, Shropshire, on 12th June 1981 it joined the growing British Airways collection at what was then the Aerospace Museum, later to become the RAF Museum, Cosford. It had first flown at Seattle, Washington, on 9th September 1960 and joined the fleet of British Overseas Airways Corporation on the 22nd. It was briefly leased to Malaysian Airlines Systems from 1971 to 1975 and on 23rd February, 1977 joined the air charter division of British Airways, Airtours. In early January 2006 it was announced that British Airways and the RAF Museum were reviewing the future status of the 'British Airways Collection' and by the summer the airliners had been dispersed. The 707 was scrapped on site during August and the forward fuselage moved to a new life at the National Museum of Flight Scotland, East Fortune. *(See colour section.)* Another -436, G-APFG, had been in use for a long time as an instructional airframe at Stansted Airport, Essex. It was broken up in early 1989 and the fuselage moved by road to one of the cavernous former airship hangars at Cardington, Bedfordshire (illustrated) for trials with smoke-hoods and other aids to cabin evacuation. Its job done, the fuselage was scrapped in April 2000 and the cockpit section is now preserved in Worcestershire.

One That Got Away: ATEL Carvair, 1983

Big John was the 12th Aviation Traders Carvair conversion, making its first flight at Stansted on 11th February 1964. Built by Douglas at Chicago in July 1947, it served the USAAF as a C-54 Skymaster and, after demob in June 1946, served PanAm and Alitalia, among others. In December 1955 Southend-based operator Air Charter acquired it as G-AOFW. Then it became a Carvair for British United Air Ferries. Leased briefly to Aviaco of Spain 1964-1965, in September 1967 ownership was transferred to British Air Ferries and G-AOFW became *Big John*. In January 1976 G-AOFW was withdrawn from use and parked up at Southend. In September 1978 CF-EPV was scrapped at Southend and *Big John* became the only intact survivor in the UK. It was announced that it would be preserved as a 'monument' to the type outside BAF's engineering base. G-AOFW was scrapped on site in November 1983. For one reason or another not even that amazing bulbous forward fuselage, elevated cockpit and swing-nose could be saved – the essence of the Carvair. A sad loss to the UK's airliner heritage. *(See colour section.)*

Historic Aircraft Museum continued from page 96

Type	Identity	Built	Arrived	Background / *current status, or fate*
Heinkel He 111 (CASA 2-111B) *	G-AWHB	1951	c Mar 1972	ex *Battle of Britain* film, Spanish AF B2I-57. # £26,000. See also Chapter 24. *Flying Heritage Collection, USA*
Lockheed (Can) Silver Star Mk.3	CF-EHB	1958	30 Nov 1973	on loan – see Chapter 12, ex Royal Canadian Navy, RCAF, 21640. *Became G-WGHB, under restoration at Norwich*
Lockheed (Can) Silver Star Mk.3	CF-IHB	1954	9 Nov 1973	on loan – see Chapter 12, ex Royal Canadian Navy, RCAF, 21261. *Became G-OAHB, G-JETT, N33VC. As G-TBRD, crashed on take-off at Duxford 6 Sep 2006.*
Mignet HM.14 'Flying Flea'	G-ADXS	1935	c Sep 1963	on loan, ex Staverton, – see Chapters 4, Southend. See also Chapter 19. *Real Aeroplane Co, Breighton, Yorks*
Mignet HM.293	G-AXPG	1972	c 1972	on loan. *Stored in Sussex*
Miles Magister I	G-AIDF	1939	c 1967	wrecked in gale at Southend 5 Sep 1967. ex RAF P6411, Church Fenton Comm Flt, 68 Sqn, 24 Elementary Flg Tng Sch, 23 Elem & Reserve FTS. *Scrapped circa 1969*
Miles Gemini 1A	G-AKGD	1947	1972	*scrapped on site, c 1974*
North American Harvard IIB	LN-BNM	1943	May 1972	ex LN-BNM, Danish AF 31-329, RCAF, 41 SFTS, FE905, USAAF 42-12392. # £6,000. See also Chapter 24. *Royal Air Force Museum, Hendon*
NAA VB-25N Mitchell *	N9089Z	1944	1966	ex Biggin Hill, USAAF 44-30861. # £6,200. *Registered as G-BKXW, stored at Booker, Bucks*
Percival Proctor IV *	NP303	1944	1967	ex G-ANZJ, RAF NP303, 23 Group Comm Flt, 4 Radio Sch. # £2,200. See also Chapter 24. *UK, current status uncertain*
Percival Proctor IV	G-AOBW	1944	19 Mar 1967	ex Stanmore, Elstree, RAF NP339, 4 and 1 Radio Schs. *Remains scrapped c 1970*
Percival Provost T.1	WV483	1953	1971	ex St Athan 7693M, 6 Flg Tng Sch. # £3,000. See Chapter 13. *Sold in the USA c 1986*
Piaggio P.166	G-APWY	1959	18 Feb 1981	ex Marconi. *Science Museum, Wroughton*
Pilatus P.2-05	G-BONE	1950	6 Aug 1981	on loan, ex Swiss Air Force U-142. *To the USA Feb 2004*
Republic F-84F Thunderstreak	FU-6	1952	14 Nov 1973	on loan, ex Belgian Air Force, USAF 52-7133. *RAF Museum, Cosford, 'deep store'*
Roe Triplane Type I	–	1964	1971	on loan. *On loan to Museum of Science and Industry, Manchester*
SAAB J29F *	29640	c 1954	13 Jun 1967	ex Swedish Air Force. *Midland Air Museum, Coventry*
Saunders-Roe Skeeter AOP.12	XL811	1959	1972	on loan, ex 9/12 Lancers, 17 Flt, 652 and 651 Sqns. *The Helicopter Museum, Weston-super-Mare*
Short Scion II	G-AEZF	1937	c 1972	on loan, fuselage frame. *Stored at Redhill, Surrey*
Stampe (SNCAN) SV-4B	G-AXYW	1946	c 1972	on loan, ex France F-BBPF. *To Australia Jun 1981*
Stampe (SNCAN) SV-4B	G-AWIW	1947	25 Oct 1974	ex Colerne – see Chapter 6, Rothmans team, F-BDCC. *Privately owned, stored at Cosford*
Stampe (SNCAN) SV-4C Coupe	G-AYLK	1949	c 1972	on loan, ex France F-BDNR. *Written off 1971*

Type	Identity	Built	Arrived	Background / current status, or fate
Stampe (AIA) SV-4C	G-AZNF	1949	c 1972	on loan, France F-BGJM, French military No.1101. *Re-registered as G-HJSS Sep 1992, airworthy, London owner*
Supermarine Spitfire XVI	TB863	1945	c 1970	on loan, ex Henlow, *Battle of Britain* film, Pinewood, *Reach for the Sky*, 3 Civilian Anti-Aircraft Co-op Unit, 17, 691, 183 and 453 Sqns. Became G-CDAN then New Zealand ZK-XVI. *Temora Aviation Museum, Australia, as VH-XVI*
Thruxton Gadfly HDW-1	G-AVKE	1967	Jan 1973	on loan, ex Thruxton. *The Helicopter Museum, Weston-super-Mare, stored*
Vickers Viscount 812	G-ATVE	1959	Jun 1972	cockpit, Channel Airways, Treffield Int, Channel, Continental Airlines USA N254V. # *To West Germany Jul 1983*
Westland Dragonfly HR.3	WG760	1951	c 1969	ex Blackbushe. *Damaged in a fire in a shed at Southend Jul 1972, scrapped*
Westland Widgeon	G-ANLW	1958	c 1982	ex Helicopter Hire. # £8,000. *Norfolk and Suffolk Aviation Museum, Flixton*
Westland Widgeon	G-APTW	1959	1976	on loan, ex Helicopter Hire. *North East Aircraft Museum, Sunderland*
Westland P.531 Mk.1	XP165	1960	Jul 1975	ex Royal Aircraft Est. *The Helicopter Museum, Weston-super-Mare*

Note: * – Illustrated in the colour sections. Aircraft marked # were entered into the 10th May 1983 auction.

CHAPTER 8

Wings of the Principality
South Wales Historical Aircraft Preservation Society and the Wales Aircraft Museum
1967 to 1996

Where is the best place to locate an aviation museum? The answer has to be an airport or airfield, preferably the former, surely? Commercial reasons abound... Good communications by road and maybe even rail. Loads of potential 'punters' either waiting for a departure, or to greet an arrival, or just wanting to watch the flying. Then there is access to the runway, allowing for the airborne delivery of new exhibits or even the occasional air event or full-blown flying display.

There are downsides... Airport directors and airfield managers are in business, there to make money and are unlikely to see the word 'heritage' or the expression 'visitor experience' very high on their 'to do' list. (Increasingly, the British public sees shopping as a leisure pursuit and most airports offer 'retail therapy' in shedloads.) Airports in particular are places of considerable flux, with building developments making demands of available acreage; car parking will take greater precedence over almost every other need. Surrounding land will have high values and rents are leases will reflect this.

There are examples of airports with an enlightened approach to viewing facilities and the exhibition of historic aircraft as a complement to the day-to-day job of running a bustling commercial enterprise. But there are museums and similar bodies who *have* learned the hard way about the fluctuations of the 'pros' and 'cons' noted above. At some point in the future, others *will* experience this. As well as this one, Chapters 4, 5, 7, 9, 10 and 20 relate to museums, or 'would-be' ones, with location at an airport or airfield as major part of the 'business plan' – if they had one, that is!

Above: Buccaneer S.1 XN928 in the WAM compound at Cardiff-Wales Airport in mid-1991.

First in Wales

On 1st March 1967 the South Wales Historical Aircraft Preservation Society was founded by Malcolm F Sketchley in Cardiff. As with other groups, see Chapter 15 on the Humberside experience for example, early collection zeal gave way to a rationalisation of the rag-tag of early airframes acquired and the acquisition of military jets. In 1975 another body, the South Wales Aircraft Preservation Society was established with the aim of starting a museum at Cardiff Airport, known locally as Rhoose. SWAPS had a great relationship with nearby RAF St Athan – see Chapter 6 – and it was there that they acquired the 'founder' airframe, the prototype Auster AOP.9. This machine, WZ662, first flown at Rearsby in Leicestershire on 19th March 1954 was a good start. 'First-of-breed' provides self-evident provenance and, in this case, the variant marked the end of Auster's series production for military customers. Today it flies in Devon and it is possible that, but for SWAPS, it might not have survived.

The prototype Auster AOP.9 WZ662 showing off its short take-off capabilities at its birthplace, Rearsby, in 1955. This was an early member of the Wales collection and today is airworthy again and based in Devon. *Auster*

Negotiations with the airport management allowed the volunteers to place airframes on site and in September 1976 a display park, the Wales Aircraft Museum, was opened to the public. This was the Principality's only dedicated aviation museum. Today, that accolade is held by the Caernarfon Airport Airworld Museum which is indeed located on an airfield. From the opening, SWAPS announced plans to establish an engine display building and, eventually, a hangar; these goals were never achieved.

Five engines

A look through the table reveals a massive list of airframes; size can matter but substance tends to endure. Over the years WAM made a name for itself through its lively acquisition policy and its imaginative repaints of some of its airframes. Of the former, there were no less than *five* Canberras (including two cockpits, one of which was a 'boiler-plate' PR.9) brought to the airport in the decade beginning 1983 and a trio Fairey Gannets materialised in the space of four years. Of the latter, in 1993 the Varsity was bedecked in Royal New Zealand Air Force colours, despite that air arm never possessing an example!

The fuselage of the Viscount 732 with 'Wales Aircraft Museum' titles was used as the gift shop for some of its time with the collection.

Two of the most significant exhibits with WAM were cockpit sections and both were saved by the direct intervention of members, and both were Avros. In the mid-1970s the forward fuselage of WB491, the last of six Type 706 Ashton purpose-built trials and test-bed aircraft, powered by four Rolls-Royce Nenes, was deposited on the south-east perimeter of Hawker Siddeley's Dunsfold airfield in Surrey. It was used for security training by the county's police force, but quickly it became evident that the gutted fuselage was unsuitable. Members of WAM recognised it for what it was and whisked it off to Cardiff in 1984. First flown at Woodford near Manchester on 2nd August 1951, Ashton 2 WB491 was delivered to the Royal Aircraft Establishment at Farnborough the following month and prepared for its turbojet testing role by Napier at Luton by installing a special cradle under the centre section. Fitted with a Rolls-Royce Conway, it took to the air as a five-jet on 20th August 1955. Later it was fitted with an Avon and in 1958 another variant of the Conway before retirement the following year.

Avro Ashton WB491 during its time with the Royal Aircraft Establishment as a test-bed – note the fifth engine under the centre section. *MAP*

Production Vulcan B.1 XA903 first flew from the same runway at Woodford on 10th May 1957 and was initially involved in trials of the Blue Steel stand-off bomb. On 3rd January 1964 it was ferried to Filton, Bristol, where Bristol Siddeley technicians readied it to become a five-jet. A Concorde powerplant, a Rolls-Royce Olympus 593, was fitted into a nacelle similar in geometry to that of the supersonic airliner's and installed where the bomb door had been. It first flew in this guise on 9th September 1966. At Cambridge in 1971 it was re-jigged a to take the Turbo-Union RB.199 turbofan that would power the Panavia Tornado and XA903 took to the air in the new guise on 19th April 1973. Its work complete the delta was retired at Farnborough on 22nd February 1979. In September 1984 the test-bed was scrapped and WAM acted swiftly to secure the nose of a second five-engined Avro test-bed.

Vulcan B.1 XA903 flying with an icing rig under the nose and a Rolls-Royce Olympus 593 engine mounted where the bomb bay would have been, circa 1966. *Rolls-Royce*

End of the line

More or less as the cockpit of Vulcan XA903 arrived at Rhoose, members of WAM were expressing worries about the future prospects at the airport. In 1989 the museum was asked to re-locate within the airport site and this was achieved over the winter. On the northern boundary British Airways had embarked upon the construction of an enormous engineering base to look after its Boeing 747 fleet and the previous WAM was to be swallowed up. The new area for WAM was smaller and the occasion was taken to rationalise the collection.

In 1991 WAM took on the legal entity Aircraft Museum (Wales) Ltd. This reflected the acquisition of the collection by Pat Collins, who had developed the Barry Island Pleasure Park. On 21st September 1995 a Westland Lynx engineering mock-up arrived and it transpired that it was the last of many airframes to be displayed at the airport. In January 1996 Mr Collins announced that WAM was to close imminently and its airframes sold or scrapped. In an interview with the South Wales Echo, Pat explained: "We have been beaten by the weather and cash problems." The 15th edition of *Wrecks & Relics* covered the closure and summed up as follows: "Plagued with site troubles... the collection here saw huge expansion in the late 1970s and early 1980s from which it never really recovered; a classic case of too much, too soon, and no hangar."

End of the line, the former WAM compound in late February 1996, Vulcan B.2 XM569 falling to the scrapman. *Colin Mears*

South Wales Historical Aircraft Preservation Society and the Wales Aircraft Museum

Type	Identity	Built	Arrived	Background / *current status, or fate*
Auster AOP.6	–	c 1947	c 1970	frame. *To Stockport APS, Handforth, c 1975*
Auster AOP.9	WZ662	1954	c 1972	prototype, ex St Athan, Bedminster, St Athan, 656 Sqn, 2 Flt. *Airworthy as G-BKVK, Exeter owner*
Auster AOP.9	–	c 1955	c 1972	fuselage frame, ex Berkswell, Midland APS. Rearsby. *Stored at Fairwood Common, believed scrapped there c 1970*
Avro Ashton 2	WB491	1951	1980	nose, ex Dunsfold, Farnborough, Royal Aircraft Est. *Newark Air Museum, Newark*
Avro Vulcan B.1	XA903	1956	1984	cockpit, ex Farnborough, RB.199 and Olympus engine test-bed, Blue Steel trials. *Wellesbourne Wartime Museum, Wellesbourne Mountford*
Avro Vulcan B.2	XM569	1963	2 Feb 1983	ex 44 Sqn. Waddington Wing, 27 Sqn, Cottesmore Wing, 27 Sqn. *Scrapped on site Feb 1996, cockpit stored at Jet Age Museum, Staverton*
BAe Jetstream 41	–	c 1990	1995	engineering fuselage mock-up, ex Hatfield, Prestwick, Jetstream 200 G-ATXJ. *To the airport fire crews by Feb 1996*

Type	Identity	Built	Arrived	Background / *current status, or fate*
Blackburn Buccaneer S.1	XN928	1962	c 1977	ex St Athan 8179M, 736, 809, 801 Sqns. *Scrapped on site Feb 1996, cockpit with private owner, Gravesend, Kent*
Dassault Mystère IVA	59	1956	24 Oct 1978	ex Sculthorpe, French Air Force. *Scrapped on site Feb 1998*
De Havilland Tiger Moth	?	?	1967	stored at Fairwood Common. *Believed scrapped c 1970*
De Havilland Vampire T.11	WZ425	1952	31 May 1973	ex Woodford, St Athan, 5 Flg Tng Sch, RAF College, 229 Op Conv Unit, Central Gunnery Sch. *Private collection, Birlingham, Worcs*
De Havilland Venom NF.3	WX788	1954	c 1977	ex Bledow Ridge, Connah's Quay, DH trials. *Cockpit at Aeroventure, Yorks*
De Havilland Venom FB.4	WR539	1956	1982	ex Cosford 8399M, Kai Tak, 28 and 60 Sqns. *De Havilland Aircraft Heritage Centre, London Colney, stored*
De Havilland Sea Venom FAW.22	XG737	1957	1977	ex Yeovilton, Fleet Requirements Unit, Sydenham, 894, 893 and 891 Sqns. *Aeropark, East Midlands Airport*
De Havilland Sea Vixen FAW.2	XN650	1961	25 Apr 1979	ex Culdrose A2612/A2639, Royal Aircraft Est – Thurleigh, 892 Sqn. *Cockpit with private owner, Spanhoe, Northants*
English Electric Canberra B.2	WP515	1951	1993	cockpit, ex St Athan, 100, 85 Sqns, College of Air Warfare, RAF College, 231 Oper Conv Unit, 109, 12 Sqns. *To Germany Jan 2005*
English Electric Canberra PR.7	WH798	1954	1984	fuselage, ex St Athan, 31, 17, 13, 80, 17, 100 and 542 Sqns. *Cockpit with Suffolk Aviation Heritage Centre, Ipswich*
English Electric Canberra PR.7	WT518	1955	1983	fuselage, ex St Athan 8691M, 31, 80 and 31 Sqns. *To the airport fire crews by 1991*
English Electric Canberra PR.9	–	?	3rd Feb 1988	cockpit, ex Brough, Boscombe Down. *On loan, Newark Air Museum*
English Electric Canberra T.17	WJ576	1953	1983	composite, ex St Athan, 306 Sqn, Swifter Flt, 231 Oper Conv Unit. *Cockpit at Boulton Paul Aircraft Heritage Project, Wolverhampton*
Fairey Gannet	?	?	c 1974	composite fuselage, ex Llangennech. *Stored at Fairwood Common, thought scrapped there*
Fairey Gannet AEW.3	XL449	1958	25 Sep 1978	ex Lossiemouth, 849 Sqn. *Scrapped on site Feb 1996, cockpit stored at Camberley, Surrey*
Fairey Gannet AS.4	XA459	1956	4 Apr 1979	ex Culdrose A2608, Lee-on-Solent, 831 Sqn. *Private owner, White Waltham, Berks*
Fairey Gannet T.5	XG883	1957	12 Apr 1983	ex Yeovilton, 849 Sqn. *Museum of Berkshire Aviation, Woodley*
Gloster Meteor T.7	WL332	1952	1977	on loan, ex Croston, Moston, Fleet Requirements Unit, Lossiemouth and Ford Stn Flts. *Stored at Long Marston, Warks*
Gloster Meteor F.8	WE925	1951	1977	fuselage, composite, ex Tarrant Rushton, 229 Oper Conv Unit, 34, 43, 92, 64, 63 and 64 Sqns. *Last recorded in East Midlands, 1999*
Gloster Meteor TT.20	WM292	1953	Oct 1982	ex Yeovilton, Fleet Requirements Unit, Kemble, 527 Sqn. *Fleet Air Arm Museum, Yeovilton*
Grunau Baby	–	?	1967	ex Swansea Gliding Club. *Stored at Fairwood Common, destroyed in a faire 1969*
Hawker Sea Hawk FGA.6	WV795	1954	c 1977	nose section, ex Culdrose A2661, Halton 8151M, Sydenham, 738, 806, 700 Sqns. *Aces High, Dunsfold, Surrey*

Type	Identity	Built	Arrived	Background / *current status, or fate*
Hawker Sea Hawk FGA.6	WV826	1954	1979	ex Fairwood Common, Culdrose A2532, Lossiemouth, 738 Sqn. *To Malta 10 Aug 1999*
Hawker Hunter F.51	E-409	1956	1979	ex Dunsfold G-9-437, Danish Air Force. *City of Norwich Aviation Museum*
Hunting Jet Provost T.3	XN458	1960	1993	ex St Athan, Halton 8334M, Shawbury, 1 Flg Tng Sch. *At public house at Northallerton, Yorks*
Lockheed T-33A	29963	1952	1978	ex Sculthorpe, French Air Force, USAF. *Scrapped on site Feb 1998*
McDonnell Phantom FGR.2	XT911	1969	1993	cockpit, ex St Athan, 92, 19 Sqns, 228 Oper Conv Unit. *Removed from the site and scrapped 1995*
NAA F-100D Super Sabre *	42160	1954	1978	ex Sculthorpe, French Air Force, USAF. *Scrapped on site Feb 1998*
Percival Proctor V	G-AHTE	1946	1975	ex Fairwood Common, Llanelli. *Under restoration at Great Oakley, Essex*
Percival Provost T.1	WW388	1954	1984	ex Llanelli, Chinnor, Chertsey, Cuxwold, Chessington, Halton, 2 Flg Tng Sch. *Private owner, Newport, Shrop*
Percival Pembroke C.1	WV753	1957	1977	ex St Athan 8113M, 207 Sqn, Southern Comm Sqn, Fighter Command, Bomber Command and Far East Comm Sqns, 81 Sqn. *To the airport fire crews by Aug 1992*
Saunders-Roe Skeeter AOP.12	XN351	1960	1980	Ex Higher Blagdon – see Chapter 11, Wroughton, 3 Royal Tank Regiment, 652 and 651 Sqns. *Privately owned, reg'd as G-BKSC, stored Ipswich area*
Slingsby Tutor glider	–	?	1967	ex Swansea Gliding Club. *Stored at Fairwood Common, believed scrapped there*
Vickers Varsity T.1	WJ944	1953	13 Apr 1976	ex 6 Flg Tng Sch, 1 Air Nav Sch, 5 FTS, 1 ANS, 2 ANS, Central Nav and Control Sch. *Scrapped on site Feb 1996, cockpit to Netherlands*
Vickers Valiant BK.1	XD826	1956	1986	cockpit, ex Abingdon, Stratford, Cosford 7872M, 543 Sqn, 232 Oper Conv Unit, 138, 90 and 7 Sqns. *The Cockpit Collection, Rayleigh, Essex*
Vickers Viscount 732	'G-WHIZ'	1955	c 1977	G-ANRS, fuselage, ex Cambrian, British Eagle, Misrair Egypt as SU-AKY, G-ANRS, Hunting, Middle East Airlines, Lebanon as OD-ACH, G-ANRS Hunting Clan. *To the airport fire crews by 1991; scrapped Feb 1996*
Vickers Viscount 802	G-AOJC	1956	1976	ex British Airways, BEA. *Broken up on site, fuselage removed Feb 1996*
Westland Dragonfly HR.3	WG718	1950	13 Jun 1979	ex Yeovilton A2531, Culdrose, Fleetlands. *Used for spares by Yorkshire Helicopter Pres Group, Elvington, 1998*
Westland Whirlwind HAS.7	XG592	1957	Jun 1976	ex Wroughton, 705, 846 and 705 Sqns. *Paintball centre, Cowbridge, Wales*
Westland Whirlwind HAR.10	XJ409	1954	13 Jun 1979	ex Wroughton, Warton SAR Flt. *Last recorded at Llanbedr, Wales, 2007*
Westland Wessex HAS.1	XM300	1962	1 Jul 1984	ex Farnborough. *Stored for the National Museum of Wales*
Westland Lynx	–	?	21 Sep 1995	engineering mock-up. *Removed from site Jan 1996*

Note: * – Illustrated in the colour sections.

CHAPTER 9

Hampshire Independence
Dan-Air Preservation Group, Lasham
1970 to 1991

Preservation activity at Lasham in Hampshire centred on two very different organisations; both of which determinedly went their own way. At the airliner engineering base on the westerly perimeter, crucial work was carried out by employees of the much-loved carrier, Dan-Air. Without them, the Airspeed Ambassador would be extinct and the precious 'population' of Avro Yorks halved. As discussed in Chapter 8, airports are not in the heritage business; neither are airlines, both function to make money. Over the decades, UK museums have been fortunate to benefit from the foresight and altruism of bosses. But this generosity is not a right. Chiefs come and go and with them policies and attitudes, airlines merge, or more often fold, with regularity.

Above: Aerial reconnaissance; courtesy of the Lasham Gliding Society: Ambassador G-ALZO in August 1986 shortly before 'The Elizabethans' descended upon it. *Alan Curry*

That being the case, we should be thankful when an organisation such as Dan-Air comes along. Bosses, flight crew, engineers and enthusiasts combined to make sure that they did what they could to help the UK's aviation heritage. By 1972 the Dan-Air Preservation Group was an active 'label' for the individuals looking after a couple of venerable, retired, 'propliners'. A decade later, DAPG announced that it had ceased operations, but individuals would continue to cherish the historic airliners. The 'group' as such was always a loose amalgam, hence the dates given in the heading extend well before, and after, its term of office.

So we should turn now to 1964 and the local Air Scouts who regularly availed themselves of the gliders on the airfield; at times camping on site. In 1955, the maintenance centre at Lasham and eventually the wholly-owned subsidiary Dan-Air Engineering Ltd was set up. On 30th April 1964, York G-ANTK flew its final service and was retired. Its capacious fuselage, and *reasonably* flat floor lent itself to becoming an unusual bunkhouse for the Air Scouts, and it was presented to them. (The last York flight ever was by G-AGNV on 9th October that year to the Skyfame Museum – see Chapter 4.) By the early 1970s, the York was suffering from the Hampshire climate and countless 'sleep overs', and its significance was well appreciated. On 7th May that year former British Overseas Airways Corporation de Havilland Comet 4 G-APDK was withdrawn and, thanks to the airline's management, the Air Scouts entered the jet age. *Tango-Kilo* became the *second* DAPG airframe. By 1979, the Air Scouts were no longer 'dorming' at Lasham and G-APDK was broken up the following year.

Comet 4 G-APDK in service as a bunkhouse for the Air Scouts at Lasham. *Jonathan Garraway*

The first aircraft deliberately preserved was the final Douglas Dakota flown by the airline, G-AMPP. Retired in September 1970, it was put on display outside the engineering offices. To confuse all and sundry, it was painted up as G-AMSU. This was not for devilment; *Sierra-Uniform* was Dan-Air's founder aircraft, starting its career in June 1953.

A moment of history came on 26th September 1971 when Ambassador G-ALZO embarked on its last revenue-earning flight from Gatwick to Jersey and return. On the 29th *Zulu-Oscar* flew a 'Champagne Charter' to Reims for airline employees and friends and then positioned to Lasham. From there the ultimate Ambassador flight was staged early in October when a Rolls-Royce Spey was flown out to Zagreb, Yugoslavia, to a stranded BAC 1-11. Returning to Lasham, it joined three others of its type (G-ALZR, G-AMAE and 'H') awaiting the scrapman's torch. By late 1972 G-ALZO was the sole survivor of the 23 built and the decision was made that it would be looked after by DAPG.

Contraction

Former RAF Comet C.4 G-BDIV was retired from Dan-Air service on 12th November 1979 and it too moved into the care of the DAPG. This was a short-lived arrangement as it was scrapped in May 1985. At the busy maintenance base, space was always at a premium and residual values for spares and/or scrap were always to be considered. Besides, in comparison to the other types, in those days the Comet was not considered an 'endangered species'.

By 1985, much thought had been given to the Ambassador and the York and they were donated to the Duxford Aviation Society. That organisation was embarking on an impressive collection of airliners to go alongside the military hardware at the Imperial War Museum at Duxford, Cambs. A team from the DAS arrived to dismantle the York ready for the road journey to its new home. For obvious reasons, they called themselves 'The Yorkies' and *Tango-Kilo* left on 23rd May 1986. When plying the airways for British European Airways, Ambassadors were known as the 'Elizabethan' Class and because of this, the DAS crew that descended upon Lasham to take apart G-ALZO were 'The Elizabethans'. Essentially the same determined bunch that worked on the York, the eight stalwarts signed the hull and painted on the legend 'Moved Faster than Epsom Salts'! The 'Lizzie' departed on 16th October 1986.

That left the 'gate guardian' Dakota. On February 28th 1991 Dan-Air Engineering Ltd was sold to FLS Aerospace. Suddenly, the 'Dak' had no relevance and it was acquired by Aces High and trucked out to North Weald, Essex, on 20th December 1991. It was exported to France the following year, for use in a theme park and by September 2005 was destroyed for a sequence in a film on the Berlin Airlift being shot in Poland. The cockpit apparently, lives on with the local enthusiast. Sales of assets like the Lasham operation helped to stave off some of the problems the airline was facing but in October 1992 came the announcement that Dan-Air had been acquired by British Airways and a fondly-remembered name disappeared.

Dan-Air Preservation Group

Type	Identity	Built	Last service	Background / *current status*, or fate
Airspeed Ambassador *	G-ALZO	1952	Oct 1971	ex Dan-Air, Handley Page, Jordan AF 108, BEA. *Duxford Aviation Society, Duxford*
Avro York *	G-ANTK	1945	30 Apr 1971	ex Dan-Air, RAF MW232, Fairey, 511 and 242 Sqns. *Duxford Aviation Society, Duxford*
De Havilland Comet 4C	G-BDIV	1962	12 Nov 1979	ex Dan-Air, RAF C.4 XR397, 216 Sqn. Scrapped May 1985
Douglas Dakota IV	G-AMPP	1944	Sep 1970	ex Dan-Air, Scottish Airlines, trooping serial XF756, RAF KK136, Military Mission Belgium, 147 Sqn, USAAF 43-49456. See main text and Note [1] below

Note: * – Illustrated in the colour sections. [1] Dakota *Papa-Papa* was painted as 'G-AMSU', Dan-Air's first aircraft and the one with which it commenced operations in June 1953.

Second World War Aircraft Preservation Society, Lasham
1979 to 2009

For 30 years, the Second World War Aircraft Preservation Society opened its collection up to the public, providing a warm and willing welcome. Throughout that time, members maintained a steadfast independence; they did things their way. With the death of Bob Coles, the leading light for most of those decades, the decision was taken to dissolve SWWAPS in October 2009. It was at once a sad, but wise, conclusion. Like so many voluntary organisations, it was not cash or know-how that was lacking; the closure reflected Bob's much-missed dynamic but more so the increasingly rare commodity of willing – and ideally younger – hands.

During its existence some pundits jibed at the title – none of the airframes could boast a 1939-1945 pedigree. But then few organisations of SWWAPS's stature and era could aspire to such gems. The collection owed its origins to founder Ralph Colombo, later to become Life President, and aviation archaeology and research of wartime airfields was central to the material amassed at his Basingstoke, Hampshire, home. It was here that the first airframe, a 1956-built Auster AOP.9, was taken on 14th August 1977 having been acquired, gale-damaged, from Thruxton.

That Hampshire airfield-cum-racetrack was considered for a while as a possible base, but in the end the choice of Lasham, near Alton, was gifted. The SWWAPS compound was on the north-east perimeter, close to the threshold of Runway 27. As well as admiring the museum, visitors had great views of the never-ceasing activities of the Lasham Gliding Society and the occasional comings and goings of airliners at the maintenance base on the west side. During the formative years of SWWAPS, the latter was run by a division of the charismatic airline, Dan-Air, and Lasham was the 'centre of gravity' of de Havilland Comet operations. (See above for more on Dan-Air.)

Above: View from a glider of the SWWAPS compound in August 1994. Clockwise from the bottom left: Sea Hawk, Starfighter, Wessex, Drover, Sea Prince, Meteor NF.13 and Meteor F.8. *Ken Ellis*
Opposite page: Lasham's Drover, during its days at Southend in August 1969. *Alan Curry*

The SWWAPS founder airframe, Auster AOP.9 XK418. *Ken Ellis*

Rare bird

SWWAPS members were the first to say that the airframes were not of earth-shattering provenance. As all were displayed outside, this was as well. The most interesting was the second to last to be acquired and unique in the northern hemisphere. Twenty-three de Havilland Australia Drover tri-motor 'bushplanes' were built at Bankstown, New South Wales, under the designation DHA-3, using elements of the DH Dove from 1948 to 1955. This machine, VH-EAS, arrived at Blackpool, Lancashire, by road on 20th September 1961 for Air Navigation and Trading who planned to operate it as G-APXX but it did not fly in the UK. Built as Mk.1 in 1952, it was delivered to QANTAS in July, being progressively upgraded to Mk.2 by 1954. From Blackpool, the Drover was roaded to Southend for the planned museum there – see Chapter 7 – arriving on 19th May 1967 and later gaining Royal Flying Doctor Service colours as 'VH-FDT'. When the contents of the Historic Aircraft Museum were auctioned on 10th May 1982 it was acquired by Doug Arnold (Chapter 13) for £1,700 and moved to Blackbushe, Hampshire. Recognising it was a rarity; SWWAPS took it on in July 1985. At the time of writing, the tri-motor is in store pending a new owner.

Among the honorary members of SWWAPS was AVM J E 'Johnnie' Johnson and warbird pioneer Spencer Flack. Here we return to Bob Coles who owned several of the exhibits under the banner of Classic Aeroplane International. Bob was employed by Hawker Siddeley and then British Aerospace and had the privilege of working under Sir Sydney Camm at the Kingston-upon-Thames design office. The bulk of his time was on the Harrier and Hawk programmes at Dunsfold, Surrey, but he cut his teeth on the Hunter and maintained a life-long love of the thoroughbred. It was Bob that managed to get Spencer Flack the Hunter F.51 that became the iconic G-HUNT – see Chapter 18 – and he had a major hand in the acquisition of the SWWAPS Starfighter. The SWWAPS Hunter was Spencer's 'spares ship' and arrived at Lasham as a 'thank you'. Bob's name can be found within the 'credits' of many a UK restoration project. When Bob died on 13th January 2009, the preservation community lost a modest yet determined man and, before the end of the year, the collection he is most associated with.

Second World War Aircraft Preservation Society

Type	Identity	Built	Arrived	Background / current status, or fate
Auster AOP.9	XK418	1956	by Jul 1979	ex Thruxton, Middle Wallop instructional 7876M, 19 MU, 654 Sqn, Light Aircraft Sqn. Private owner, Devon
De Havilland Vampire T.11	XE856	1954	Oct 1981	ex Welwyn Garden City, Woodford, Chester, St Athan, 219 Sqn, North Weald Stn Flt, 226 OCU. Bournemouth Aviation Museum, Hurn, registered as G-DUSK
De Havilland Australia Drover II 'VH-FDT'		1952	1985	See main text and Chapters 7 and 13. Stored, Booker, Bucks
Gloster Meteor F.8 *	WH291	1951	15 May 1980	ex Kemble, 229 OCU, 85 Sqn, CAW, 257 Sqn. See also Chapter 12. Stored, Booker, Bucks
Gloster Meteor NF.13	4X-FNA	1953	1981 / 1982	ex Israel, IDF-AF, WM366, A&AEE, RRE – composite. Stored, Enstone, Oxfordshire
Hawker Hunter F.51	E-423	1956	1979	ex Elstree, Bittesell, Dunsfold G-9-444, Dan AF, Esk 724. Stored, Enstone, Oxfordshire
Hawker Sea Hawk FGA.6	WV798	1954	1981	ex Chertsey – see Chapter 14, Culdrose A2557, FRU, 801, 803 and 787 Sqns. Stored, Booker, Bucks
Lockheed F-104G Starfighter	22+35	1962	19 Aug 1988	ex Luftwaffe Manching, JbG34, KE+413, DD+105. Cold War Jets, Bruntingthorpe, Leics
Percival Prentice 1	G-APIT	1947	1984	ex Biggin Hill, Southend, VR192, 1 ASS, 6 FTS, CFS, 2 FTS, Blackburn. Stored, pending disposal
Percival Sea Prince C.1	WF137	1950	by Jul 1979	ex Yeovilton, Culdrose Stn Flt, Shorts Ferry Unit, Arbroath Stn Flt, 781 Sqn. Stored, Booker, Bucks
Westland Wessex HAS.3	XM833	1962	4 Feb 1983	ex Wroughton. North East Aircraft Museum, Sunderland
Westland Whirlwind HAR.9	XN309	1959	Jul 1981	ex Faygate, Culdrose inst A2663, Wroughton, 705 Sqn. Last known in Cork, Ireland, circa 1992
Westland Whirlwind HAR.10	XP360	1962	6 Mar 1980	ex Fawkham Green, Central Flying Sch, 225 Sqn. Paint ball arena, Herefordshire

Note: * – Illustrated in the colour sections.

CHAPTER 10

Scottish Warbirds
Strathallan Aircraft Collection
1970 to 1988

The can be no better way to start the story of the incredible Scottish warbird collection than to quote from introduction within the first edition of the pocket-sized official guide published in 1974. "The Strathallan Aircraft Collection was begun as recently as 1970 – almost by accident! Sir William Roberts only wanted to obtain a Hurricane when G-AWLW was advertised as before for sale in the magazine *Flight*, along with two two-seat Spitfires (G-AVAV and G-AWGB) and a quantity of spares. This was in December 1969, and the aircraft had participated in the marking of the *Battle of Britain* film. As the vendor was unwilling to accept offers for individual aircraft, after much negotiation the whole package was bought, and the Collection had started. In April 1970 the three aircraft were flown to Shoreham Airport, near Brighton, for general overhaul. Some of the spare parts were also transported to Shoreham. Later, in the summer of 1970, one of the Spitfires (G-AWGB) was sold and shipped to Canada, and now flies under the appropriate registration CF-RAF. In 1971 it was decided to base the aircraft at Strathallan airfield, and the Spitfire was flown to Strathallan in December of that year..."

Above: Lancaster G-BCOH engine-running at Strathallan. *via Dick Richardson*

Right: A ceremony was held to mark the opening up of the Comet to the public. Left to right: Dick Richardson, Major General Peter de Havilland, Sir William Roberts. *via Dick Richardson*

Spitfire two-seater G-AVAV at Elstree with Samuelson Films, circa 1967. This was one of the two that came as a 'package' with Hurricane G-AWLW

Sir William James Denby Roberts had an extensive farm estate, complete with airstrip, at Combwell Priory, near Flimwell in Kent, and it was there that the nascent collection was first assembled. The Priory was not the only property in Sir William's name; the family had owned the stunning Strathallan Castle since 1910. Located to the north of Auchterarder in Perthshire, Scotland, amid lush woodland and within the gentle vale of the River Earn, the estate also boasted a private airstrip in between the castle and the river. During the late 1960s this had been developed into an unlicensed airfield with a 3,280ft grass runway – 28 / 10 – and became the home of the Scottish Parachute Club. Also on site was Strathallan Air Services Ltd, trading as Strathair, an aero engineering company. All the ingredients for a flying museum were there. Early in 1972, Sir William decided to take over the operation of the airfield at Strathallan and to move his warbirds there. This must have been an emotive conclusion as his brother, David, had operated the charter side of Strathair, flying Piper Aztec 250 G-APXN. Among its work, the company flew Scottish shellfish to southern England and into Europe. Tragically, on 24th June 1971 David was killed while piloting Xray-November in a crash on the edge of the estate. The parachute club still operates from Strathallan and has awarded a trophy in honour of David.

Wisely, Sir William decided that if he was to fly his newly-acquired Spitfire and Hurricane he would need to get some hours of experience in a North American Harvard – the ideal intermediary aeroplane. To this end, he purchased G-AZBN in the Netherlands in April 1972. This needed the attention of the engineers at Strathallan and it was totally refurbished. Not long after discovering Bravo-November, Sir William found Texan G-AZJD and he snapped that up as well. From October 1969, Sir William had become the owner of 1966-built Aero Commander 200 G-AWYH and he used this on the long 'commute' between Kent and Pethshire. This sleek machine, the first of its type in the UK, was previously registered to Douglas Arnold Aviation and Shipping Company of Fairoaks, Surrey – it is a small world, see Chapter 13. When shiny Texan Juliet-Delta was rolled out at Strathallan, Sir William took to it and it was in this that he mostly flew between the two locations; the Aero Commander taking a back seat.

Flying museum

As noted above, having gone from one to five warbirds, the seeds had been planted and very quickly a full-blown collection blossomed. A search was started for others and – as will be seen from the table the 1970s witnessed an acquisition spree. To go with this a huge hangar was commissioned and this was ready by 1977. This impressive structure allowed the workshop, previously in buildings alongside, to move so that the majority of the airframes were under the same roof. From an enthusiasts' point of view this was manna from heaven as before aircraft being worked on were not available for public inspection. Entering the 'big hangar' allowed a close look at the airworthy 'fleet', inspection of machines under restoration and a glimpse of things to come in the form of fuselages of types in the 'pending tray' arranged along the side of the building.

That as many of the collection as possible be kept in airworthy trim, or brought up to those standards was part and parcel of the decision to 'go public' in 1970. Days when some of the collection would be informally flown were regular and in 1973 the first full airshow was staged. This was well greeted and did not just rely on the in-house performers, with military participation and other displays. These were to remain a major part of Strathallan's calendar.

The Shuttleworth Collection down at Old Warden, Bedfordshire, had established this formula since the late 1950s. As shown in Chapter 4, Skyfame at Staverton in Gloucestershire had started off in this manner from the 1961, though by the 1970s these were more toned-down affairs. So, while the team at Strathallan had some experience to tap into, the concept of regular shows at a flying museum was still a novelty in the UK. Adding to the small number of full-time staff, a volunteer support organisation, the Strathallan Aircraft Society, was established. To widen the appeal of a visit to the aerodrome, a 'Nostalgia Room' was opened allowing a non-aviation trip down memory lane.

Part of the 'pending tray' within the display hangar at Strathallan in June 1977; Spitfire XIV NH904 later became G-FIRE – see Chapter 18. *Tim R Badham*

All of this and much, much more was the remit of Strathallan's general manager, the genial and indefatigable Dick Richardson. Chapter 3 made mention of Lancaster PA474 and Chapter 5 detailed its move from Henlow in Bedfordshire to Waddington, Lincs, on 18th August 1965. At that time Dick was a Chief Tech on a servicing team in Hangar 4, looking after a four-engined Avro bomber of another generation – the Vulcan. The first Lancaster operation had been staged by 44 Squadron from Waddington on 3rd March 1942 and when PA474 took up residency, that unit was flying Vulcan B.1s from the base.

Dick explains why the Lancaster came to Waddington: "The Station Commander, Gp Capt Arthur 'Bootsie' Griffiths, was keen to get his hands on the 'Lanc' and offered it a home so that it was looked after in readiness for its proposed move to the RAF Museum. Of course the only real was to keep an aeroplane in good shape is to fly it and 'Bootsie' was keen to do this while captaining the aeroplane! One day a mate said to me, 'they've lumbered me with the 'Lanc', Dick'. I said 'I'll look after it' and went to see the Officer Commanding the Mechanical Engineering (Aircraft) Squadron who was delighted to have a volunteer to look after it." On 7th November 1967 PA474 was test flown after a full restoration and it became very much in demand. Dick: "So the occasional display turned into a fairly regular trip hither and thither and soon the aircraft was doing over 50 hours during the summer months. In due course, with Sqn Ldr John Stanley as captain and Flt Lt Ken Sneller as co-pilot we did airshows all over the UK and I stayed with the aeroplane until I left the RAF in 1971 to go down to 'Willie' Roberts's place. Happy days and it was this operation which convinced me that old aeroplanes were the things I wanted to be with. (Having become so popular at airshows, and already having the iconic Mk.I R5868 at Hendon, the RAF Museum relinquished its tenure on Lancaster PA474. It went on to join the Battle of Britain Memorial Flight, at Coltishall, on 20th November 1973. From Strathallan, Dick went on to work for Charles Church – Chapter 25 – and for a long time has run the wonderful aerodrome at Popham, Hampshire.)

Catalogues and publicity hand-outs for Strathallan.

General Aircraft Cygnet G-AGBN under the Lancaster's wing in the 'big' hangar, September 1977.

Well-rounded collection

Sir William was after a well-rounded collection and while he had started with a Hurricane and Spitfires at the 'sharp-end' of warbirds, he was also looking for more practical light aircraft classics of the 1930s through to the 1950s. As well as a goodly selection of de Havilland Moth types, he and his team are to be congratulated on the choice of the Miles M.18, the Fokker Instructor and particularly the General Aircraft Cygnet and the twin-engined Reid and Sigrist Desford Trainer which was called Bobsleigh when it was modified for prone-pilot trials.

One of several imports from Australia, the Dragon during its service with the RAAF.

With a new nose section for a pilot in prone position, Reid and Sigrist Desford VZ728 prior to delivery to RAE Farnborough, summer 1951.

Two heavyweights were also acquired for static display with the intention of allowing the public the chance of inspecting their interiors. The first of these hit the headlines when it arrived; de Havilland Comet 2R XK655 touched down on 21st August 1974 only for its starboard main undercarriage to collapse in the process. Built for British Overseas Airways Corporation in 1953, it was extensively modified for use by 51 Squadron flying electronic reconnaissance sorties monitoring Soviet radio traffic and other 'spook' activities. On 3rd May 1976, the Comet was joined by another specially-modified machine, Avro Shackleton T.4 VP293 a long time servant of the Weapons Flight of the Farnborough-based Royal Aircraft Establishment. This earned fame from its name, *Zebedee*, and several theories were put about as to the origin of this. The most prominent of these was that in an era of high-performance jets and tricycle undercarriages, mastering a large, lumbering four-engined tail-dragger was only achieved after the embarrassment of bounce after bounce on landing! For those of a more recent pedigree, Zebedee was a character in the cult BBC series *The Magic Roundabout* who had a spring instead of legs.

Comet 2R XK655 shortly after its delivery to Strathallan, September 1974. *Roy Bonser*

An Avro Anson was firmly on the 'shopping list' and in 1972 Kemps Aerial Surveys stopped flying two 'Annies' and three purely civilian Avro XIXs and they were parked out at their base at Thruxton, Hampshire, facing an uncertain future. In a situation similar to that of acquiring the Hurricane, the whole fleet (and a Belgian-registered 'spare') made the trek to Scotland. One, *Hotel-Victor*, was flown as part of the warbird 'fleet', one went on to became a source of components in the restoration of T.21 G-BFIR while *Kilo-Xray* embarked upon a painstaking restoration at Woodford and today flies with the Shuttleworth Collection.

Of the Roberts warbirds, the Mosquito took a fair time to return to airworthy condition at West Malling in Kent, flying up to Strathallan in November 1975. A tragic blow to the fortunes of this superb machine was the death of Neil Williams on 11th December 1977. He was a pilot of outstanding abilities and considerable experience on type – see Chapters 5 and 13. The restoration team set to work on the Westland Lysander and it made its first flight at its new home in December 1979. The Hudson from Australia would have been a very welcome sight displaying in UK skies, but would have been eclipsed by an airworthy Fairey Battle.

Anson C.19 G-APHV of Kemps Aerial Surveys parked up at Thruxton, 1972.

Repainted in RAAF wartime colours, the Hudson in the display hangar.

Battle I 1899 under restoration at Strathallan in June 1976. *Ken Ellis*

Roar of the Lancaster

Victory Aircraft at Malton in Canada had come into being to produce Lancaster Mk.Xs for the war effort and the name of this industrial combine expressed beliefs in what the bomber could achieve. Test flying in early 1945, KB976 crossed the Atlantic in May 1945 to join 405 'Vancouver' Squadron RCAF fleetingly at Gransden Lodge, Huntingdonshire, before the unit moved to Linton-on-Ouse in Yorkshire, but did not embark on 'ops'. It returned to Canada after only the briefest of times in the UK and by 1946 was in storage at its birthplace. In 1953 it started a new phase of its career, having been converted for the maritime reconnaissance role as a Mk.10(AR) and it flew on until it was struck off charge on 25th May 1964. It was the last RCAF Lancaster flying and it was ferried to Calgary, Alberta, to join an air museum. It January 1970 it was up and running again, as CF-TQC, having been acquired by Northwest Air Lease of St Albert for conversion into a fire-bomber. This work did not take place and by 1972 it was languishing, prospects uncertain.

Lancaster 10(AR) CF-TQC ready for the ferry flight from Calgary in January 1970 ready for an intended new life as a fire-bomber.

Lancaster G-BCOH during its ferry flight to the UK, 1975. *via Dick Richardson*

    With Dick Richardson's RAF background caring for an airworthy Avro Lancaster, it was not surprising that the team at Strathallan savoured the opportunity to fly *another* example within the UK. Their researches into likely candidates settled on Canada. Dick first clapped eyes on KB976 on 10th April 1974. Bringing it up to a state whereby it could be ferried to the UK was a gargantuan task. UK registered as G-BCOH and carrying the name *Spirit of Caledonia*, the 'Lanc' was ferried from Edmonton to Toronto on 6th May 1975. The following day, captained by P A Mackenzie DSC DFC of British Caledonian, a former Pathfinder Force Lancaster pilot, *Oscar-Hotel* started its second eastwards crossing of the Atlantic, routing via Gander and Reykjavik, arriving at Glasgow on the 20th. It touched down amid much celebration at Strathallan on 12th June.

    Restoring, certificating and operating any of the fleet was a costly and time-consuming process, but the Lancaster took things to a new level. Work to bring it up to UK flight status continued and engine runs were soon being achieved. There was incredible interest in the aircraft and visitors were permanently asking when it would fly. Writing to the author in June 1982, Dick Richardson noted: "If it flies or not remains to be seen. It all depends on what the Civil Aviation Authority require us to do, whether 'Willie' [Roberts] can afford to fly it when airworthy, and most certainly it all depends on the completion of our new, longer, landing strip. About £1,000 per hour is probably *our* cost to fly it; so it's not cheap." We will learn more about the story of KB976 in Chapters 13 and 25.

Trimming down

In the spring of 1981 auction house Christie's announced that it would be staging a sale at Strathallan at 2.30pm precisely on 14th June 1981. This sent shockwaves around the enthusiast world, but to many it had an air of inevitability about it. Visitor figures were not as good as had been hoped for and the costs of looking after a 'live' museum had continued to spiral upwards. A trim down was vital if the rest of the collection was to survive. Included in the sale was Aero Commander 200D G-AWYH, plus engines and aircraft spares. The machines put 'under the hammer' are denoted in the table. Presiding of the sale was the Hon Patrick Lindsay – see Chapter 21. In an interesting twist, the Hurricane – flying 'star' of the collection – was sold for £260,000 to the Davies Trust. This was a Roberts family administered undertaking and the fighter was to stay on at Strathallan. (That sum of money in present-day values would be just over £1 million.) In May 1984 the Hurricane departed to Canada, but was destroyed in a hangar fire in February 1993.

Sir William, writing in the third and last edition of the guide book in 1984, explained some of the pressures the collection was under and why the sale was necessary. "Aircraft which are to fly, be they old or new, have to be maintained to certain standards. These standards are rightly very high, and are generally as laid down by the Civil Aviation Authority and other similar organisations. Over the years it was becoming increasingly difficult and costly to maintain aircraft to those standards *and* still have time left in which to continue with the restoration of other aircraft... It seemed better to concentrate on a lesser number of aeroplanes, and at the same time broaden the appeal of the collection."

Two more airframes, the BA Swallow and an unrestored Tiger Moth, G-ANTS, were entered in the Christie's sale at Duxford on 29th July 1985 – netting £5,000 and £4,200 respectively. This injection of cash would not last long and on 30th September 1988 the hangar doors were shut for the final time. In its day, Strathallan had been a vibrant, imaginative pioneer helping to keep a wide variety of classics flying and helping to put others into hands that would get them back into the skies.

The remainder of the aircraft were disposed of, but Sir William kept three – the Lysander, Magister and Swordfish – within the estate, perhaps hoping that they would form the caucus of a resurrection at some point. On 15th September 1990 the Lysander and the Swordfish were entered into the Sotheby's auction at the company's London salesroom, but did not reach their reserves. Today these machines are airworthy, with the Shuttleworth Trust and the Royal Navy Historic Flight, respectively. Magister R1914 is still cherished in store with the Strathallan estate.

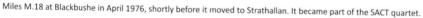

Miles M.18 at Blackbushe in April 1976, shortly before it moved to Strathallan. It became part of the SACT quartet.

There was an ironic sequel to the grand sale of 14th July 1981. Concerned that the Strathallan Collection faced oblivion, a body called the Scottish Aircraft Collection Trust (SACT) was established and it acquired four of the inmates. On 8th August 1981 this quartet – the Hornet Moth, the Miles M.18, the Prentice and the Desford – all moved by road to Perth's Scone airfield, where they were to be restored to flying condition. SACT extended its repertoire on 26th May 1983 when Beech 18 G-BKRN flew in from Prestwick, but this moved off to Cranfield, Bedfordshire, in March 1987 – see Chapter 17. During SACT's tenure only the M.18 reflew, on 26th May 1983. This organisation barely outlasted the set-up it was designed to 'save', winding up its operations in 1989.

Magister R1914 is still kept on the Strathallan estate.

Strathallan Aircraft Collection

Type	Identity	Built	Arrived	Background / *current status, or fate*
Avro Anson C.19/2	VM360	1947	5 Feb 1973	G-APHV, ex Thruxton, RAF VM360, Defford, Aeroplane & Armament Exp Est. *National Museum of Flight Scotland, East Fortune*
Avro Anson C.19/2	G-AWRS	1946	5 Feb 1973	ex Thruxton, RAF TX213, Western Comm Sqn, 22 Gp Comm Flight, Officer Cadet Training Unit, 18 Group, 2 TAF, 2 Group Comm Flts, 527 Sqn, Central Signals Est, 61 Group, Reserve Command Comm Flts. *North East Aircraft Museum, Sunderland*
Avro XIX Series 2	G-AGWE	1946	16 Jan 1973	ex Thruxton, RAF TX201 – no service. See also Chapter 20. *Last reported in Florida, USA, 1998*
Avro XIX Series 2	G-AHIC	1946	16 Jan 1973	ex Thruxton, RAF TX242 – no service. *Broken up for spares, Castle Donington, 1979*
Avro XIX Series 2	G-AHKX	1947	22 Jan 1973	ex Thruxton. # £600. *Airworthy, on loan to Shuttleworth Collection, Old Warden*
Avro XIX Series 2	G-AYWA	1947	1974	ex Thruxton, Belgium OO-VIT, OO-DFA, OO-CFA. *Musée Royal de l'Armée, Brussels, Belgium*
Avro Lancaster Mk.10(AR)	KB976	1945	12 Jun 1975	G-BCOH, CF-TQC, RCAF KB976, RAF, 405 Sqn. *See Chapter 25 for more*
Avro Shackleton T.4 *	VP293	1951	3 May 1976	ex Royal Aircraft Est – Farnborough, Maritime Op Tng Unit, 206, 42 Sqns. Auctioned 29 Jul 1985 £5,000. *Scrapped on site Feb 1990, cockpit preserved*

Type	Identity	Built	Arrived	Background / current status, or fate
BA Swallow II	G-ADPS	1935	Oct 1976	ex Sandown. See also Chapter 26. *Airworthy, Devon owner*
Bristol Bolingbroke IVT	9940	1942	19 Dec 1972	ex Canada, RCAF. # £18,000. *National Museum of Flight Scotland, East Fortune*
Bristol Bolingbroke IVT	10201	1942	1985	ex Canada, RCAF. *Under restoration to return to flight, as G-BPIV, Duxford*
Bristol Sycamore HR.3	WA576	1951	1974	ex Halton 7900M, Royal Aircraft Est, Aeroplane & Armament Exp Est, G-ALSS. # £300. *Dumfries and Galloway Aviation Museum, Dumfries*
De Havilland Puss Moth	VH-UQB	1930	1974	ex Australia, G-ABDW. # £7,500. *National Museum of Flight Scotland, East Fortune*
De Havilland Tiger Moth	G-ANTS	1939	2 Mar 1972	ex Mintlaw, RAF N6532, Bomber Command Comm Flt, Wyton and Benson Stn Flts, 22 Reserve Flg Sch, 22 Elementary Flg Tng Sch, 11 Elementary & Reserve Flg Tng Sch. Auctin 29 Jul 1985 £4,200. *Hong Kong owner, no further details*
De Havilland Tiger Moth	G-AOEL	1939	12 Dec 1975	ex RAF N9510, 7 Flg Tng Sch, 2 Glider Unit, 11, 1 and 7 Reserve Flg Schs, 7 Elementary Flg Tng Sch. *National Museum of Flight Scotland, East Fortune*
De Havilland Tiger Moth	G-APGL	1944	1971	ex Mintlaw, RAF NM140, Light Aircraft Sch, Air Obs Post Sch, 14, 8 Reserve Flg Tng Sch, 8, 3, 22 and 3 Elementary Flg Tng Sch, Tarrant Rushton Stn Flt. # £2,600. *Stored, Baxterley, Warks*
De Havilland Tiger Moth	DF155	1942	3 Apr 1970	G-ANFV, ex Mintlaw, RAF DF155, 25 Reserve Flg Sch, 28 Elementary Flg Tng Sch. # £19,000. *Airworthy, Scottish owner*
De Havilland Dragon	VH-ASK	1938	1973	ex Australia, RAAF A34-13. # £7,000. *National Museum of Flight Scotland, East Fortune*
De Havilland Leopard Moth	G-AIYS	1935	Jul 1977	ex Iraq YI-ABI, Egypt SU-ABM. See also Chapter 26. # £28,000. *Airworthy, Hertfordshire owner*
De Havilland Hornet Moth	G-ADMT	1936	Jan 1976	ex Southampton. # £6,000 – to SACT. *Airworthy, Norwich onwer*
De Havilland Dragon Rapide	G-ALXT	1944	4 Aug 1975	ex Staverton, Ceylon 4R-AAI and CY-AAI, RAF NF865, Metropolitan Comm Sqn. £8,000. *Science Museum, Wroughton, Wilts*
De Havilland Moth Minor	G-AFOZ	1939	1971	ex RAF W7975, 30 Oper Tng Unit, 225 Sqn, G-AFOZ. *Fatal crash at Turnhouse 3 May 1975*
De Havilland Moth Minor	G-AFPN	1939	15 May 1976	ex Denham, RAF X9297, Empire Air Armaments Sch, 1 Air Armament Sch, 7 Air Gunnery Sch, G-AFPN. # £17,000. *Airworthy, Welshpool owner*
De Havilland Mosquito TT.35 *	RS712	1945	9 Nov 1975	G-ASKB, ex West Malling, *Mosquito Squadron*, West Malling, Henlow, *633 Squadron*, 3 and 1 Civilian Anti-Aircraft Co-op Units. # £100,000. *Displayed at Oshkosh, USA, as N35MK*
De Havilland Comet 2R	XK655	1953	21 Aug 1974	ex Wyton, 51 Sqn, BOAC G-AMXA. *Scrapped on site Jul 1990*

Type	Identity	Built	Arrived	Background / *current status, or fate*
De Havilland Vampire T.11	XD403	1954	Apr 1973	ex 4, 1, 7, 8, 5 and 4 Flg Tng Schs. *Private owner, Errol, Scotland*
De Havilland Vampire T.11	XD547	1954	1971	pod, on loan, ex Milngavie, Central Air Traffic Control Sch, 8 Flg Tng Sch, Tangmere Stn Flt, 263 Sqn. *Dumfries and Galloway Aviation Museum, Dumfries*
Fairey Swordfish II	W5856	1939	Aug 1977	ex USA, Royal Canadian Navy, Fleet Air Arm – no service. *Royal Navy Historic Flight, as G-BMGC, Yeovilton*
Fairey Battle I	1899	1940	5 Nov 1972	ex Canada, RAF R3950 – no service. See Chapter 25. *Brussels Museum, Belgium*
Fairey Firefly AS.6	WD833	1950	9 Dec 1974	ex Royal Australian Navy, 723 Sqn. # £22,000. *To USA, becoming N833WD*
Fokker S.11 Instructor	G-BEPV	1948	7 Jan 1977	ex Netherlands PH-ANK, Netherlands Navy 174, Neth Air Force E-31. *Airworthy, based Spanhoe, Northants*
General Aircraft Cygnet 2	G-AGBN	1941	21 Jun 1975	ex Biggin Hill, RAF ES915, Maintenance Command Comm Sqn, 52 and 52 Oper Tng Units, 23 Sqn. # £7,000. *National Museum of Flight Scotland, East Fortune*
Grumman TBM-3W Avenger	045	1944	18 May 1976	G-BTBM, ex Netherlands Navy P-102, US Navy 85650. # £7,800 – see Chapter 13. *Airworthy as N452HA, USA*
Hawker Hurricane XII *	'P3308'	1942	Apr 1970	G-AWLW, ex Canada CF-SMI, RCAF 5588. *Canadian Warplane Heritage as C-GCWH, 4 May 1984, destroyed in hangar fire, Hamilton, Canada, 15 Feb 1993*
Hawker Sea Hawk FGA.6	XE340	1955	24 Nov 1982	on loan, ex Wroughton, Staverton, Lee-on-Solent, Brawdy, 801, 898, 897, 800 Sqns. *Spares for the Royal Navy Historic Flight, Yeovilton*
Kay Gyroplane	G-ACVA	1934	1987	on loan, ex Perth, Glasgow. *National Museum of Scotland, Edinburgh*
Lockheed Hudson IV	A16-199	1942	Mar 1973	G-BEOX, ex Australia Adastra Surveys, VH-AGJ, RAF FH174. # £16,000. *RAF Museum, Hendon*
Miles Monarch	G-AFJU		1976	acquired for pares, ex Lasham, RAF X9306, Ferry Tng Unit, Service Ferry Pilots Pool, G-AFJU. # £50. *Reading owner, under restoration in France*
Miles Monarch	G-AFLW	1938	Jun 1976	ex Booker, Rolls-Royce – Hucknall. # £2,600. *Stored White Waltham, Berks*
Miles Magister	R1914	1939	1975	G-AHUJ, ex Aboyne, RAF R1914, 137, 604 Sqns, Middle Wallop Stn Flt, 604 Sqn. *Still stored on the Strathallan estate*
Miles M.18 Mk.II	G-AHKY	1939	Jun 1976	ex Blackbushe, RAF HM545, Miles U-0224, U-8. # £3,500 – to SACT. *National Museum of Flight Scotland, East Fortune*
Miles Messenger 2A	G-AJOC	1946	Nov 1973	ex Dunottar. # £1,800. *Ulster Folk and Transport Museum, Holywood, stored*
North American Harvard IIb	FT391	1943	2 Apr 1972	G-AZBN, Netherlands PH-HON, Neth AF B-97, USAAF 43-13132. # £20,000. *Airworthy, Surrey owner*

Type	Identity	Built	Arrived	Background / current status, or fate
North American AT-6D Texan	G-AZJD	1943	17 Jul 1972	ex France F-BJBF, Netherlands Air Force H-9, RAF EX958, USAAF 41-33931. *Airworthy in Spain*
North American T-6G Texan	14526	1951	Jan 1981	ex Flimwell, USAAF. # £450. *Registered as G-BRWB, under restoration in Denmark*
Percival Prentice	VS356	1948	30 Sep 1975	G-AOLU, ex Biggin Hill, Ireland EI-ASP, G-AOLU, RAF VS356, Central Flg Sch, 2, 22 Flg Tng Schs. # £1,200 – to SACT. *Under restoration Montrose, Scotland*
Percival Provost T.1	WV493	1953	23 Jun 1976	G-BDYG, ex Halton 7696M, 6 Flg Tng Sch. # £16,000. *National Museum of Flight Scotland, East Fortune*
Pilcher Hawk replica	–	1983	1985	ex BBC Glasgow. *Last reported stored in Glasgow, 1995*
Reid and Sigrist Desford Tnr *	VZ728	1945	Jun 1975	G-AGOS, ex Thruxton, Royal Aircraft Est VZ728, G-AGOS. # £5,500 – to SACT. *Leicester Museums, stored Snibston*
Rolls-Royce TMR	XJ314	1953	Jun 1982	on loan, ex Hayes, South Kensington. *Science Museum, London*
Royal Aircraft Factory SE.5A rep	'F5447'	1987	1987	on loan, G-BKER. *Airworthy, Scottish owner*
SAAB Safir	G-ANOK	1954	1985	ex East Fortune, Sweden SE-CAH. *Stored at Yarrow, Scotland*
Short Scion	G-ACUX	1934	Jan 1974	ex Australia VH-UUP, G-ACUX. # £10,000. *National Museum of Flight Scotland, East Fortune*
Supermarine Spitfire Tr.9	MJ772	1944	Dec 1971	G-AVAV, Irish Air Corps 159, Vickers G-15-172, RAF MJ772 340, 341 Sqns. *Sold in the USA 13 Dec 1974, airworthy as N8R*
Supermarine Spitfire Tr.9	ML407	1944	2 Mar 1972	ex Elstree, Irish Air Corps 162, Vickers G-15-175, RAF 332, 485, 349, 341, 485 Sqns. *Carolyn Grace, G-LFIX, based at Bentwaters, Suffolk*
Supermarine Spitfire Tr.9	PV202	1944	Apr 1970*	ex Irish Air Corps 161, Vickers G-15-174, RAF 412, 33 Sqns. Later G-BHGH, G-TRIX. *Historic Flying, G-CCCA, based at Duxford*
Supermarine Spitfire Tr.9	TE308	1944	Apr 1970*	G-AWGB, ex Irish Air Corps 163, Vickers G-15-176, RAF – no service. Later CF-RAF, C-FRAF, N92471. *Bill Greenwood, Aspen, USA airworthy as N308WK*
Supermarine Spitfire FR.XIV	NH904	1945	17 Jan 1977	ex Flimwell (arrived there 9 Sep 1971), Henlow, Valley, Belgian Air Force SG-108, RAF NH904, 610, 414 Sqns. Became G-FIRE – see Chapter 18. *Airworthy in the USA as N114BP*
Westland Lysander III *	'P9441'	1942	14 Feb 1972	G-AZWT, ex RCAF 2355. *Flies as 'V9367' with Shuttleworth Collection, Old Warden*
Westland Whirlwind HAS.7	XG594	1957	1982	on loan, ex Wroughton, 771 Sqn. *Fleet Air Arm Museum, Yeovilton*

Note: * – Illustrated in the colour sections. Arrival dates are at Strathallan, unless marked*. Aircraft marked # were entered into the auction of 14th June 1981.

CHAPTER 11

West Country Idyll
Torbay Aircraft Museum, Higher Blagdon
1972 to 1988

Among all of the aviation museums that have graced the United Kingdom, you would be hard pressed to find one with a more delightful setting than the Torbay Aircraft Museum. To that accolade you can add a warm welcome at what was a beautifully appointed collection aiming to appeal to *all* visitors. Drop in at any time and you would find 'buffs' mingling with former wartime aircrew and families looking for a diversion from the buckets and spades of the Torbay beaches.

Born in Lincolnshire, Keith Fordyce was surrounded by aviation during his formative years and became a lifelong aviation enthusiast. He was a 'disc jockey' for Radio Luxembourg by 1955 and in August 1963 was the first host of ITV's *Ready, Steady, Go!* From the 1970s he concentrated on radio work, pioneering *Sounds of the Sixties* from 1979 and also fronting the quiz *Beat the Record*. He went on to become a regular on Devon local radio with a loyal following for his informal, relaxed and 'chatting over the fence' style.

He became a private pilot and in the late 1960s he and his wife Ann began a search for a suitable venue for one of his dreams – to run an aviation museum. Their quest came to an end in 1969 when they moved into Higher Blagdon and discovered the adjacent Barton Pines, a farm with extensive outbuildings surrounded by six acres of lush countryside. The crumbling structures, owned by the well-known Devonian Whitley family, dated from around 1900 and served as a stable for the South Devon Hunt. At its height, 50 hunters and hundreds of hounds were kept at Barton Pines. The stable block became the museum's cafeteria and provided shelter for some of the airframes while the aircraft park was originally the site of a large wooden building that served as kennels.

In April 1971 Keith and Ann, trading as Torbay Aviation Ltd, acquired Barton Pines and set to the task of establishing a museum with the ambitious target of opening up for that year's holiday season. Located off the main Paignton to Totnes road and just 15 minutes drive Torbay, it was well located for 'trade' from not only the beaches, but for much of south Devon, with Exeter and Plymouth and the A30 arterial road not far away. Barton Pines and the area around it had been designated an area of outstanding natural beauty and it certainly was a stunning site to visit with great views of the countryside as well as a wonderful mixture of airframes and superbly detailed supporting displays.

Above: Meteor T.7 WF877 against the wonderful backdrop of Barton Pines, 1977. *Ken Ellis*

Front cover of the regularly revised Torbay guidebook plus publicity hand-outs.

With Keith in the role of curator and Ann as commercial director, the pair recruited Wally Ellis as aircraft manager and a wide range of friends and contacts to bring their dream together. Keith explained to the author that when acquiring exhibits for the collection he made sure that he had a copy of *Wrecks & Relics* on his desk and showed me his well-thumbed third edition. The Torbay Aircraft Museum was opened to the public on 5th June 1971 and truly offered something for everyone. The small staff worked hard to provide changing displays – one on the 'Red Baron' proved to be particularly popular and included a purpose-built full-sized Fokker Dr.I static replica as the centre-piece. Non-aviation exhibitions were also staged to make sure that all of the family found something of interest.

Flying in

Occasionally, the tranquillity of the area was briefly exchanged for the clatter of rotor blades, the museum team maintaining a helipad within the grounds. This played host to the Westland-built Sioux AH.1s of the 'Blue Eagles' display team in 1974. Two of the exhibits flew into the site, the first arriving just after Barton Pines had been acquired by the Fordyce family. This was de Havilland Tiger Moth G-ANSM which had a strong West Country background. Built at Hatfield for the RAF as R5014, it was taken on charge in March 1940. It went on to serve with 18 Elementary Flying Training School at Fairoaks, Surrey, from November 1940 to June 1945 and 6 Flying Training School, Ternhill, Shropshire, 1947 to 1949. It ended its RAF career as a 'hack' at Hemswell, Lincolnshire, in February 1954. 'Demobbed' in June 1954 it took on the civil registration G-ANSM and joined the circuit at Whitchurch with the Bristol and Wessex Aeroplane Club in August the following year. It moved with the club to Lulsgate – Bristol Airport – until it became a tug with Devon and Somerset Gliding Club at North Hill and Dunkeswell. Acquired by Torbay Aviation Ltd *Sierra-Mike* was flown into Barton Pines in April 1971 by Keith and was exhibited statically during the museum's first year. After that it was dismantled for restoration.

Probably to help raise further funds to help with the running of the museum G-ANSM was returned to its former home at Dunkeswell in late 1980 and there work continued. *Sierra-Mike's* return to the air was completed in the workshops at Old Warden, Bedfordshire – the home of the Shuttleworth Collection – where a non-standard Gipsy Major 10 (with an extra 10hp of 'poke') was fitted. The Tiger re-flew in early 1982. Since 1999 it has been base at Sibson, near Peterborough.

The other exhibit to make an airborne arrival at Barton Pines used the helipad and made RAF history in doing so. Built on the north Devon coast at Weston-super-Mare, Bristol Sycamore HR.14 XG544 was ready for collection by the RAF on 14th December 1956, entering service at Leconfield in Yorkshire on air-sea rescue duties with 275 Squadron in February 1957. It served in this role until October 1961 when XG544 briefly joined 72 Squadron, then flying the twin-rotor Bristol Belvedere HC.1 from Odiham in Hampshire. In January 1964 it moved to Northolt on the western edge of London flying with the Metropolitan Communications Squadron which took the 'number-plate' of 32 Squadron in February 1969.

On 11th August 1972 XG544 was flown to Upavon for a special mission. At the Wiltshire base the helicopter was the centrepiece of a reception chaired by ACM Sir Harry Burton. Guest of honour was Raoul Hafner, the Austrian-born rotorcraft pioneer who had designed the Sycamore. (For a while his first practical helicopter, the R.II Revoplane, was displayed at Barton Pines.) After lunch, pilot Sqn Ldr John Perry DFC, navigator Flt Lt Sam Booker and passenger Keith Fordyce, boarded XG544 and took off from the lawn of the Officers' Mess bound for the Torbay Aircraft Museum via a flypast at the Westland factory at Yeovil, Somerset. Touching Down on the 'H' at Barton Pines XG544 had completed the last ever flight in RAF service by a Sycamore, bring to an end 20 years of faithful service by the type.

Sycamore HR.14 at Northolt in 1970 with 32 Squadron. *MAP*

Under the hammer

Although it was evident that the Torbay Aircraft Museum was run with passion by all who were involved in it, it was nevertheless a business and during 1988 the reluctant decision was made that it was no longer viable. Sotheby's were called in and a sale of the airframes and artefacts was staged at the auctioneer's Billingshurst, Sussex 'out-station' on 19th October 1988 with viewing having taken place at Barton Pines the previous week.

Seventeen aircraft were 'hammered' with yields ranging from £220 for the wingless former school playground Anson C.19, to £5,200 for the Chipmunk T.10. Torbay was one of the first museums in the UK to make effective use of the full-scale replicas built for the film *Battle of Britain*, released in 1969. There was vigorous bidding for the Hurricane, Messerschmitt and Spitfire, netting £13,500 for the trio but this fell below the reserve. Other lots included a Bedford OY fuel tanker with reached £400, a Rolls-Royce Avon turbojet on a stand at £800 and a wonderful Lister Autotruck with trailer, for £200.

Torbay displayed three full-scale replicas that had starred in the 1969 film ' Battle of Britain' – the Messerschmitt Bf 109. *Sotheby's*

The museum's Provost duo. *Roy Bonser*

Messenger G-AKEZ at Higher Blagdon prior to taking on 1944 RAF camouflage. *Roy Bonser*

The Chipmunk inside the converted stable block. *Sotheby's*

De Havilland Chipmunk

Painted in 'Invasion stripes' and camouflage as Field Marshal Montgomery's runabout 'RG333' the museum's Miles Messenger fetched £480. This machine was built by Miles at Newtownards, Northern Ireland, in September 1947. It was first used by a Nottingham-based company later flying from Netherthorpe, Blyborough, Yeadon and Castle Donington. *Echo-Zulu's* last flight was on 15th September 1968 by which stage it had clocked up 1,410 hours.

The *Battle of Britain* replicas were sold via private treaty to become exhibits at the rapidly expanding Kent Battle of Britain Museum at Hawkinge. A major investor in the auction was Snowdon Mountain Aviation, the company taking the Anson, Dove, Dragonfly, Provost WV679, whole Sea Hawk and the Varsity procedure trainer. These were for the Caernarfon Air Museum which opened at Llandwrog airfield on 11th May 1989. Snowdon Mountain's Ray Mackenzie-Blythe was another who used *Wrecks & Relics* as a reference work for his 'shopping list'.

Keith and friends hoped to be able to carry on with a slimmed-down collection of exhibits at a new, more central, location in the Torbay area. This proved impossible and the last major artefact, the Sea Hawk cockpit, was offered for sale 1992. The logic regarding the setting and the location was good, but tourist requirements in the Torbay and south Devon catchment area meant that museums were no longer high on the 'must do' list. Nevertheless, in its time, the Torbay was one of the UK's most charismatic venues and there are many visitors who have fondest memories of time spent there.

As this book reached the layout stage, the sad news came through that Keith Fordyce died following a long illness on March 27, aged 83. Fittingly, as this was typed *Sounds of the Sixties* was piping out of Radio 2, courtesy of Brian Matthew. Obituaries paid tribute to Keith's pioneering radio and TV work and all gave testament to what a warm, endearing character he was. Only a few of the 'nationals' noted his role in Britain's aviation heritage. I hope that this chapter goes some small way to countering that. Blue skies, Keith.

Torbay Aircraft Museum

Type	Identity	Built	Arrived	Background / *current status, or fate*
Avro Avian III	G-EBZM	1928	1973	on loan from Northern APS (The Aeroplane Collection). ex Peel Green, Lymm, Liverpool, Huyton, Manchester, Hesketh Park. *Museum of Science and Industry, Manchester*
Avro Anson C.19	TX235		1979	ex Andover School, Shawbury, Training Command Comm Sqn, Fighter Command Comm Sqn, Debden Stn Flt, Flying Training Command Comm Sqn, 64 Group Comm Sqn, 2 Group Comm Sqn, Gibraltar Comm Flt. *Air Atlantique Class Flight, Coventry, stored for spares*
BA Swallow II	G-AFGE	1938	Jun 1972	Briefly on loan. Ex Goodwood, impressed as BK894, served with Central Landing Est, Royal Aircraft Est, G-AFGE. *Airworthy in Wiltshire*
Bristol Sycamore HR.14	XG544	1956	11 Aug 1972	ex 32 Sqn, Metropolitan Comm Sqn, 72, 118, 228 and 275 Sqns. *Noted in Zurich, Switzerland, Aug 2004*
Colditz Cock glider replica	–	?	1974	On loan, from the BBC. *Imperial War Museum, stored*
De Havilland Tiger Moth *	G-ANSM	1940	Apr 1971	ex Devon and Somerset Gliding Club, RAF R5014, 6 FTS, 18 EFTS. *Airworthy at Sibson*
De Havilland Dove 6	G-ALFT	1948	1975	ex Civil Aviation Flying Unit – Stansted. *Scrapped at Caernarfon, March 2004*
De Havilland Vampire T.11	XE995	1955	3 Mar 1973	ex Woodford, St Athan, 8 FTS, 5 FTS, 32 Sqn. *Scrapped in Kent, circa 1995*
DH Sea Venom FAW.21 *	XG629	1956	May 1971	ex Culdrose, Aircraft Direction School, 831 and 893 Sqns. *Privately owned, Stone, Staffs*
DH Canada Chipmunk T.10	WB758	1950	21st Oct 1972	ex 71 MU Bicester, 2030 Sqn ATC Sheldon 7729M, Oxford University Air Sqn, Transport Command Comm Flt, 14 Reserve Flying Sch. *Sold to private owner and eventually broken up for spares*
Desoutter I	G-AAPZ	1929	May 1971	On loan from Shuttleworth Collection. *Airworthy at Old Warden, Beds*
Elliotts of Newbury Primary		?	Jun 1971	On loan. Ex Sunderland Flying Club. *No other details*
Focke-Achgelis Fa 330A-1	100545	c 1943	Jun 1971	On loan. Ex Cranfield, RAE Farnborough, Germany. See also Chapter 3. *Fleet Air Museum, Yeovilton*

Type	Identity	Built	Arrived	Background / current status, or fate
Fokker Dr.I static replica	'425/17'	1978	1978	built locally. *Kent Battle of Britain Museum, Hawkinge*
Gloster Meteor T.7	WF877	1951	1 Feb 1974	ex Flight Refuelling – Tarrant Rushton, Chilbolton, Folland, Gloster, 96 Sqn, Meteor Flt Wunstorf, 11 Sqn. *Private owner, reg'd as G-BPOB, stored at Duxford*
Hafner R-II Revoplane	–	1933	11 Aug 1972	ex Shuttleworth – Old Warden, Yeovil, Filton, Austria. *The Helicopter Museum, Weston-super-Mare*
Hawker Hurricane static rep	'L1592'	1968	1971	ex *Battle of Britain* film. *Kent Battle of Britain Museum, Hawkinge*
Hawker Sea Hawk FB.5	WM961	1954	May 1971	ex Culdrose A2517, Fleet Requirements Unit, 802 and 811 Sqns. *Caernarfon Air Museum, Llandwrog*
Hawker Sea Hawk FGA.4	WV843	1954	1971	cockpit, ex Fleetlands, crashed 31 Aug 1956, 738 Sqn. *Current status unknown*
Messerschmitt Bf 109 static rep	'6'	1968	1971	ex *Battle of Britain* film. *Kent Battle of Britain Museum, Hawkinge*
Miles Messenger 2A	G-AKEZ	1947	May 1971	ex Castle Donington. *Sold to private owner and sold in New Zealand Jan 2006*
Percival Proctor IV	G-ANYP	1944	Mar 1972	ex Brooklands Tech Coll, Wiltshire School of Flying, NP184, Yatesbury, Maintenance Command Comm Flt. *Sold off to private collector, no details*
Percival Provost T.1	WV605	1954	1971	On loan from Shuttleworth Collection. Ex Macclesfield College, 6, 3 and 22 Flying Training Schools. *Norfolk and Suffolk Aviation Museum, Flixton*
Percival Provost T.1	WV679	1954	20 Dec 1971	ex 1 SoTT Halton 7615M, 2 Flying Training School. *Wellesbourne Wartime Museum, Wellesbourne Mountford*
Pitts S-2A travelling airframe	'G-RKSF'	?	1977	*Returned to publicity company 1990*
Royal Aircraft Factory SE.5a rep	–		20 Jul 1981	built as a project by a Torbay school. *Sold in the USA circa 1997*
Saunders-Roe Skeeter AOP.12	XN351	1960	May 1971	On loan from Shuttleworth Collection. Ex Wroughton, 3 Royal Tank Regiment, 652 and 651 Sqns. See also Chapter 8. *Privately owned, reg'd as G-BKSC, stored Ipswich area*
Supermarine Spitfire replica	–	1968	1971	ex *Battle of Britain* film. *Kent Battle of Britain Museum, Hawkinge*
Vickers Varsity T.1 cockpit	–	?	1971	Procedure trainer, ex Oakington. *Caernarfon Air Museum, Llandwrog*
Westland Dragonfly HR.3 *	WN499	1953	Jun 1971	ex Blackbushe, Culdrose Station Flight. *Yorkshire Helicopter Pres Group, Elvington*
Westland Whirlwind HAR.3	XJ393	1954	Mar 1972	ex Lee-on-Solent, Arbroath A2538, RRE, A&AEE. *Scrapped at Pulborough, W Sussex, 1993*
Westland Whirlwind HAS.7	XN299	1959	1979	ex Culdrose, Joint Weapons Establishment – Old Sarum, Fleetlands, 847, 848 Sqns. *Tangmere Military Aviation Museum, Tangmere*

Note: * – Illustrated in the colour sections.

ONES THAT GOT AWAY

Armstrong Whitworth Scimitar, 1958

Armstrong Whitworth at Whitley, near Coventry, kept several airframes long after they should have been discarded for pure commercial reasons. The one that survived into the 21st century is the Royal Aircraft Factory SE.5A that now graces the Shuttleworth Collection at Old Warden in Bedfordshire. Sadly, this was not the case with AW-built treasures. In October 1958 the fuselage of a single-seat biplane was jettisoned from Whitley and moved to the famous scrapyard of R J Coley and Sons at Hounslow, Middlesex, never to be seen again. This was G-ADBL, the second of two AW.35 Scimitar fighters aimed at the requirement that was ultimately won by the Gloster Gladiator. A refinement of the AW.16, G-ADBL first flew at Whitley on 18th March 1935. Four Scimitars were sold to the Royal Norwegian Air Force, but nothing else came of the type. *Beer-London* flew on as 'hack' for AW but was retired, probably in 1937. It was stored dismantled at Whitley and by 1948 was noted at Baginton, Coventry Airport, as a bedraggled fuselage with many panels missing. At that point, it had another decade ahead of it before it faced oblivion. *MAP*

CHAPTER 12

'Royalist Air Force'
Ormond-Haydon-Baillie,
Haydon-Baillie Aircraft and Naval Collection
1973 to 1977

Flushed with the success of having ferried a Hawker Sea Fury across the Atlantic in the autumn of 1973, its dashing and gifted pilot was talking to the press at his point of arrival, Southend in Essex. He explained that the naval fighter, and the jet trainer he had brought over a fortnight before, was part of a 'squadron' he was assembling. He was passionate that these machines would not lie still in a hangar; they would be flown and displayed for the joy of all. Banter developed that he was trying to rival the Royal Air Force, but the former Flight Lieutenant was adamant that that was not the case, his was a sort of 'Royalist Air Force'. That phrase stuck and it epitomised a vibrant, gifted and very dedicated pilot – Flt Lt Ormond Adare Haydon-Baillie.

The story of what was officially called the Haydon-Baillie Aircraft and Naval Collection is one of massive potential, tragically cut short. Along with a passenger, Ormond was killed in West Germany on 3rd July 1977 while flying his latest acquisition, Cavalier-modified Mustang I-BILL.

British born, Ormond joined the Royal Canadian Air Force in 1964 and quickly shone out as a talented pilot. He served with 434 'Bluenose' Squadron working to introduce the Canadair-built Northrop CF-5 Freedom Fighter into service. His talents were later harnessed into test and evaluation flying, including service at the Central Experimental and Proving Establishment, Cold Lake, Alberta. Two types he flew extensive during this time were Silver Stars, Lockheed T-33A 'T-Birds', and swept-wing Sabres, both built by Canadair.

Above: Bearing the initials of its owner, Ormond Haydon-Baillie's Sea Fury at Duxford in June 1974, shortly after its arrival from Southend.

All the while, he was tracking down interesting aircraft and flying a wide range of types. He left the RCAF in 1973 intent on returning to the UK with his 'squadron' – then comprising three airworthy machines, a Sea Fury and a pair of Silver Stars and two long flightless Fairchild-built Bristol Bolingbroke IVTs plus tons of supporting spares. Also, Ormond and his brother, Wensley, had been scouring the planet looking for other likely additions; there was much 'in the pipeline'.

Canadian recruits

Ormond discovered former Royal Australian Navy Sea Fury FB.11 WH589 at Bankstown, New South Wales, in January 1969. He arranged for it to be shipped to California on no less a vessel than the aircraft carrier USS *Coral Sea*. Once unloaded, a workshop prepared the fighter and Ormond conducted the first flight in June 1970. Now Canadian registered as CF-CHB and with the call-sign *Jolly 1*, the WH589 was subjected to a major restoration at its new home at Cold Lake. Bedecked in an RAF wartime colour scheme and Ormond's initials – 'OH-B' – as its code-letters the Sea Fury became a common sight at US and Canadian air events and it was entered into the famous air races at Reno, Nevada, in 1971. Much of the work required on *Hotel-Bravo* was carried out by its owner, this included a hectic month rebuilding the engine at Beale Air Force Base, California, following a forced-landing. 'OHB' was never scared of getting his hands dirty and was capable of intense, hard graft.

A small portion of the Blenheim airframe and engine cache inside a hangar at Duxford after coming through the docks at Harwich, 1974.

Meanwhile, he had heard of a cache of Bolingbrokes in open storage in Manitoba and set about investigating. These were versions of the of the famous Bristol Blenheim, built under licence for the RCAF by Fairchild Aircraft Ltd at Longueil, Port Quebec. A deal was struck with owner Wes Agnew, including two airframes, loads of spares and 23 Bristol Mercury radials. Ormond was heavily involved in stripping this lot down during August 1973 and trucking them off for shipment to Harwich docks in the UK.

He had also secured three Silver Stars, as mementos of his jet flying with the RCAF. One of these, CF-IHB, was painted in striking gloss black colours with a knight's helmet and plumes on the nose. It was painted so in honour of 414 'Black Knight' Squadron that flew Silver Stars (among other types) on electronic warfare simulation missions out of North Bay, Ontario. The all-silver CF-EHB was eventually registered in the UK as G-WGHB – the initials of his brother, Wensley. The third, N12420, had been acquired as a back-up for the other two, but was also destined to fly in the UK.

The 'silver' Silver Star, G-WGHB, outside the World War One era hangars at Duxford, June 1974.

With the Bolingbroke hulks on the high seas, Ormond embarked upon an intensive period in which he ferried the two Silver Stars and the Sea Fury to their new base at the Historic Aircraft Museum at Southend, Essex – see Chapter 7. During November 1973 he crossed the Atlantic *five* times, three at the helm of historic aircraft. On the 9th, he touched down at Southend in the 'Black Knight' amid a warm welcome from his elder brother and two sisters and a barrage of press. Then it was on to a British Overseas Airways Corporation Boeing 707 back to Canada and the Sea Fury. He was back at Southend on the 24th, the piston-engined fighter having been fitted with two over-load drop tanks for the epic journey. The first two eastbound trips had been solo but for the final excursion, Ormond was joined on the BOAC 'Jumbo' by family friend Merlin Hay, Lord Hay of Errol, who took the back seat in Silver Star CF-EHB. They arrived at Southend on the 30th.

Opening up Duxford

The stay at Southend was not to last. Ormond had learned that the Imperial War Museum had established a store of airframes and other large artefacts at Duxford airfield, just outside of Cambridge. Always persuasive, he managed to gain accommodation for the Blenheim project and for the 'T-Birds' and Sea Fury. The trio hopped across from Essex on 9th May 1974 in an operation like the transatlantic crossing of the year before, but without the Boeings and the jetlag! Ormond's 'squadron' became the first of what was to become the UK's warbird 'Mecca'.

Keeping to the Canadian theme, the Avro Canada CF-100 Canuck was acquired from Cranfield – see Chapter 3. Five redundant Canadair Sabres previously in use for contract target-towing work for the Luftwaffe were secured, as was a Gloster Meteor F.8 from the RAF at Kemble, Glos. A huge coup had been the acquisition, dismantling and shipping of a variety of Supermarine Spitfires that had been eking out their last days as surface decoys on Indian Air Force bases. Stores for all of these had been set up at Hemel Hempstead, Herts, and at the Royal Naval Aircraft Yard at Wroughton, Wiltshire. Other Spitfires were in the process of dispatch when the tragic news of Ormond's death broke.

Wensley organised the winding down of the collection over the next couple of years. As will be seen from the table, many went on to fly again or become museum pieces. Ormond would have been pleased with that outcome. Wensley became a major collector of what has become known as 'Concordalia' – anything to do with the Anglo-French supersonic airliner. By early 1990 Wensley had turned his attentions to another high-Mach machine, the superlative English Electric Lightning. Establishing a store near Southampton he acquired the P.1B development prototype XA847 from Henlow, Beds, and two-seat T.55 XS422 from Boscombe Down, Wiltshire. He also renewed contact with the then flightless Silver Star that carried his initials, G-WGHB. He entered negotiations with British Aerospace at Warton, Lancashire, for the stock of former Royal Saudi Air Force Lightnings that had been 'traded in' as part of the kingdom's huge Panavia Tornado order. Three two-seat T.5s and eleven F.53 fighters were carefully dismantled, put into containers and stored in Warrington, Cheshire, pending a decision on their future. By 1996 all had been moved on, many joining museums; G-WGHB is under restoration to fly again in a Norfolk workshop.

As will be seen in Chapter 16, the Blenheim project was taken on by Graham Warner and this led to the fulfilment of one of Ormond's many dreams, that an example of Bristol's 'Forgotten Bomber' would fly again. In his 1996 book *Spirit of Britain First*, Graham paid tribute: "Ormond was a dynamic and charismatic leader, always at the hub of the activity at Duxford. His infectious enthusiasm and single-minded determination inspired his helpers; he cut through red tape incisively and delighted in brow-beating bureaucrats. His obvious love of flying was soon shared by his team, and the great interest it aroused was noted by others as Duxford... Together they did much to establish the basis of the unique and highly successful combination of a major national museum working closely with privately-owned, live exciting flying aircraft that has made Duxford the internationally acclaimed major public attraction it is today."

One of the former Indian Air Force airfield decoys brought back to the UK by 'OHB' was Mk.XIV NH749. It was restored to fly at Cranfield, Beds, as G-MXIV and first flew on 9th April 1983. It is illustrated, along with Warbirds of the Great Britain's Mustang G-PSID, at Woodford in June 1985 before it was exported to the USA the following year. *Alan Curry*

Ormond-Haydon-Baillie, Haydon-Baillie Aircraft and Naval Collection

Type	Identity	Built	Arrived	Background / *current status, or fate*
Avro Canada Canuck Mk.4 *	18393	1955	29 Mar 1975	G-BCYK, ex Cranfield – see Chapter 3, RCAF, 440, 419, 409 Sqns. *Imperial War Museum, Duxford*
Bristol Bolingbroke IVT	9893	1942	1974	ex Canada, Hartney – Manitoba, RCAF. See Chapter 16. *Stored, for static restoration for IWM, Duxford*
Bristol Bolingbroke IVT	10038	1942	1974	ex Canada, Hartney – Manitoba, RCAF. See Chapter 16. *Became G-MKIV, crashed 21 Jun 1987, in use for spares at Duxford*
DH Canada Chipmunk T.10	G-BCYJ	1951	1975	ex RAF WG307, Birmingham Univ Air Sqn, Primary Flg Tng Sch, Central Flg Sch, Aircrew Officers Tng Sch, PFS, 1 Initial Tng Sch, 12, 9 Air Experience Flts, Aberdeen, Manchester, Queens, Durham, Queens UASs, Binbrook Stn Flt, Leeds, Southampton UASs, 5, 18 Reserve Flg Sch, 1 Basic Flg Tng Sch. See Chapter 16. *Sold in South Africa 2004*
DH Canada Chipmunk T.10	WP963	1953	1976	ex RAF Halton 8341M, 229 Oper Conv Unit, Old Sarum Stn Flt, Sch of Land-Air Warfare. *Sold in the USA 1978*
Gloster Meteor F.8	WH291	1951	10 Feb 1976	held in store at 5 MU Kemble; ex 229 OCU, 85 Sqn, CAW, 257 Sqn. See also Chapter 9. *Stored, Booker, Bucks*
Hawker Sea Fury FB.11 *	WH589	1951	9 May 1974*	G-AGHB, ex CF-CHB, Southend – see Chapter 7, ex Canada, Cold Lake, Australia, WH589, Royal Aus Navy 724 Sqn. See Chapter 18. *Registered as N895HW, Washington State, USA*
Lockheed (Canadair) Silver Star Mk.3	G-WGHB	1958	9 May 1974*	ex CF-EHB, Southend – see Chapter 7, ex Royal Canadian Navy, RCAF, 21640. *Under restoration at Norwich*
Lockheed (Canadair) Silver Star Mk.3 *	G-OAHB	1954	9 May 1974*	ex CF-IHB, Southend – see Chapter 7, ex Royal Canadian Navy, RCAF, 21261. *Became G-JETT, N33VC. As G-TBRD, crash on take-off at Duxford 6 Sep 2006*
Lockheed (Canadair) Silver Star Mk.3	N12420	1954	1976	ex USA, RCAF 21200. *Written off in accident, Sebring, USA 9 Jul 1979*
NAA P-51D Mustang *	I-BILL	1944	26 Jun 1977	ex Florence – Italy, USA, N6851D, N16S, N7720C, USAAF 44-74694. *Fatal crashed at Mainz-Finthen, West Germany 3 Jul 1977*
NAA (Canadair) Sabre 6	01+03	1953	1978	held in store at Wroughton; ex Dornier, Luftwaffe KE+104, BB+284, JD+103. *Airworthy Wyoming, USA as N80FS*
NAA (Canadair) Sabre 6	D-0113	1954	1978	held in store at Wroughton; ex Dornier, Luftwaffe 01+02. BB+163, YA+043. *Last reported at Mojave, USA as N81FS 1988*
NAA (Canadair) Sabre 6	D-9538	1953	1978	held in store at Wroughton; ex Dornier, Luftwaffe BB+170. *Became USA N1039C, N82FS, N186JC – fatal crash in New Jersey, 30 Jun 1999*
NAA (Canadair) Sabre 6	D-9540	1954	1978	held in store at Wroughton; ex Dornier, Luftwaffe 01+02. BB+185. *Ditched off Tampa Bay, USA c 1983, as N83FS*

Type	Identity	Built	Arrived	Background / *current status, or fate*
NAA (Canadair) Sabre 6	D-9541	1954	1978	held in store at Wroughton; ex Dornier, Luftwaffe JB+240. *Became USA N1039L, N89FS, Canada C-GBUI, airworthy as N186PJ, Hillsboro, Oregon, USA*
Supermarine Spitfire VIII	'T17'	1944	1977	held in store at Wroughton; ex Indian Air Force inst airframe Jaipur, RAF MT719 17 Sqn. *Became Italy I-SPIT, G-VIII, airworthy in Texas, USA as N719MT*
Supermarine Spitfire XIV	MV370	1945	1977	held in store at Hemel Hempstead, Herts; ex India Nagpur, Indian AF inst T44, IAF, RAF MV370, no service – became G-FXIV, see Chapter 24. *Luftfahrtmuseum, Germany*
Supermarine Spitfire XIV	NH749	1945	1977	held in store at Hemel Hempstead, Herts; ex India Patna, Indian Air Force, RAF NH749 – no service. *Airworthy, USA as N749DP*
Supermarine Spitfire XVIII	HS649	1945	1977	held in store at Hemel Hempstead, Herts; ex India Kalaikunda, Indian Air Force HS649, RAF TP298 – no service. *Static at the National War and Resistance Museum, Overloon, Netherlands*

Note: * – Illustrated in the colour sections. * Flown into Southend initially, dates given here are arrival at Duxford. The following Spitfires were acquired in India but are *believed* to have been redirected while being shipped: Mk.XIV MV262 (Indian 'T42') – see Chapter 13 and 25; Mk.XIV SM832 – see Chapter 13 and 25; Mk. XVIII TP276 (Indian HS653) direct to the USA, not yet airworthy; Mk.XVIII TP280 (Indian HS654) direct USA, then to UK as G-BTXE, airworthy in the USA as N280TP; Mk.XVIII TP298 (Indian HS662) direct to the USA, crashed in USA as N41702 19 May 1994.

CHAPTER 13

Market Forces
Warbirds of Great Britain
1973 to 1992

In the yard of auctioneers Christie's South Kensington sales room a dismantled Spitfire IX was causing a lot of interest. It was 31st October 1986 and the fighter as one of four airframes going 'under the hammer' along with an array of aeronautica. Paying a lot of attention to BR601 was Doug Arnold, the doyen of Warbirds of Great Britain. A big man, he was well known for speaking his mind and was on record as disliking seeing his business covered in the aviation press. I still wanted to introduce myself to him. He was gruff and brief, but when I asked if he would be bidding, he said: "Spitfires are always special." And he moved on. The former South African Mk.IX reached £70,000 and the following month, it was noted arriving at Bitteswell in Leicestershire. He made no fanfare about the transaction.

Accompanying this narrative is a vast table chronicling an enterprise with global reach. What became known as Warbirds of Great Britain was a private collection, but its extent and lack of public 'image' was a powerful magnet for enthusiasts. There were moments early on at Blackbushe when it looked as though a museum of some description might open, but this was not to be. So, as a private collection, why is WoGB in *Lost Aviation Collections of Britain*? Well, its sheer scope and that it was based at several very public aerodromes, for a start. Also, WoGB aircraft appeared at far more air displays that they are given credit for. There are other reasons, it was the first warbird operation to restore Spitfires and other types on what could be called an 'industrial' level. As it expanded, the sheer size of WoGB's operation pump-primed all of the nascent warbird community – giving it 'critical mass'. Take a look at that table again, WoGB brought to the UK a series of fabulous aircraft, some of which the public got to appreciate on the wing. Still more joined museums – Hendon solved elements of its 'shopping list' through WoGB – or went to other restorers and owners and fly today. All this was down to persistence and a shrewd eye for a deal.

Above: One of the first signs of change at Bitteswell was the putting up of an 'airport' sign. *Roy Bonser*

Collecting airfields

These skills did not stop at the sourcing a rare airframe at the right price in a timely manner. Douglas William Arnold was also astute when it came to property. Initially trading in light aircraft at Fairoaks in Surrey as Douglas Arnold Aviation and Shipping Company – see Chapter 1 – and then as Fairoaks Aviation Services, a very successful agency for the Britten-Norman BN-2 Islander utility twin was established. The company moved to Blackbushe in Hampshire by 1974. Located on the A30 trunk road to the west of Camberley, it boasted a control tower and an increasingly ramshackle 'terminal' building with capacious, if pot-holed, car park at the roadside. As the number of warbirds increased, lines of Dakotas, Junkers and Mitchells attracted great interest. Parking a B-17 Flying Fortress so close to the road was a powerful attention magnet. But the greatest interest was within the new hangar structures that were built on the north western edge, out of sight and out of reach. Here was the extensive workshop and the storage area for the smaller types. These now form a part of the huge car auction complex that has been developed at the western end of the airfield.

When the framework for these big structures was going up there was a lot of speculation that they were for museum purposes. In use by 1981 they had transformed the investment appeal of the airfield. This all paid off in 1984 when it was announced that the whole site had been acquired by British Car Auctions. There were initial fears that this would bring an end to flying at Blackbushe, but the new owners were also aircraft operators and aviation and other forms of commerce have flourished side-by-side there ever since.

After use in the film 'Hanover Street', TB-25N Mitchell N9115Z flew to Blackbushe in mid-979. It was repainted as 'Marvellous Milly' for static use in another film – 'Eye of the Needle'.

Negotiations were already in hand with British Aerospace regarding the former Armstrong Whitworth assembly and flight test airfield at Bitteswell. On 28th November 1984 it was announced that Warbirds of Great Britain, in the form of Bitteswell Ltd, had acquired the site for over £3 million. Doug Arnold declared that he would like to see wider employment possibilities, noting that an airliner repair and overhaul facility was a possibility. In the spring of 1985 the WoGB fleet began to arrive, some flying in; most arriving by the seemingly endless lorry loads.

No sooner had it started than it was all over. On 22nd January 1986 the MFI group of companies announced that it had bought the airfield from Bitteswell Ltd and the whole site would be developed into the giant distribution and warehousing complex that it is today. So WoGB was set to move again. The last aircraft to fly out was Spitfire IX NH238, departing on 28th November 1987. From that autumn most of the dismantled aircraft were moved to the appropriately named Spitfire Hangar at Biggin Hill and later in the year, the 'flyers' started to accumulate at Hangar 100 at Bournemouth's Hurn airfield. During the moves to and from Bitteswell considerable rationalisation of the aircraft held took place.

With Doug Arnold hitching a ride on the fork-lift, Spitfire IX NH238 'D-A' is towed down the Lutterworth Road and on to Bitteswell airfield to make the last aircraft departure on 28th November 1987. *Roy Bonser*

Then, in early November 1992 came the news that Doug Arnold had died. The once huge WoGB fleet was dispersed with incredible speed. Some aircraft initially travelling to the Netherlands, but others found keen purchasers within the UK warbird movement. The Arnold family continued to hold some airframes and it is believed there is still a small store in Berkshire. However, that is a story beyond the remit of this book.

Spitfire 'factory'

Defining the 'founder' aircraft of the collection is somewhat problematical, but Doug Arnold had always expressed an interest in Spitfire XVI SL721 and on 28th March 1973 he took delivery of it at Leavesden in Hertfordshire. This machine had been famous during its days with the Metropolitan Communications Squadron at Northolt to the west of London as the pale blue 'hack' of Air Chief Marshal Sir James M Robb and it carried his initials, 'J-MR' on the fuselage sides. Imported from the USA in airworthy condition, it quickly gained another set of initials, 'DA', on its flanks. This was not to be the only Spitfire that carried those letters – Mk.IX NH238 and Mk.XVIII SM969 also having that honour. One of the former West German target-tug Sea Fury T.20s went one better, carrying 'DW-A' briefly during its stay at Blackbushe.

Ormond Haydon-Baillie – see Chapter 12 – had pioneered India as a source of Spitfires and WoGB took on several of his airframes and went on to unearth more. At Blackbushe, under the careful watch of Dick Melton, a workshop was established and a restoration schedule established. With ever-changing priorities resulting from the exceptional rate of acquisitions, only two were to take to the air with WoGB: Mk.IX NH238 on 6th May 1984 and Mk.XVIII SM969 on 12th October 1985. A third, Mk.XVI TE356, was contracted out and first flew from East Midlands Airport on 16th December 1987.

Spitfire XVI SL721 wearing the rank insignia and initials of Air Chief Marshal Sir James M Robb, circa 1950.

A sneak look inside the Blackbushe Spitfire workshop, 1983.

Spitfire XVI TE392 on the gate at Hereford in August 1970. It was part of the RAF Museum's 'gate guardians for exhibits' exchange with WoGB. *Stuart Howe*

From far and wide

India was also where the B-24 Liberator was located. This was a major recovery operation and the fuselage was flown into Stansted Airport, Essex, on board a HeavyLift Short Belfast in May 1982. Already mentioned are the bright-red Sea Fury T.20S two-seaters that were acquired from retirement at Lübeck in West Germany. Swiss Air Force disposals were also carefully monitored, resulting in a pair of Pilatus P.2 trainers arriving in 1981 to be followed by a quartet of P.3s a decade later. Yugoslavia produced two P-47 Thunderbolts and a Messerschmitt Bf 109G.

It was in Spain where acquisitions took on a much larger scale. Surplus stocks of the Spanish Air Force changed the skyline at Blackbushe with lines of Douglas C-47 Skytrain and CASA-built Junkers Ju 52 transports. Along with these was a CASA-built, Merlin-engined, version of the Heinkel He 111 bomber that arrived in June 1976. WoGB were negotiating for another and it was due to arrive late the following year. As a reminder that flying historic aircraft has an element of risk, even for the most experienced, CASA 2-111B G-BFFS never made it to Blackbushe. Flown by Flt Lt Neil Williams, it departed Cuatro Vientos, near Madrid, on 11th December but impacted on high ground near Escorial, killing its superbly gifted pilot, a master of warbirds and a lyricist when it came to aerobatic flight. He was just 43.

Another aspect of WoGB is the tantalising prospect of ones that got away. Even the tenacious Doug Arnold had to admit defeat at times. In December 1979 two out-of-sequence registrations firmly got the attention of enthusiasts: G-MUST a Commonwealth Aircraft-built Mustang Mk.22 and G-SMIT a Messerschmitt Bf 109G-6. Both were in Australia and they stumbled in the face of that country's export rulings. Around the time of Doug's passing, a B-17G Flying Fortress and a P-63A Kingcobra were reported to have been close to arrival in the UK. Then there must have been many three-cornered, or even more complex trades, where an airframe went straight to another vendor without appearing at any of WoGB's bases; all to enable another exotic type to join the collection.

A pair of former Spanish Air Force C-47 Skytrains parked out at Blackbushe in August 1978.

Lightning N505MH 'Miss Behavin' shortly after delivery to WoGB direct at Biggin Hill base in May 1989.

Thunderbolt G-BLZW on delivery to The Fighter Collection at Duxford, 18th September 1985.

Sections of Lancaster X KB889 leaving Bitteswell for the Imperial War Museum at Duxford on 14sh May 1986. *via Roy Bonser*

Warbirds of Great Britain

Type	Identity	Built	Arrived	Background / *current status, or fate*
Avro Lancaster Mk.10(AR)	KB976	1945	1990	G-BCOH, ex Bedford, Woodford, Strathallan – see Chapter 10, CF-TQC, RCAF KB976, RAF, 405 Sqn. *See Chapter 25 for more*
Avro Lancaster X	KB889	1944	1984	G-LANC, ex Canada – Niagara Falls, RCAF, 428 Sqn. *Imperial War Museum, Duxford*
Avro Lincoln B.2 *	RF342	1946	11 Nov 1983	ex Southend – Chapter 7, Cranfield, G-APRJ / G-36-3, Napier G-29-1, G-APRJ, RF342, Telecommunications Flg Unit, Defford. See also Chapter 25. *Majority with Australian National Aviation Museum, stored. Nose at Flying Heritage, Seattle, USA*
Beech T-34A Mentor	N34AB	?	1990	ex US Navy 33340. *Return to the USA c 1994 – no further details*
Bell P-63A Kingcobra	N52113	1942	May 1988	ex USA, USAAF 42-69097. *Became G-BTWR fatal crash, Biggin Hill 3 Jun 2001*
Boeing N2S-5 Kaydet	G-AWLO	1943	c 1975	ex Farnborough, Kenya 5Y-KRR, VP-KRR, USAAF 42-17400. *Airworthy, Hertfordshire owner*
Boeing B-17G Flying Fortress *	G-FORT	1944	12 Jun 1984	ex France F-BEEC, South Africa ZS-EEC, F-BEEC, USAAF 44-85718. *Airworthy, Lone Star Flight Museum, Texas, as N900RW*
Consolidated PBY-6A Catalina	G-BPFY	1944	Mar 1990	ex North Weald, USA N212DM, UK G-BPFY, N212DM, G-BPFY, Canada C-FHNH, France F-ZBAV, USA N5555H, N2846D, US Navy 64017. *Israeli Defence Force/Air Force Museum, Hazerim, Israel*
Consolidated B-24J Liberator	KH191	1944	6 May 1982	ex India, Jalahalli, Indian Air Force T18 and KH191, RAF KH191 8 Sqn. *Airworthy with the Collings Foundation, USA as N224J*
Curtiss P-40N Warhawk	N9950	1944	1991	ex USA, USAAF 44-7983. *Believed stored in the UK*

Type	Identity	Built	Arrived	Background / *current status, or fate*
De Havilland Mosquito TT.35	RS709	1945	28 Nov 1979	G-MOSI, ex USA N9797, Skyfame – Chapter 4, *Mosquito Squadron*, G-ASKA, Bovingdon, *633 Squadron*, RAF 3/4 Civilian Anti-Aircraft Co-op Unit, 236 Op Conv Unit. *National Museum of the USAF, Dayton, Ohio, as 'NS519'*
De Havilland Comet 4C	G-BDIT	1961	8 Jun 1981	ex Dan-Air, RAF C.4 XR395 216 Sqn, Aeroplane & Armament Exp Est. *Scrapped on site Aug 1984*
De Havilland Vampire T.11	XD599	1953	28 Nov 1980	ex Staverton, Stroud, Central Air Traffic Control Sch, RAF College, 1 Sqn. See Chapter 23. *Sywell Aviation Museum, Northants*
DH Australia Drover II	'VH-FDT'	1952	1983	ex Southend – see Chapter 7, Squires Gate, G-APXX, Australia VH-EAS. See also Chapter 9. *Stored, Booker, Bucks*
DH Canada Beaver AL.1	XP812	1961	1982	composite airframe, ex Arborfield, Middle Wallop, Army Air Corps. *Became G-BMGE, sold in the USA as N5217G, Oct 1985*
Douglas C-47A Skytrain	G-BFPT	1942	1978	ex Spanish Air Force T3-65, Spain EC-ASE, USA USAAF 42-100805. *Cancelled as sold in the Yemen Sep 1978*
Douglas C-47B Skytrain	G-BFPU	1943	1978	ex Spanish Air Force T3-49, USA N86449, USAAF 43-49431. *Burnt out in the Sudan on delivery to Yemen, Sep 1978*
Douglas C-47B Skytrain	G-AFPV	1945	1978	ex Spanish Air Force T3-40, USAAF 45-1087. *Cancelled as sold in the Yemen Sep 1978*
Douglas C-47A Skytrain	G-BFPW	1944	1978	ex Spanish Air Force T3-40, USA N73855, USAAF 44-77272. *To the USA as N3753N Aug 1980*
Douglas C-47A Skytrain	G-BGCE	1942	1978	ex Spanish Air Force T3-2, USA N86453, USAAF 43-16130. *To the USA as N37529 Apr 1980*
Douglas C-47A Skytrain	G-BGCF	1943	1978	ex Spanish Air Force T3-33, USA N73855, USAAF 44-77272. *To the USA as N3753C Apr 1980*
Douglas C-47A Skytrain	G-BGCG	1943	1978	ex Spanish Air Force T3-27, USA N49V, NC50322, USAAF 43-15536. *To the USA as N5595T Jan 1980*
Fleet 80 Canuck	CS-ACQ	1946	1979	ex Portugal, Canada CF-DQP. *Nearing completion of restoration as G-FLCA, Coventry 2011*
Focke-Wulf Fw 190A-5	1227	1943	30 Aug 1991	ex Booker, USSR, Luftwaffe, crashed 19 Jul 1943. *Became G-FOKW; to USA as N19027 first flown after restoration in Arizona 1 Dec 2011*
Fokker S.11-1 Instructor	G-BIYU	1950	23 May 1981	ex Netherlands PH-HON, Neth Air Force E-15. *Airworthy with Thirsk-based owners*
Gloster Meteor TT.20	WM167	1952	1 Dec 1975	ex Royal Aircraft Est – Llanbedr, Farnborough, RAF 228 Sqn, Colerne St Flt, 228 Oper Conv Unit. See Chapter 23. *Airworthy as G-LOSM with Air Atlantique at Coventry*
Grumman FM-2 Wildcat	N909WJ	1941	30 Dec 1990	ex USA, US Navy 16203. *Believed airworthy, USA*
Grumman TBM-3W Avenger	045	1944	31 Jul 1981	G-BTBM, ex Strathallan – see Chapter 10, Netherlands Navy P-102, US Navy 85650. *Airworthy as N452HA, USA*
Grumman F8F-2 Bearcat	N800H	1945	30 Dec 1990	ex USA N2YY, N7827C, US Navy 121752. *Airworthy as N800H, Seattle USA*
Hawker Hurricane IV	KZ321	1942	1983	G-HURY, ex Israel, Yugoslav Air Force, RAF KZ321 6 Sqn. *Airworthy as CF-TPM with Vintage Wings, Canada*

Type	Identity	Built	Arrived	Background / *current status, or fate*
Hawker Sea Fury T.20S	G-BCKG	1951	15 Aug 1974	ex West Germany D-CAFO, Hawker G-9-57, Fleet Air Arm WG652, 759 Sqn, Culdrose and St Merryn Stn Flts. *Airworthy in the USA as N62143*
Hawker Sea Fury T.20S	G-BCKH	1949	9 Aug 1974	ex West Germany D-CAMI, D-FAMI, Hawker G-9-24, Fleet Air Arm VX300, 736, 766, 782 Sqns. *To USA as N46990, later N62147, airworthy at Chino, USA, as N924G*
Hawker Sea Fury T.20S *	G-BCOV	1950	9 Aug 1974	ex West Germany D-CACE, Hawker G-9-62, Fleet Air Arm VX302, no service. *To USA as N613RD, then N51SF*
Hawker Sea Fury T.20S	G-BCOW	1949	11 Oct 1974	ex West Germany D-CACO, Hawker G-9-64, Fleet Air Arm VX281, 738 and 736 Sqns. See Chapter 18. *To USA as N8476W then N281L; airworthy with Royal Navy Historic Flt, Yeovilton as G-RNHF*
Heinkel He 111 (CASA 2-111B) *	G-BDYA	1949	18 Jun 1976	ex Spanish Air Force T8B-124. *To the USA as N72615 and written off 10 Jul 2003*
Junkers Ju 52 (CASA 352L) *	G-BECL	1950	30 Jul 1976	ex Spanish Air Force T2B-212. *Airworthy in France as F-AZJU*
Junkers Ju 52 (CASA 352L)	G-BFHD	1951	4 Jul 1978	ex Spanish Air Force T2B-255. See Chapter 26. *National Air and Space Museum, Udvar Hazy Center, Dulles, USA*
Junkers Ju 52 (CASA 352L)	G-BFHE	1952	4 Jul 1980	ex Spanish Air Force T2B-273. *Airworthy in South Africa as ZS-AFA*
Junkers Ju 52 (CASA 352L)	G-BFHF	1952	Jun 1978	ex Spanish Air Force T2B-275. *Aviodrome, Netherlands*
Junkers Ju 52 (CASA 352L)	G-BFHG	1951	Jun 1978	ex Spanish Air Force T2B-262. *Fantasy of Flight, Florida, USA*
Lockheed F-5G Lightning	N505MH	1944	16 May 1989	G-MURU, ex USA N62350, USSAF 44-53186. *Airworthy with Evergreen, McMinville, USA as N505MH*
Messerschmitt Bf 109G-10	9644	1942	Apr 1979	ex Yugoslavia, Yugoslav Air Force 9644, Bulgaria, Luftwaffe 610937. *Airworthy with Evergreen, McMinville, USA as N109EV*
Messerschmitt Bf 109G-14	T2-124	1942	1979	ex USA, Luftwaffe 610824. *To USA as N109MS. National Museum of the USAF, Dayton, USA, on loan*
Messerschmitt Bf 109 (HA.1112 Buchón)	G-AWHG	1958	1973	ex Leavesden, Battle of Britain film, Spanish AF C4K-75. *Airworthy in Germany with the Messerschmitt Foundation as D-FWME*
North American Harvard IIb	FT323	1943	c 1979	G-AZSC, Netherlands PH-SKK, Neth Air Force B-19, RAF FT323 – no service, USAAF 43-13064. *Airworthy at Goodwood*
NAA TB-25N Mitchell	N9115Z	1944	1979	ex *Hanover Street*, USAAF 44-29366. *RAF Museum Hendon*
NAA TB-25N Mitchell	N9455Z	1944	1981	ex Dublin, *Hanover Street*, USAAF 44-30210. *March Field Museum, Attwater, USA*
NAA TB-25N Mitchell	N9494Z	1944	c 1979	ex *Hanover Street*, USAAF 44-30925. *Became G-BWGR, Musée Royal de l'Armée, Brussels, Belgium*
NAA P-51D Mustang *	N166G	1944	11 Nov 1979	G-PSID, ex USA N3350, N335J, N6171C, USAAF 44-63788. *Airworthy in France as F-AZFI*

Type	Identity	Built	Arrived	Background / *current status, or fate*
NAA P-51D Mustang	N314BG	1944	1986	ex USA, Canada C-GZQX, CF-BAU, USA N51N, N169MD, N6337T, RCAF 9567, USAAF 44-73140. *Believed airworthy, USA*
NAA P-51D Mustang	N513PA	1944	Feb 1992	ex USA N6311T, Canada CF-MWN, USAAF 44-73435. *Airworthy in Mexico as XB-HVL*
NAA TF-51D Mustang	N7097V	1944	Feb 1992	ex USA, Israeli Air Force 39, RCAF 9257, USAAF 44-74859. *Current status unknown*
Percival Provost T.1	WV483	1953	Jun 1983	ex Southend – Chapter 7, St Athan 7693M, 6 Flg Tng Sch. *Sold in the USA c 1986*
Pilatus P.2-05	U-125	1948	Jun 1981	ex Swiss Air Force. *Became G-BLKZ, accident 31 May 2008, stored Duxford*
Pilatus P.2-05	U-143	1950	Jun 1981	ex Swiss Air Force. *Became G-CJCI – see Chapter 25, sold in Germany Aug 2008*
Pilatus P.3	A-804	1956	6 Apr 1991	ex Swiss Air Force. *Sold in USA Sep 1992 as N321RD*
Pilatus P.3	A-811	1956	6 Apr 1991	ex Swiss Air Force. *Sold in the USA as N328RD*
Pilatus P.3	A-849	1957	6 Apr 1991	ex Swiss Air Force. *Sold in the USA as N487RD*
Pilatus P.3	A-862	1957	6 Apr 1991	ex Swiss Air Force. *Sold in the USA as N500K*
Republic P-47D Thunderbolt	N47DE	1945	11 Nov 1979	G-BLZW, ex USA, Peru Air Force 122, USAAF 45-49205. *Airworthy in USA as N47RP*
Republic P-47D Thunderbolt	13021	1944	1985	ex Yugoslavia, Yugoslav Air Force 13021, USAAF 44-90438. *Airworthy in the USA as N647D*
Republic P-47D Thunderbolt	13064	145	1985	ex Yugoslavia, Yugoslav Air Force 13064, USAAF 45-49295. *RAF Museum Cosford, as 'KL216'*
Sopwith Pup replica	N5180	1960	c 1975	G-APUP, on loan, ex Old Warden. *RAF Museum, Hendon*
Supermarine Spitfire IX	BR601	1942	Nov 1986	ex Cape Town, South African Air Force 5631, RAF BR601, 165, 316, 454 and 64 Sqns. *Lone Star Flight Museum, Texas, as N601FF*
Supermarine Spitfire IX	NH238	1944	Dec 1983	G-MKIX, ex USA N238V, Belgium OO-ARE, Belgian Air Force SM-36, Netherlands Air Force H-60, RAF NH238 – no service. *Believed stored in the UK*
Supermarine Spitfire PR.XI	PL983	1944	Oct 1987	ex East Midlands, Stonebroom, Duxford, Old Warden, Vickers G-15-109, US Embassy NC74138, RAF PL983, 2 and 1 Sqns. *Became PL983, fatal crash in France 4 Jun 2001, stored, Duxford*
Supermarine Spitfire XIV	MV262	1945	c 1979	ex OHB – See Chapter 12, India, Indian Air Force, RAF MV262 – no service. *Became G-CCVV – see Chapter 25. Under restoration at Booker, Bucks, as N808U*
Supermarine Spitfire XIV	MV293	1945	c 1979	G-SPIT, ex India, Bangalore T20, Indian Air Force, RAF MV293, 8 Sqn RIAF. *Airworthy at Duxford with The Fighter Colln as 'MV268'*
Supermarine Spitfire XIV	NH799	1944	c 1979	ex India, Indian Air Force, NH799, 9 Sqn RIAF. *Became G-BUZU. Airworthy in New Zealand as ZK-XIV*
Supermarine Spitfire XIV	SM832	1945	c 1979	G-WWII, ex OHB – see Chapter 12, India, Indian Air Force, RAF SM832. *See Chapter 25. Airworthy with Chino Warbirds as N54SF, USA*
Supermarine Spitfire XVI	RW386	1945	c 1983	G-BXVI, ex St Athan, Halton 6944M, 604 Sqn. *Airworthy in Sweden as SE-BIR*

Type	Identity	Built	Arrived	Background / *current status, or fate*
Supermarine Spitfire XVI	SL721	1945	28 Mar 1973	G-BAUP, ex Leavesden, USA N8R, Beaulieu, Worthing, RAF SL721, Central Flg Sch, 31 Sqn, Metropolitan and Fighter Command Comm Sqns. *Became USA N8WK, N721WK, airworthy in Canada with Vintage Wings as C-GVZB*
Supermarine Spitfire XVI	TE356	1945	1986	G-SXVI, ex Leeming, Cranwell, Little Rissington, Central Flg Sch, 2 Civilian Anti-Aircraft Co-op Unit, 34 and 695 Sqns. *Airworthy with Evergreen, McMinville, USA as N356EV*
Supermarine Spitfire XVI	TE392	1945	Aug 1984	ex Hereford 7000M, Wellesbourne Mountford, Church Lawford, 2 Civilian Anti-Aircraft Co-op Unit, 34, 695, 595, 164, 65 and 126 Sqns. *Lone Star Flight Museum, Texas, as N97RW*
Supermarine Spitfire XVIII	HS877	1945	c 1979	G-BRAF, ex India, Indian Air Force HS877, RAF SM969. *To the USA as N969SM Oct 2008*
Supermarine Seafire III	PP972	1946	1987	G-BAUR, ex France, Aéronavale, Fleet Air Arm PP972, 767 and 809 Sqns. *Believed stored in the UK*
Vought F4U-4 Corsair	N49092	1944	19 Feb 1988	ex USA, Florida, Honduran Air Force 615, US Navy 97280. *To USA as N712RD, damaged at Oshkosh 29 Jul 1999, stored*
Vought FG-1D Corsair	N55JP	1944	1988	ex USA, Museum of Science and Tech, New Zealand, RNZAF NZ5648. *Became G-BXUL; airworthy in New Zealand as ZK-COR*
Westland Lysander IIIa	V9281	1942	1979	G-BCWL, ex Booker, Booker, Canada, RCAF. See Chapter 26. *Fantasy of Flight, Florida, USA*

Notes: * – Illustrated in the colour sections. Additionally six, possibly more, former Indian Air Force Tempest IIs were imported to Bitteswell by February 1986, but all had moved on by mid-year. Three Folland Gnat T.1s were noted leaving Bitteswell by road in Dec 1987 – no further details.

CHAPTER 14

Lakeside Diversion
Thorpe Park
1973 to 1987

Over 400 acres of former gravel pits were transformed by 1975 into a themed leisure site, Thorpe Park, near Chertsey in Surrey. This was run by Leisure Sport Ltd, a division of Hall Aggregates Ltd. One of the themes adopted was aviation history with a small airstrip and 'period' hangars and a whole series of reproduction aircraft, some static, some taxiable, and some flying. The flying examples toured the airshow 'circuit' as well as making appearances at the water park. From the earliest days, three former Fleet Air Arm machines, a Sea Hawk, a Sea Vixen and a Whirlwind were displayed statically, but these had moved on by 1981.

The static replicas were both convincing and substantial. Two were powered, enabling them to taxi during demonstrations on the lakes. Fairey Marine was contracted by Amicus to build a full-scale, taxiable, reproduction of a Vickers Type 60 Viking amphibian for the 1974 film *The Land That Time Forgot*. Powered by a converted motor car engine, it was painted in the colours of the Argentine Navy as 'R-4'. After filming it was moved to Thorpe Park, floated and occasionally taxied. Today it is displayed at the Brooklands Museum, Weybridge. The other powered replica was a Hansa-Brandenburg W.29 floatplane reproduction painted in Imperial Germany Navy colours and powered by 1330cc Ford motor car engine and specially commissioned by Leisure Sport.

Great War on the wing

Among the flying replicas was a Fokker D.VII built in West Germany by Williams Flugzeugbau, powered by a 200hp Ranger and flight tested as D-EAWM and painted in the bold red and white colours of Ernst Udet. In August 1981 the parasol monoplane Fokker D.VIII replica was involved in a fatal accident near White Waltham in Berkshire. The decision was taken to stop the 'travelling circus' and the 'flyers' – apart from one. After the decision to stop flying *Papa-Lima* started a nomadic life, moving to Land's End, Sandown and, from April 1985, to a workshop in Hampshire for a major rebuild. It emerged from there to serve with the Old Flying Machine Company at Duxford and, from December 1990, with the Great War Combat Team at North Weald. It was exported to Italy in July 1996.

The 'flyer' that Leisure Sport retained was water-based, a scaled-down version of a Supermarine S.5 Schneider Trophy floatplane. Created by the Thruxton-based Aviation Design Bureau it was launched on to the water at Thorpe Park on 13th June 1975. Powered by a 120hp Rolls-Royce/Continental O-240A, it was first flown at Calshot, Hants, on 28th August – where the RAF High Speed Flight clinched the Schneider Trophy in perpetuity in 1931. The S.5 suffered a landing accident at Thorpe Park on 18th September 1982; the pilot was OK but *Fox-Fox* was badly damaged and it was sold off.

At the end of the 1987 season it was decided that the space taken up by the Great War aerodrome and the Schneider Trophy hangars and slipway could be better employed. The auction house Christie's included the remaining 'statics' and the second Sopwith Camel 'flyer' in the sale of 1st October 1987. Despite the aviation element of Thorpe Park having only a brief existence, the site itself has gone on from strength to strength. Today it calls itself: 'The nation's thrill capital'!

Above: Line-up on the Great War airfield, May 1980. Left to right: Fokker Dr.I, Sopwith Camel, Fokker D.VII, Airco DH.2, Albatros D.V and Bristol M.1C. *Peter Green*

The impressive static replica Supermarine S.6, on its beaching trolley. Leisure Sport

Publicity poster for the 1981 air display at Thorpe Park.

The Vickers Viking taxiable replica afloat at Thorpe Park.

Thorpe Park

Type	Identity	Built	Arrived	Background / *current status, or fate*
Albatros D.Va replica	'5397/17'	1978	1978	G-BFXL *Fleet Air Arm Museum, Yeovilton*
Bristol M.1C static replica	'C4912'	1976	1978	# *No details*
Curtiss R3C-2 static replica	'3'	1978	1978	floatplane #. *Planes of Fame, Chino, USA*
De Havilland (Airco) DH.2 replica	'5894'	1978	1978	G-BFVH *Airworthy, Lincolnshire owner*
De Havilland DH.2 static rep	'5964'	1976	1977	*Last known in Rugby, 1999*
De Havilland Tiger Moth	N9191	1939	Jul 1976	G-ALND, floatplane, ex 19 Elementary Flg Tng Sch, Duxford Stn Flt, 6 Coastal Patrol Flt. *Airworthy, South Wales owner*
De Havilland Sea Vixen FAW.2	XP919	1963	23 Jun 1975	ex Halton 8163M, 766, 899 Sqns, Aeroplane & Armament Exp Est. *Scrapped Aug 2006 Walpole, Suffolk*
Deperdussin 1913 static replica	'19'	1979	1979	floatplane, # *Sold in the USA*
Fokker D.VII replica	-	1978	1978	G-BFPL, ex Germany D-EAWM. *Last known in Italy*
Fokker D.VII static replica *	'5125'	1975	1975	# *Last known on display in a restaurant in Orlando, USA*
Fokker D.VIII replica	-	1980	1980	G-BHCA *Fatal crash 21 Aug 1981*
Fokker Dr.I replica *	'1425/17'	1976	1976	G-BEFR *Fatal crash 20 Jul 1995*
Fokker Dr.I static replica	'1/17'	1978	1978	# *Last known on display in a restaurant in Orlando, USA*
Hansa-Brandenburg W.29 rep	'2292'	1979	1979	taxiable, floatplane. *Sold prior to auction, no other details*
Hawker Sea Hawk FGA.6	WV798	1954	16 May 1975	ex Culdrose A2557, FRU, 801, 803 and 787 Sqns. See Chapter 14. *Stored, Booker, Bucks*
Hawker Hunter F.51	E-430	1956	1980	ex Dunsfold, Hawker G-9-448, Danish Air Force. *Gatwick Aviation Museum, Charlwood*
Macchi M.39 static replica	-	1979	1979	floatplane, #. *Planes of Fame, Chino, USA*
Royal A/c Factory SE.5A static rep	'B4863'	1975	1976	# *Last known on display in a restaurant in Orlando, USA*
Sopwith Baby static replica	-	1978	1978	floatplane, # *Lightwater Valley Theme Park, North Stanley, Yorks*
Sopwith Camel replica *	'C1701'	1969	Mar 1977	G-AWYY, ex USA N1917H. *Fleet Air Arm Museum, Yeovilton*
Sopwith Camel replica	'B7270'	1977	Oct 1977	G-BFCZ #. *Brooklands Museum, Weybridge*
Sopwith Triplane static replica	'N5492'	1977	1977	*Fleet Air Arm Museum, Yeovilton*
SPAD XIII replica	'S3398'	1978	Nov 1978	G-BFYO, ex D-EOWM. *Imperial War Museum, Duxford*
Supermarine S.5 replica *	'N220'	1975	Jun 1975	G-BDFF – *see text*
Supermarine S.6 static replica	'S1595'	1979	1979	# *Planes of Fame, Chino, USA*
Vickers Viking taxiable replica	'R4'	1974	1976	ex *The Land That Time Forgot*. *Brooklands Museum, Weybridge*
Westland Whirlwind HAS.7	XM665	1958	16 Dec 1974	ex Wroughton, Fleetlands, 829, 847, 848, 737 Sqns, 700H Flt. *Museum of Flight, Nowra, Australia*

Note: * – Illustrated in the colour sections. Aircraft marked # were entered into the auction of 1st October 1987.

ONES THAT GOT AWAY

De Havilland Flamingo, 1954

With only 16 built and most put into wartime communications work, it is amazing that any examples of R E Bishop's shapely DH.95 twin-engine 12-17 seat airliner survived into the 1950s. The prototype first flew from Hatfield on 28th December 1938 but the type was already largely swallowed up by the pressing needs of massive re-armament. The longer-term survivor, G-AFYH first flew on 29th November 1940 and was issued the following day to the Fleet Air Arm, joining 782 Squadron as BT312, carrying the name *Merlin VI*. It served on until it was demobbed in October 1946 and was acquired by Southern Aircraft at Gatwick for reworking and hopeful sale. It was acquired by the Redhill-based British Air Transport and was delivered to the airline on 25th May 1947. It saw little service and was retired and stored in a hangar at Redhill. Forgotten, it survived all the way through to May 1954 but then, with the closure of the airfield (it later re-opened), it was axed. So near yet so far...

CHAPTER 15

On the Road Again
Humberside Aviation Museum and the
Bomber County Aviation Museum
1975 to 2003

Established during the hey-days of the UK's amateur preservation movement, the Humberside Aircraft Preservation Society came into being in 1975. Its path of collecting, expanding and ultimately forming a museum reflected the progress of many other similar bodies; some still with us, others gone by the wayside. Critical to this was a building of suitable size to act as a store and a workshop. The use of a substantial wartime building on the former Goxhill airfield, west of Barton-upon-Humber, was obtained from a helpful landowner. Here the HAPS volunteers assembled an eclectic array of airframes gleaned from the surrounding area, plus engines, turrets and the produce of a series of aviation archaeology digs. This was all typical of the time.

All the while, the team had their eyes upon Elsham Hall, some seven miles to the south-west. Here was a good venue looking to expand its attractions and it was a stone's throw from the former Bomber Command airfield of Elsham Wolds. (The latter was to be bisected by the A15 trunk road as it wended its way to connect with the impressive Humber Bridge; which opened to traffic in June 1981.) Negotiations bore fruit and in late 1976 the Humberside Aviation Museum was opened in the grounds of the hall; the site at Goxhill was kept on as a store for some time beyond that.

Above: Dismantling Dassault Mystère IVA 101 at the USAF base at Sculthorpe in Norfolk, ready for the journey to Cleethorpes, September 1981. Financed by the Americans, the USAF over-saw the disposal or decommissioning of the former French Air Force fleet. *Christian Brydges*

The move occasioned a rethink of aims and some of the airframes accepted early on were transferred to other groups. This was again typical of the 'learning curve' of the time. Initial potential exhibits comprised incomplete light aircraft, including a pair of Auster fuselage frames and a cache of Miles Messenger and Gemini hulks. Included in this was Messenger 2A G-AJFF which had been acquired after reference to the 5th edition of *Wrecks & Relics*. Appealing and probably cheap, if not free of charge, such 'wreckage' offered immediate 'aircraft' for the blossoming collection. However, it soon became clear that restoration to presentable static condition would take considerable time, effort and expenditure. In the case of the plywood construction Miles types, the skills involved were well beyond the HAPS crew and they did well to recognise this. The Austers eventually went into hands that may one day out them back in the air; Messenger G-AKBM helped keep a fellow example flying; other Miles machines went to Sandy Topen's expanding Vintage Aircraft Team – see Chapter 17.

Gemini 7 G-AKHZ at Coventry in July 1961. Acquired by HAPS in 1977, this airframe currently forms the basis of a restoration project in Cheshire. *Roy Bonser*

Seaside attraction

A Westland Dragonfly helicopter, acquired from the fire school at Stansted, Essex, became the first 'heavy metal' for the collection and from mid-1979 further more weather-tolerant airframes began to arrive; a ubiquitous de Havilland Vampire T.11 and a hybrid Hawker Hunter. Elsham Hall was excellent as a launch pad for HAM, but space would prove to be restrictive for larger types. Eyes turned to Cleethorpes, south of Grimsby. In 1977 the Marineland and Zoo, close to the South Promenade, closed its doors and by 1981 was being developed as a leisure park. (It is today the home of the bustling Pleasure Island Theme Park.) For the developers of the site, an aircraft park was an ideal extension to the plans and another move was on the cards for HAPS. Lorry loads made the trip eastwards from Elsham and the former reptile and tropical house was turned into a museum and there was plenty of space outside. The name was changed to Bomber County Aviation Museum and it was open to visitors from 1981.

The new venue allowed for expansion of airframes – another classic element of the 1970s and 1980s – and three English Electric Canberras, another Vampire, a former French Air Force Dassault Mystère, a Westland Whirlwind and a Wessex arrived over the next four years. The barrel-nosed Canberra T.19 radar operator trainer, one of just five such conversions, was of note, but by far and away the most important aircraft preserved at this time was also one of the collection's smallest. This was a genuine pre-war Mignet HM.14 Pou du Ciel, or 'Flying Flea' to use its adopted British name. BCAM volunteers picked it up from an Air Training Unit across the other side of the Humber at Brough and it was only after it arrived on the

South Promenade that its true provenance was confirmed. It had been built at Anlaby, Hull, by T Leslie Crosland faithfully following page-by-page the book *The Flying Flea – How to Build It* by the ebullient Frenchman Henri Mignet. Powered by a Scott A.2S Flying Squirrel two-cylinder, registered as G-AEJZ and carrying the builder's initials 'TLC', it flew from either Hedon or Brough aerodromes, gaining its Authorisation to Fly on 29th May 1936. It was put into store before the outbreak of World War Two and eventually passed to the ATC unit. Today, it is proudly looked after by the team at Aeroventure at Doncaster.

A family gathering around Leslie Crosland's Flying Squirrel-powered 'Flying Flea', circa 1936. *via Christian Brydges*

Canberra T.19 WJ975 in the grounds of the former Cleethorpes Zoo, August 1983. *Alan Curry*

Salvaged from the fire school at Stansted, the hulk of Dragonfly HR.5 WP503 was always going to present a challenging restoration. *Alan Curry*

Bomber base

By 1987, it was clear that BCAM's tenure at Cleethorpes was coming to an end and move No.3 was looming. The search for a new home started all over again. An offer of a compound within the former domestic site at what had been RAF Hemswell, to the east of Gainsborough, was more than the volunteers could have hoped for. Either side of the A631 the classic buildings of an 'Expansion Period' RAF Station survive and have found other uses. Opened in January 1937, Hemswell throbbed to the sounds of Hampdens, Wellingtons, Lancasters, Lincolns and Canberras of Bomber Command. It was the 'set' for much of the ground-based sequences in Michael Anderson's 1954 film *The Dam Busters*, starring Richard Todd and Michael Redgrave.

Among the new roles the base had been put to, it was – and is – a thriving antiques centre with most of the accommodation 'H-blocks' and the guardroom hosting hundreds of dealers. Located on a former Bomber Command base, with more than a hint of 'Dam Busters' allure, with plentiful footfall from visitors who could be 'diverted' to see the collection, BCAM had found a venue of great potential.

The move, achieved in full by 1989, gave rise to another rationalisation and several airframes were disposed of, or broken up for spares. Now based well inland, the opportunity was taken to change name from Humberside Aircraft Preservation Society to Hemswell Aviation Society. The site offered a secure, fenced-in, aircraft park with space for a small display within a wooden building that also acted as workshop and store. New airframes arrived at Hemswell, a loaned Lightning F.1A giving way to an F.3 in due course, plus a Provost T.1 and a Jet Provost T.4. BCAM settled down to a well-deserved period of stability and in 1994 a long-term renewal of the lease was secured.

Sadly, by 2003 a number of circumstances came together to persuade the team that it was time to throw in the towel. High among the considerations was another 'learning curve' that haunts all groups as they gain longevity. With total reliance on volunteers, 'new blood' was becoming a rare commodity and the workload was being shared by an ever smaller bunch with, to quote one of them, an: "average age heading for three-figures!" It was with considerable sadness that Hemswell was vacated, but all could look back on nearly three decades of endeavour, underlined by phenomenal resilience in the face of three changes of base; all of this was no mean achievement.

Humberside Aviation Museum and the Bomber County Aviation Museum

Type	Identity	Built	Arrived	Background / current status, *or fate*
Auster 5	G-AKWT	1944	1975	ex Stroxton Lodge, crashed 7 Aug 1948, RAF MT360, 26 and 175 Sqns, 121 Wing, 181, 80, 486, 19 Sqns. *Stored near Newark, Notts*
Auster J/1N Alpha	G-AIJI	1947	1975	ex Kirmington, damaged 12 Jan 1975. *Stored near Newark, Notts*
Bristol Babe static replica	'G-EASQ'	1970	28 Jul 1981	ex Selby. *Bristol Aero Collection, Kemble, Glos*
Bristol Sycamore HR.14	XG506	1955	19 Nov 1983	ex Misson, 1 Sch of Tech Tng – Halton 7852M, Helicopter Dev Unit, Metropolitan Comm Sqn, 72, 118, 225, 118 and 275 Sqns. *Scrapped for spares for other projects at Doncaster, Yorks, 2001*
Dassault Mystère IVA	101	c 1956	19 Sep 1981	ex Sculthorpe, French AF. *Scrapped at Doncaster, early 2006*
De Havilland Vampire T.11	XD375	1953	1979	ex Duxford, Winterbourne Gunner 7887M, 4 and 1 Flying Training Schools, 3 CAACU, 73 Sqn. *Scrapped in Yorkshire Aug 1998*
De Havilland Vampire T.11	XD445	1953	29 Aug 1981	ex Woodford, Hawarden, St Athan, 4 and 5 FTS, Bückeburg Stn Flt. *Private collection, Staffordshire*
English Electric Canberra PR.7	WH796	1954	14 Nov 1982	cockpit. ex Macclesfield, St Athan, Wyton Stn Flt, 58, 13, 58, 100, 542, 82 and 542 Sqns. *To scrapyard at Stock, Essex, circa 1991*
English Electric Canberra B.6(M)	WH946	1954	24 Apr 1984	ex Macclesfield, Ewyas Harold, Coningsby Stn Flt, 76, 21, 542 and 617 Sqns. *Scrapped circa 1989*
English Electric Canberra T.19	WJ975	1953	24 Jul 1983	ex Cambridge, 100, 7, 100, 85 Sqns, West Raynham Target Facilities Flt, 228 Operational Conversion Unit, 44, 35 Sqn, 231 OCU. *Scrapped upon closure, cockpit to Aeroventure, Doncaster*

Type	Identity	Built	Arrived	Background / current status, *or fate*
English Electric Lightning F.1A	XM192	1961	29 Jun 1996	On loan. Ex Binbrook, Wattisham 8413M, Wattisham Target Facilities Flt, 226 Op Conv Unit, 111 Sqn. *Thorpe Camp Visitor Centre, Woodhall Spa*
English Electric Lightning F.3	XP706	1963	30 Jan 1999	ex Strubby, Binbrook 8925M, Lightning Tng Flt, 11, 5 Sqns, LTF, 23, 11, 74 Sqns. *Aeroventure, Doncaster*
Hawker Hunter GA.11	WT741	1955	1979	ex Bitteswell, Coventry, Kemble, 738 Sqn, RAF F.4, 118 Sqn. See Note [1]. *Cockpit at Aeroventure, Doncaster*
Hunting Jet Provost T.4	XP557	1961	20 Jan 1996	ex Firbeck, Bruntingthorpe, 1 Sch of Tech Tng Halton 8494M, 6 Flying Tng Sch, RAF College. *Dumfries and Galloway Aviation Museum, Dumfries*
Mignet HM.14 'Flying Flea'	G-AEJZ	1936	28 Jul 1982	ex Brough *Aeroventure, Doncaster*
Mignet HM.14 'Flying Flea'	'G-AFFI'	1973	22 Feb 1981	ex Nostell Priory, Rawdon. *Yorkshire Air Museum, Elvington*
Miles Messenger 2A	G-AHUI	1946	1976	ex Handforth, Wolverhampton. *Forming the basis of a complex restoration by The Aeroplane Collection at Hooton Park, Cheshire*
Miles Messenger 2A	G-AJFF	1947	21 Jan 1976	ex Egham. *Used in G-AHUI – above*
Miles Messenger 2A	G-AKBM	1947	1975	ex Immingham, Weston-super-Mare. *Reduced to spares circa 1978*
Miles Gemini 1A	G-AKER	1947	1977	cockpit, ex Tattershall. See Chapter 17. *Reduced to spares by 1996*
Miles Gemini 7	G-AKHZ	1947	1977	ex Handforth, Sywell. See chapter 17. *Forming the basis of a complex restoration by The Aeroplane Collection at Hooton Park, Cheshire*
Percival Provost T.1	WW388	1954	1996	ex Firbeck, Long Marston, Cardiff-Wales, Llanelli, Chinnor, Chertsey, Cuxwold, Chessington, 1 Sch of Tech Tng – Halton 7616M, 2 Flying Tng Sch. *Stored in Shropshire*
Stewart Ornithopter	–	1975	4 May 1981	On loan from Alan Stewart. *Thought stored at Louth, Lincs*
Westland Dragonfly HR.5	WP503	1953	16 Jun 1976	ex Stansted, Royal Aircraft Est – Thurleigh, North Coates, Lee-on-Solent, Lossiemouth Stn Flt. *Sunk into diving lake at Capernwray, Lancs, Apr 1996*
Westland Whirlwind HAR.10	XP339	1961	28 Oct 1984	ex Macclesfield, Hadfield, Pryton Hill, 32, 103 and 225 Sqns. *To West Germany Jun 1987*
Westland Wessex HAS.1	?	?	20 Nov 1982	forward fuselage. Ex Holme on Spalding Moor, Royal Aircraft Est – Farnborough. *Thought scrapped circa 1989*

Notes: [1] Complex composite, complex history! Initially based upon the mis-match of the GA.11 cockpit with the bulk of former Danish Air Force T.7 ET-273. On 1st May 1983 the noseless FGA.9 XG195 arrived from Macclesfiled and this, plus bits from XG297, formed the basis. Additionally, a Supermarine Swift procedure trainer cockpit was exhibited during the Hemswell days – this is now on show at the Newark Air Museum, Notts.

CHAPTER 16

Driving Passion
Graham Warner and the
British Aerial Museum of Flying Military Aircraft
1978 to 1989

The British Aerial Museum came into being as a 'handle' by which a growing collection of historic aircraft could be identified. BAM's founder airframes were the two Canadian-built Bolingbroke IVTs brought to Duxford by Ormond Haydon-Baillie in 1974 – see Chapter 12. These two machines were melded into one and became one of the most challenging restorations to flight ever undertaken in the UK. In 1987 this wonderful aircraft flew again, only to crash 31 days later. Nobody would have blamed the essentially volunteer team from going down the pub and never returning. But they went about procuring *another* airframe and started again...

This story should be known chapter and verse by *Wrecks & Relics* readers and that epic restoration gets scant detailing here as it is beyond the scope of this book. Currently, Blenheim G-BP1V is recovering from an accident suffered on 18th August 2003. Restoration is being carried out under the aegis of Blenheim (Duxford) Ltd and some of the 'faces' that worked on the original project are still involved. This time, *India-Victor* will fly with a short nose as a Mk.I and, as ever, will delight thousands every time it displays. It will continue act as a memorial to all Blenheim 'people', aircrew, ground crew, constructors and repairers who made the type the versatile and vital warplane it became. It will also serve as tribute to a small band who have exhibited tremendous skill and shown remarkable resilience by bringing a Blenheim to the skies – twice.

The Genesis of all of this is man who decided that a forlorn set of corroded parts and faded yellow fuselage sections deserved a chance to fly again. With respect to everyone else involved in this unique project, this is about Graham Arthur Warner.

Above: Blenheim 'V6028' during its all-too-short flying life, on an early sortie out of Duxford.

Inspiration and competition

In the late evening of April 20, 1943 a force of 339 aircraft of RAF Bomber Command set off on a 600-plus mile journey to Stettin (now Szczecin) on the sprawling estuary of the River Oder wending its way to the Baltic. The raid turned out to be one of the most successful of the 'Battle of the Ruhr'; the city was left devastated, 13 industrial complexes had been hit including a large chemical plant. That said, 13 Avro Lancasters, 7 Handley Page Halifaxes and a Short Stirling failed to return: 147 aircrew, killed, missing or prisoner. For Bomber Command that was a low level of sacrifice.

Merlin-engined Halifax II HR712 of 102 Squadron was airborne from its base at Pocklington at 21:34 hours. Job done and en route home, it was hit by flak 4 hours and 52 minutes after leaving its Yorkshire base and crashed into the waters off Nyborg, Denmark. The captain and flight engineer survived to be picked up by a boat, to spend the rest of the war as prisoners. The five other crew members perished and were buried with military honours at Nyborg's New Cemetery. Among them was the just 20-year old bomb-aimer, 1318828 Sgt Alex F Warner – Graham's elder brother.

Alex had volunteered to join the RAF in 1941 and he inspired Graham to join the Air Training Corps and a life-long interest in aviation was sparked. The loss of Alex was an incalculable loss for the Warner family. They were to share this anguish with the relatives of the 55,573 men of Bomber Command – including many Blenheim aircrew – who died during the war.

Graham was not put off flying and joined the RAF at 17, gaining his 'wings' when he was 19 on North American Harvards at 4 Flying Training School, Heany, Southern Rhodesia. He went on to fly Avro Lincolns as a second pilot and Gloster Meteor and de Havilland Vampire single-seat jets.

Graham Warner seated in the 'Storch', MS Criquet G-BIRW. *Duncan Cubitt – Key Publishing www.flypast.com*

On leaving the RAF, he decided to deal in cars with the ultimate aim of becoming a racing driver – it was known as 'Racing on Sunday, selling on Monday'. Graham's middle brother, Kennett, was a design draughtsman with Connaught Engineering involved in the company's racing and sports cars, and the pair had entered some sprints and hill-climbs. In 1954, Graham joined the sales staff of Performance Cars on London's Great West Road, then – aged 26 – he opened his own small showroom on the Fulham Road in 1956. This was The Chequered Flag, and soon large premises in Chiswick beckoned. 'The Flag' was destined to become a legend in the world of classic cars and racing. Graham's first contest was at Brands Hatch in 1958 behind the wheel of a black-and-white Austin-Healey 100S – he came second. In the next three years he went on to win over 50 races.

In June 1959 Graham bought 1946-built de Havilland Canada Chipmunk G-AKDN – which also acquired the black and white house colours. After that the brothers shared a Cessna, but running 'The Flag' was all-compelling and Graham made little use of either machine. [The Chipmunk was the eleventh built in Canada and used by de Havilland as prototype for the T.10 for the evaluation at Boscombe Down that led to the RAF's order, ultimately for 740, built in the UK from 1949 to 1953. Graham sold *Delta-November* in January 1961; it is still airworthy.] By the late 1970s, The Chequered Flag had more or less withdrawn from motor sport, but the temptation of historic car racing proved too much. Through this Graham met and sponsored former racing driver and BRM devotee Robs Lamplough. Another phase of his life was about to unfold.

Invite to Blenheim Palace

Robs had learned to fly at the RAF College Cranwell and combined his love of fast cars with a globe-trotting quest to acquire and restore classics with wheels or wings. Like Ormond Haydon-Baillie he had seen the potential of Duxford and moved his cache of former Israeli Defence Force/Air Force North American P-51 Mustangs and Supermarine Spitfires there for restoration, plus some of his flying 'warbirds', including Beech D.17 'Staggerwing' N18V, Hispano Buchón N48157 (see Chapter 24) and Yakovlev C-11 *Moose* G-KYAK. Graham was intrigued to hear of this side of Robs' interests and in 1978 took up an invite to come and see for himself. It was at this point that he 'discovered' the Blenheim airframes, parts, engines and what-have-you. Sadly, by then they were inert, because Ormond had been killed the previous year in a Mustang in West Germany. The plight of this stalled restoration began to gnaw away at Graham. Eventually he contacted Wensley Haydon-Baillie, who was over-seeing the dispersal of his brother's collection. Ormond had been able to get the use of the former armoury, Building 66, but from then on forever known as 'Blenheim Palace'. Previously, Graham could only peer through the windows into this workshop, now he could inspect it in detail.

Enquiries were made about the feasibility of the Blenheim flying and Graham contacted the former 'Black Knight' support team to see if things could continue. Then he made the leap and became the owner of both airframes, all of the engines and spares via The Chequered Flag. (He also bought the OHB Chipmunk, re-acquainting himself with the type and using it to renew this pilot's licence. Other 'Chippies' were to follow later.) Atypical of most warbird owners, Graham bought a restoration project *before* getting his hands on a 'flyer'.

John Gullick was Ormond's crew chief and he was keen to see the Blenheims move forward again. The young team that had been working within Building 66 comprised: John Romain, William Kelly, Robert Jackson, 'Beans' Smith. The former will need no introduction to readers and was then an apprentice with British Aerospace at Hatfield. John went on to become the managing director and chief pilot of BAM's successor, the Aircraft Restoration Company. Today, ARC and its associate company, Historic Flying, occupy an expanding complex at the east end of Duxford with a large staff of full-time engineers in a major and modern workshop. The company is also a renowned specialist in classic and warbird aircraft operation. There are many other names that could be mentioned, but their story is emblazoned in Graham's two books that cover the incredible restorations – *The Forgotten Bomber* (1991) and *Spirit of Britain First* (1996).

One of the Blenheims as found by Ormond Haydon-Baillie in Canada in 1973.

Informal amalgam; enforced take-over

With a major project up and running, Graham had got the 'bug' and started to acquire other aircraft. As noted at the beginning the title British Aerial Museum, and the suffix 'of Flying Military Aircraft', came about very much as an after-thought to give the expanding venture a name that, to use a present-day interpretation did 'what it says on the can'. Along with Robs and another motor racing friend, Anthony Hutton, BAM became a loose grouping according to ownership and types: Robs and Tony's machines became the Fighter Wing Display Team of BAM, while Graham's evolved as the Bomber/Recce Wing.

Tony flew a Harvard and Yak C-11 G-AYAK and was at home flying on the UK or US airshow circuit. He later took on one of the Canadian air survey Beech 18s that Graham acquired from Prestwick, see below. Robs' collection continued to grow and the Fighter Wing Display Team began to take on an ethos all of its own. Eventually he re-located to North Weald in Essex, building his own hangar there and achieving some exceptional restorations. His 'fleet' is currently being wound down, his former Israeli P-51D G-BIXL *Miss Helen* licking her wounds following a heavy landing at Duxford in July 2008. Anthony also moved, expanding his Harvard duo into the four-ship Harvard Formation Team. He also established the innovative 'Squadron' flying centre and maintenance facility at North Weald, which is still the hub of classic aircraft flying at the famed Essex airfield.

With an exceptionally complex and challenging restoration taking shape in 'Blenheim Palace', Graham's choice of aircraft for his 'wing' of BAM were of a more practical nature, but of great interest. Three liaison types with short take-off and landing characteristics arrived in short order and were flown at airshows: two French-built Criquets, radial-engined Fieseler Fi 156 Storchs, a French twin-finned Broussard and the Auster AOP.9 'raced' single-handedly to Australia by intrepid Army Air Corps pilot Major Mike Somerton-Rayner.

Close-up of the fin and rudder of Auster AOP.9 G-AXRR with Australia flight charted. It departed Gatwick on 18th December 1969 and, 23 airfields, 18 days and 141 flying hours later arrived at Sydney. *Alan Curry*

The Broussard at Duxford in its Moroccan Air Force colours.

During the summer of 1982 a pair of Beech 18s arrived from storage at Prestwick in Scotland having last been used by an air survey organisation. *Golf-Lima* was restored and was ideal for twin-ratings and as a 'stepping stone' to the Blenheim – it was also airshow item in its own right. Then came another project, also from Canada and with the same powerplant as the Blenheim, the Bristol Mercury nine-cylinder radial. This was a Westland Lysander III which would have added considerably to the liaison theme.

Then in 1984 The Chequered Flag, Graham's classic and new car dealership that was giving him the wherewithal to operate the BAM 'fleet' faced an enforced take-over. Graham found that the company had been sold from under him and 28 years of respected trading and competing came to an end. This was a devastating enough blow, but the Blenheim was 'on the books' of the company and the new owners had no need for a World War Two warrior as an asset. Tenders went out inviting interested parties to bid for it with a deadline of April 1985. Graham was successful – he had effectively bought back his own property! The other airframes were in Graham's name alone. The Blenheim could continue, but this was a watershed in how things would be. ARC came into being and this marked the metamorphosis from personal collection to a more planned, managed business.

Chipmunk T.10 WG307 on circuits at Duxford, June 1981.

Cathartic 31 days

On 22nd May 1987 the moment came. The patient, skilled and engaging John Larcombe AFC was set to test fly G-MKIV and so turn it into the only one of its breed to have flown since the late 1940s. 'Larks' became BAM's chief pilot in 1980, he was exceptionally skilled and a gifted instructor. Among the types he had flown in the RAF were English Electric Canberra jet bombers; Folland Gnat advanced jet trainers and Handley Page Victor tankers and in his airline career, he captained Boeing 707s, Douglas DC-10s and Lockheed TriStars. (Tragically, 'Larks' was killed when The Fighter Collection's Bell RP-63C Kingcobra N62822 encountered serious engine troubles in France on 4th June 1990. It seems that John stayed with the stricken craft to avoid a village in its flight path.)

Emotions were high before the Mercuries started and turned to euphoria when John returned from the successful maiden flight. I remember a call from an ecstatic Graham Warner telling me *India-Victor* was about to go and to get myself down to Duxford. Key Publishing's Ford Sierra allowed me to break the world land speed record between the *FlyPast* offices and the guardroom at Duxford. The 'jobsworths' at the gate were only doing their job – though I was not overly appreciative of that at the time – and it seemed to take forever to get through and find the Blenheim ticking quietly as those lovely radials cooled down. All around were entranced – they'd done it!

The attention of the press had no sooner died down than it erupted again – for the worst of reasons. Thirty-one days later – 21st June – with another pilot in command, the Blenheim crashed at 13:45 during a display at Denham, ending up on the golf course. The pilot attempted a touch-and-go on the runway despite it being agreed that in the display sequence there would be no landing *of any sort*. I spoke to a shaken and disconsolate Graham the following day and was amazed to find that his over-riding concern was that nobody was killed or badly injured. The pilot, along with John Romain and John 'Smudge' Smith had had miraculous escapes. Graham's stoicism was breath-taking.

A moment of stupidity and the Blenheim was no more. Graham summed up feelings in *Spirit of Britain First*: "John Romain and I in particular were devastated at the destruction of the Blenheim, for it had been the central focus of our lives. We had both lost our sense of purpose and direction, and felt initially that we couldn't face the prospect of climbing up on that first square and starting the struggle all over again." But they did...

'A Blenheim *will* fly again' was the title of the hand-out of the appeal launched at a press conference on 29th June. The Blenheim Society was launched, holding its inaugural meeting in November 1987, and fund-raising ventures were set in train by the society, individuals and organisations. A search for a new airframe centred upon Strathallan – see Chapter 10 – and Bolingbroke IVT 10201, soon to be G-BPIV, arrived by road on 21st January 1988. Graham turned his energies toward raising funds, via his two already mentioned books and the incredible, definitive *The Bristol Blenheim – A Complete History* published by Crécy in 2002 and appearing as a second edition three years later. (And still available –see the rear of this book for contact details!) He is also the very active president of the Blenheim Society.

The deep consideration that allowed the team to do it all again extended to reflection of how things would be run. The need to generate income was paramount and it was clear that the future lay with ARC run as a business, with the Blenheim's renaissance as part of its remit. Of the remainder of the BAM fleet, the first Morane-Saulnier Criquet had been delivered to the Museum of Flight at East Fortune in Scotland on 9th November 1982 and others were disposed of in due course. The Lysander project was dropped and the airframe sold to the Imperial War Museum and a contract secured for ARC to restore it to static display condition. Graham ploughed the funds from these sales back into 'Blenheim II'.

Jacobs R-755A powered Criquet F-BJQC on the ramp at Duxford shortly after arrival, October 1988. It was painted in Luftwaffe colours and cleverly adopted the codes 'TA+RC' for The Aircraft Restoration Company. *Ken Ellis*

The complete static restoration of Lysander G-LIZY in the colours of Special Duties 'agent-droppers' 161 Squadron, prior to its installation Duxford's 'AirSpace' hall. *Ken Ellis*

So, the informal amalgam of kindred spirits that arose from a meeting at Duxford in 1978 evolved into a major force in the operation and restoration of historic aircraft. As Graham commented to me during the writing of this book, with the second Blenheim in hand, ARC was established and at that point "BAM really just faded away." While that concludes the subject of this chapter, BAM, we need to take this extraordinary story a little further...

It was with great pride and emotion that Graham watched a *second* first flight when 'Hoof' Proudfoot eased G-BPIV *Spirit of Britain First* into the air at Duxford on 18th May 1993. The aircraft went on to enjoy a very active life, attending many airshows and other events, at last providing the team that created it and a very appreciative public, with the glorious sight of a Blenheim in its element.

While returning to base on 18th August 2003, *India-Victor* suffered problems and the resulting crash landing meant that a major rebuild was needed. Up to this point, Graham was both owner and financier of this iconic aircraft but he now faced a difficult decision and came to a remarkable conclusion. "I realised that I could not fund the third rebuild, or face raising such a large sum, so that the only way to return it to the skies would be to present the aircraft in its damaged condition, together with a substantial donation, to Blenheim (Duxford) Ltd [a subsidiary of ARC] formed for that purpose." Throughout each twist and turn, at each point Graham and those around him had one over-riding aim – to protect the Blenheim above all else. When the Blenheim flies again an odyssey that started in Manitoba in 1974 will enter a new phase.

Graham Warner inspecting the starboard engine with Colin Swann at work on the other side, Duxford, 1985. *Alan Curry*

British Aerial Museum

Type	Identity	Built	Arrived	Background / *current status, or fate*
Auster AOP.9 *	XR241	1962	May 1983	G-AXRR, ex Shuttleworth – Old Warden, St Athan, Army Air Corps 1 Wing HQ, 654 Sqn. *Airworthy with Essex owner*
Beech 18 3TM *	G-BKGL	1952	5 Jul 1982	ex Prestwick, Canada CF-QPD, RCAF 5193. *Private owner, airworthy at Duxford*
Beech 18 3TM *	G-BKGM	1952	11 Aug 1982	ex Prestwick, Canada, CF-SUQ, RCAF 2324. *To Tony Hutton on US register as N5063N Apr 1984, painted as 'HB275'. Restored as G-BKGM Sep 2009, Sidmouth owner*
Bristol Bolingbroke IVT	9893	1942	1978	ex OHB – see Chapter 12, Canada, Hartney – Manitoba, RCAF. *Stored, for static restoration for IWM, Duxford*
Bristol Bolingbroke IVT	10038	1942	1978	ex OHB – see Chapter 12, Canada, Hartney – Manitoba, RCAF. *Became G-MKIV, crashed 21 Jun 1987, in use for spares at Duxford*
DH Canada Chipmunk T.10 *	WG307	1951	Sep 1981	G-BCYJ, ex OHB – see Chapter 12, RAF WG307, Birmingham Univ Air Sqn, Primary Flg Tng Sch, Central Flg Sch, Aircrew Officers Tng Sch, PFS, 1 Initial Tng Sch, 12, 9 Air Experience Flts, Aberdeen, Manchester, Queens, Durham, Queens UASs, Binbrook Stn Flt, Leeds, Southampton UASs, 5, 18 Reserve Flg Sch, 1 Basic Flg Tng Sch. See Chapter 16. *Sold in South Africa 2004*
Max Holste Broussard	G-BJGW	1958	Aug 1981	ex France F-BMMP, French Army No.92. *Sold in France Jul 1991 as F-GHNU*
Morane Saulnier Criquet *	G-BIRW	1947	Apr 1981	ex Belgium OO-FIS, France F-BDQS. *To Museum of Flight, East Fortune, 9 Nov 1982*
Morane Saulnier Criquet *	G-BPHZ	1960	14 Oct 1988	ex France F-BJQC. *To Aero Vintage, Duxford, 2003, airworthy*
Westland Lysander IIIA	G-LIZY	1940	1983	ex Canada, RCAF 1558, RAF V9300, no service. *Restored for the Imperial War Museum, Duxford, from 1988 – displayed as 'V9673'*

Note: * – Illustrated in the colour sections.

CHAPTER 17

Jet Determination
Vintage Aircraft Team,
Lincoln Field Vintage and Historic Aircraft Collection,
the Cranfield Historic Aircraft Society
1977 to 1996

Those familiar with the Vintage Aircraft Team will probably share certain memories. The over-riding one would be the fascinating 'encampment' at Cranfield, Bedfordshire, and its series of canvas hangars, the largest of which was known as the 'VAT-Cave'. In the days of the Popular Flying Association and its annual gathering at Cranfield, the VAT enclosure would be a centre of intense fascination – what *was* lurking in there? From this came another image: an eclectic array of aircraft, most incomplete, or unfinished; the majority de Havilland twin-boom jets.

While the Cranfield set was fascinating, it was not the only base and VAT was not the only name under which activities fell. Cranfield and Duxford shared the honours for the first venue, with Vampire T.11 WZ507, of which more anon, using both while Duxford became home to the static jets. In late 1982 the T.11, Vampire FB.5 VZ304 and Gloster Meteor NF.14 WS760, along with the two former Ormond Haydon-Baillie Silver Stars, took part in a BBC political drama, *The Aerodrome*, which was screened in December 1983. All of the aircraft donned black overall, an overly intricate 'roundel' and big, white codes beginning with an intimidating 'Z' on the nose. Set in 1930s Britain, the country was run by an authoritarian dictatorship with access to highly-advanced technology – hence the jets. This regime was building a fortress-like airfield alongside a township. Among the cast was Richard Briers and the interplay of locals and the monolithic military men was the nub of the plot. As well as Duxford, Little Rissington in Gloucestershire was used for some of the flying and building-background sequences. Not long after this, VAT's presence at Duxford waned.

Above: VAT flagship, Vampire T.11 WZ507 (G-VTII) shortly after its arrival at Duxford, June 1981.

Most of the restoration projects and the airframe 'pending tray' by then had moved to Bushey, Hertfordshire. Here a volunteer organisation, the Lincoln Field Vintage and Historic Aircraft Collection – which really rolls off the tongue – was formed. Meanwhile Cranfield remained as the base for the airworthy Vampire and received from 1984 a number of former Vampires and Venoms from the Swiss Air Force; these were to form the backbone of VAT's stock in trade for much of its existence. It was to here that the cache of former 3/4 Civilian Anti-Aircraft Co-operation Unit Vampire T.11s held in dismantled store at Keevil, Wiltshire, for many years was brought although very few sets of wings seem to have made the transition.

This is a good point to remind readers that VAT undertook restorations, operated aircraft or held in them in store for a series of other operators – for example Aces High, Butane Buzzard Aviation and Source Classic Jet. One of the Aces High airframes was Lightning F.2A G-BNCA which was stored on behalf of the film specialist operator. It was scrapped at Cranfield in December 1994 at the same time as the 'fleet' acquired by Arnold Glass was also 'processed'. If all of these aircraft were to be added to the table it would swell it considerably. Co-located and associated with VAT at Cranfield for a short while in the late 1980s was Militair Ltd and its aircraft are also not given here. It may well be that other machines listed in this table were not owned by VAT and as such I should point out that ownership is not to be inferred by an airframes' appearance in the table.

An example of the aircraft handled by VAT for others, former Swiss Air Force Venom FB.50 J-1523 at Cranfield in July 1984; it was destined for Source Classic Jet as G-VENI. *Alan Curry*

In 1985, VAT and LFV&HAC had to leave the site at Bushey but it was to be 1991 before the site was finally vacated. From 1985 operations were consolidated at Cranfield and during that year LFV&HAC disbanded only to reform as the Cranfield Historic Aviation Society. In 1990, building developments at Cranfield meant that the 'VAT-Cave' and its surrounding structures had to go. At this point VAT underwent a thorough rationalisation of the airframes it owned and the residue moved through to Bruntingthorpe in Leicestershire from early 1992. Sadly, this did not beckon a new dawn; in 1996 VAT ceased to function and its aircraft were dispersed.

Jet pioneers

So in the space of nearly 20 years, there were four bases, with Cranfield doubling alongside Duxford and Bushey. Another location could be added to the list and that was Carlisle in Cumbria where VAT had a 'detachment' from 1977 through to early 1980. In January 1977, Meteor NF.14 WS832 arrived to join the small collection of the Solway Aviation Group. The Meteor was presented by VAT's leading light, the hard-grafting and ever-adaptable Alexander 'Sandy' Topen. His eyes had been on Solway's Vampire T.11 WZ507 and determined that it was in very good condition and that it could be restored to flying trim. Last in service with the Central Air Traffic Control School at Shawbury, Shropshire, WZ507 had flown to Carlisle and was struck off RAF charge on 9th May 1969.

In a hangar at Carlisle, a team led by Sandy and involving several volunteers from the Solway group worked away on the Vampire. On 9th January 1980 it was placed on the civil register as G-VTII – taking the 'Is' as 1s this stands for Vampire T.11 – to John Chillingworth, Sandy Topen and John Turnbull. On 17th February *Double-India* flew for the first time and became the first private civilian restored and operated former military jet in the UK. At that time, it was only the second of its type flying in Britain, the other being the Central Flying School's XH304, run in conjunction with Meteor T.7 WF791 as the 'Vintage Pair'. Hard on the heels of Sandy in the jet 'stakes' was Spencer Flack – more of that in Chapter 18. VAT's Vampire was ferried to Duxford in the early summer of 1981. Today it is operated by the Vampire Flying Group at North Weald in Essex, and has to have established some record for longevity for a jet 'warbird'.

Venom FB.54 G-BLKA at Cranfield in 1985, in RAF Suez markings as 'WR410'.

The many hurdles encountered and surmounted during transforming WZ507 to G-VTII meant that Sandy and VAT had amassed considerable experience in restoring and operating classic jets. Hence the work carried out for other organisations for the rest of VAT's existence. Two other aircraft were returned to flight for VAT under its own aegis. Former Swiss Air Force Venom FB.54 J-1790 touched down at Cranfield from Dubendorf on 5th July 1984 and on 1st December that year, now as G-BLKA and wearing RAF colours it flew again, going on the airshow 'circuit' the following year. In 1988 Jet Provost T.3 XN637, as G-BKOU, joined the two de Havilland 'twin-boomers' well ahead of the flood of the type on to the civil register after the RAF disposed of the venerable trainer.

The third of the Cranfield jet trio, Jet Provost T.3 XN637 inside the 'VAT-Cave' 1987.

Vintage Aircraft Team, Lincoln Field Vintage and Historic Aircraft Collection, the Cranfield Historic Aircraft Society

Type	Identity	Built	Arrived	Background / *current status, or fate*
Auster J/1 Autocrat	G-AIBR	1946	1980	fuselage, ex Duxford, Sywell, Gamston. *Airworthy, Norwich owner*
Auster J/1N Alpha	G-AKJU	1946	1988	ex Southend, RAF TW513, Aeroplane & Armament Exp Est. *Airworthy as G-TENT, Chichester area*
Auster AOP.9	XK416	1957	1981	G-AYUA, ex Luton, Sibson, Middle Wallop 7855M, Army Air Corps 651 Sqn. *Stored, Nottinghamshire owner*
Auster AOP.9	XP248	1959	1987	ex Wroughton, Marlborough 7822M, Old Sarum, Middle Wallop, 651 Sqn. *No details*
Auster AOP.9	XP283	1959	1978	fuselage, ex Shoreham, Middle Wallop 7859M, 654 Sqn. *Last known Warwickshire owner 1996*
Beagle Terrier 1	G-AVCS	1952	1 Sep 1983	ex Cranfield, Finmere, RAF WJ363, Odiham Stn Flt, 1900 Flt. *Under restoration, Lisburn, Northern Ireland*
Beagle Terrier 2	G-AYDW	1946	1981	ex G-ARLM, Army Air Corps / RAF TW568, Light Aircraft Sch, Air Observation Post Sch, 227 Op Conv Unit, 43 Op Tng Unit. *Stored, Devon*
Beech D.18S	G-BKRN	1952	1987	ex Scottish Aircraft Collection Trust, Perth – see Chapter 10, Prestwick CF-DTN, RCAF instructional A675, RCAF 1550. *Under restoration to fly, Bruntingthorpe*
De Havilland Tiger Moth	G-AMTK	1939	1981	ex Rochester, Croydon, RAF N6709, 2 Glider Sch, 6 and 1 Elementary Flg Tng Sch, 34 Elem and Reserve Flg Tng Sch, 11 and 1 Reserve Flg Tng Sch, 1 Elem Flg Tng Sch, 12 Radio Sch, 9 Elem Flg Tng Sch. *Hertfordshire owner, stored*
De Havilland Tiger Moth	G-ANEH	1939	1981	ex Didcot, RAF N6797, 11 and 1 Reserve Flg Sch, 1 Elementary Flg Tng Sch, 12 Radio Sch, 9 EFTS, 9 Elem & Reserve Flg Tng Sch. *Airworthy, Oxfordshire owner*
De Havilland Tiger Moth	NL985	1944	1981	ex Leamington Spa, Finningley and Colerne – see Chapter 6, Cwmfelinfach 7105M, 9 Fg Tng Sch, 2 Grading Sch, London Univ Air Sqn, Queens Univ Air Sqn, 11 and 5 Reserve Fg Schs, Birmingham Univ Air Sqn, 16 and 14 Elementary Flg Tng Schs. See also Chapter 17. *Salisbury owner, registered as G-BWIK and believed under restoration*
De Havilland Vampire FB.5 *	VZ304	1950	1980	ex Carlisle 7630M, 3 Civilian Anti-Aircraft Co-op Unit, 249 Sqn. *Scrapped at Bushey, 1991*
De Havilland Venom FB.50	J-1632	1956	5 Jul 1984	G-VNOM, ex Swiss Air Force. *Norfolk owner, stored*
De Havilland Venom FB.54	'WR410'	1957	5 Jul 1984	G-BLKA, ex Swiss Air Force J-1790. *De Havilland Aircraft Heritage Centre, London Colney*
De Havilland Vampire T.11	WZ415	1952	1983	ex Keevil, 3/4 Civilian Anti-Aircraft Co-op Unit, 226 OP Conv Unit, Aeroplane & Armament Exp Est. *Scrapped at Leavesden 1993*
De Havilland Vampire T.11	WZ416	1952	1982	ex Hatfield, 1 Flg Tng Sch, Central Flg Sch, RAF College, Central Gunnery Sch, Handling Sqn. *Stripped for spares and scrapped 1983*

Type	Identity	Built	Arrived	Background / *current status, or fate*
De Havilland Vampire T.11 *	WZ507	1953	1980	G-VTII, ex Central Air Traffic Control Sch, 5 and 8 Flg Tng Schs, 229 Oper Conv Unit. First flown at Carlisle 17 Feb 1980. *Vampire Preservation Group, airworthy, North Weald*
De Havilland Vampire T.11	WZ616	1953	1983	ex Keevil, 3/4 Civilian Anti-Aircraft Co-op Unit, West Raynham Instrument Rating Flt, Wattisham Stn Flt, 111 Sqn, 229 Op Conv Unit. *Reported sold in the USA 1987*
De Havilland Vampire T.11	XD375	1953	1978	ex Winterbourne Gunner 7887M, 4 and 1 Flying Training Schools, 3 CAACU, 73 Sqn. *Scrapped in Yorkshire Aug 1998*
De Havilland Vampire T.11	XD459	1954	1983	ex Keevil, 3/4 Civilian Anti-Aircraft Co-op Unit, 229 and 233 Oper Conv Units, 151, 253 and 56 Sqns. *Aeroventure, Doncaster, Yorks*
De Havilland Vampire T.11	XH328	1956	1983	ex Keevil, 3 Civilian Anti-Aircraft Co-op Unit, 14 Sqn RNZAF, 60 Sqn. See Chapter 23. *Norfolk owner, stored*
De Havilland Vampire T.11	XH329	1956	1983	ex Keevil, 3/4 Civilian Anti-Aircraft Co-op Unit, Acklington and Biggin Hill Stn Flts. *Stored Greenford, Gtr Lon*
De Havilland Vampire T.11	XK632	1956	1983	ex Keevil, 3/4 Civilian Anti-Aircraft Co-op Unit, Central Flg Sch. *Scrapped at Denham, circa 1998*
DHC Chipmunk T.10	WD356	1951	1981	ex Nostell Priory, Aldergrove 7625M, Queens Univ Air Sqn. *To Canada 1999*
DHC Chipmunk T.10	WD386	1951	1992	ex Tenby, St Athan, 1 Flg Tng Sch, Oxford Univ Air Sqn, 22 Reserve Flg Sch, 2 Basic Flg Tng Sch. *In Northern Ireland 2007*
DHC Chipmunk T.10	WP845	1952	28 May 1992	ex Stroud, Northhumblerland Univ Air Sqn, Air Officer Tng Sch, Primary Flg Sch, AOTS, Initial Tng Sch, 7 Air Experience Flt, Home Command Comm Sqn, London Univ AS, RAF College, 14 Reserve Flg Sch. *To Canada 2001*
English Electric Lightning F.2A	G-27-239	1962	28 Oct 1987	G-BNCA, ex Warton, 8346M, RAF XN734, Rolls-Royce, Aeroplane & Armament Exp Est. *Scrapped Dec 1994*
Gloster Meteor NF.14	WS760	1954	1980	ex Brampton 7964M, Upwood, 1 Air Nav Sch, 64 Sqn, 237 Op Conv Unit. *Transferred to Meteor WS760 Group, 1985. Displayed Aeropark, East Midlands Airport, Castle Donington*
Hawker Hunter T.7	XL578	1958	3 Apr 1992	ex St Athan, 1 Tactical Weapons Unit, TWU, 229 Op Conv Unit. *Private owner, Woodhall Spa, Lincs*
Hunting Jet Provost T.3	XN637	1961	1978	G-BKOU, ex Winterbourne Gunner, 3 Flg Tng Sch. *Airworthy, North Weald, Essex*
Lockheed T-33A *	'91007'	1952	1987	G-TJET, ex Danish Air Force DT-566, USAF 51-8566. Re-registered as G-NASA. *To the USA Nov 1996*
Miles Magister	G-AIUA	1940	1981	ex Old Warden, Duxford, Felthorpe, RAF T9768, 10 Air Gunnery Sch, 7 Flg Instructor Sch, 15 Elementary Flg Tng Sch, Wyton Stn Flt. *Wings World War Two Remembrance Museum, Balcombe, West Sussex*

Type	Identity	Built	Arrived	Background / *current status, or fate*
Miles Magister	G-ANWO	1938	1983	ex Old Warden, Duxford, Felthorpe, RAF L8262, 21 Pilot Advance Flg Unit, Central Flg Sch, 17 Service Flg Tng Sch, RAF College, 2 and 6 Flg Instructor Sch, Coltishall Stn Flt, 5 and 8 Elementary Flg Tng Sch, 29 Elementary and Reserve Flg Tng Sch. *Bury, Lancs, owner, stored*
Miles Messenger 2A	G-AHUI	1946	1982	ex Caistor, Elsham Hall and Goxhill – see Chapter 15, Handforth, Wolverhampton. *Forming the basis of a complex restoration by The Aeroplane Collection at Hooton Park, Cheshire*
Miles Messenger 2A	G-AJFF	1947	1982	ex ex Caistor, Elsham Hall and Goxhill – see Chapter 15, Egham, Elstree, Swanton Morley. *Used in G-AHUI – above*
Miles Gemini 1A	G-AKER	1947	1982	cockpit, ex Elsham Hall – see Chapter 15, Tattershall. See Chapter 17. *Reduced to spares by 1996*
Miles Gemini 1A	G-AKGD	1947	1983	ex Southend. See Chapter 17. *Used in The Aeroplane Collection composite project, Hooton Park, Cheshire*
Miles Gemini 7	G-AKHZ	1947	1982	ex Elsham Hall – see Chapter 15, Handforth, Sywell. See Chapter 17. *Forming the basis of a complex restoration by The Aeroplane Collection at Hooton Park, Cheshire*
North American Harvard II	1513	1941	1981	ex East Ham, Portuguese Air Force 1513, South African AF 7426, RAF EX884 no service, USAAF 41-33857. *Under restoration as G-CCOY, Bruntingthorpe*
Percival Provost T.1	WV495	1953	15 Mar 1991	ex Booker, St Merryn, Tattershall Thorpe, Strenshall, Halton 7697M, 6 Flg Tng Sch. *Sold in the USA 1992*
Percival Provost T.1	XF914	1956	1982	ex Castle Donington – see Chapter 20, Barton, Connah's Quay, Shawbury, Flg Tng Command Comm Flt, Central Flg Sch, Glasgow and London Univ Air Sqns. *To the USA 1993*
SPP Super Aero 45	G-AYLZ	1957	1982	ex Southend, Andrewsfield, 9M-AOZ, F-BILP. *Currently registered, Surrey owner*

Note: * – Illustrated in the colour sections. At different times, several Tiger Moth fuselages and dismantled airframes were also to be found at Bushey, Cranfield and Bruntingthorpe – all have remained anonymous.

CHAPTER 18

Elstree's 'Air Force'
Spencer Flack
1977 to 1994

Effortless was the only way to describe it... Bright red Beech Baron 55 G-FLAK, carrying the name *Red Baron* on the nose, sizzled across the finishing line. When the race officials had huddled and checked their clipboards, the obvious result was announced: Spencer Flack had won the 1990 Schneider Trophy air race at 228.1mph. *FlyPast* was heavily involved in air racing in those days, sponsoring Terry Hiscock and his Beagle Pup 150 G-AXIF *Susie II*. We'd managed 28th position, thrashing around the Solent and across Bembridge aerodrome on the Isle of Wight. When I found Spencer to ask him how he achieved such consistent lap times and lyrical flying patterns, he beamed his usual wry smile, pointed at the other competitors and said: "That's for them to find out and for me to perfect". Not modest but far from boastful, Spencer worked hard, played hard and made sure that whatever it was he was doing he had the edge over everyone else.

Part of that hard graft had been the creation of a very successful plant hire company and off-shoots. As with several other chapters, deciding just *when* Spencer's aeronautical ventures came under the catch-all of 'collection' took some pondering. There was a lot of activity before the arrival of the two-seat Sea Fury, but that Centaurus-powered beast carried the legend 'Elstree Air Force' under its owner's name by the cockpit. Its then we'll settle on – that's when the quantum leap was made...

Above: G-HUNT at Yeovilton in August 1980 – it is first season it caused a sensation where-ever it went. *Tim R Badham*

Spencer, wearing a Reno air races cap, with John Swain, his air race crew-chief. *via John Swain*

Biplanes and bigger things

The son of an acclaimed RAF pilot, Spencer learned to fly in a Piper Cherokee at Elstree in 1973 and before long he was Chairman of Elstree Aero Club. His first foray into a 'classic' was in 1975 when he acquired Dornier-built Bücker Bü 133 Jungmeister G-AXMT which had been delivered new to the Swiss Air Force in 1938 and he kept it until 1981. He also acquired a Stampe SV-4 and with this two-seater he was tutored on how best to handle a biplane and aerobatics by Neil Williams – more of this gifted pilot in Chapters 5, 10 and 13 – and 'Manx' Kelly, founder and leader of the Stampe-equipped Rothmans Aerobatic Team, 1970 to 1974. This was typical of Spencer – find the best, learn from them and be prepared to pass such skills on to others.

In 1976 Spencer followed up a lead that the Spanish Air Force was disposing of a series of locally-built Bü 131 Jungmann training biplanes. (The air force knew them as E3Bs, the builder, CASA, designated them 1-131s.) He put his money down on a batch of ten and they were registered as G-BECT, 'U, 'V, 'W, 'X, 'Y, G-BEDA, 'B, 'C and G-BSRF. He organised an "Elstree expeditionary force" to go get them and bring them back. In September 1976 he flew the volunteer pilots out in his plant hire company's twin-turboprop Beech King Air C90 G-BBKN. Only six Jungmann made it back, the keen pilots leaving a trail of broken biplanes along the way. Spencer finally abandoned the Elstree exodus and returned with more skilled pilots who got the job done. It was bad luck that G-BSRF was one of the aircraft written off, it had been specially registered to carry the initials of Spencer Robert Flack! The venture was far from a financial debacle, on the day the six surviving biplanes made it to Elstree, three of them were sold for cash! The next batch was dismantled and crated for the journey to Hertfordshire!

By the end of 1976 Spencer had set his mind on bigger things and he was beginning to formulate the idea of restoring a warbird – or more – to fly and display on the airshow 'circuit'. He needed a 'stepping stone' and for this and turned to Warbirds of Great Britain at Blackbushe – see Chapter 13. He came away with two-seat former target-tug Sea Fury T.20S G-BCOW and it was registered to him in February 1977. Spencer had plans for a recently active single-seater and was also following up on a 'from scratch' restoration project. But in the summer of 1977 those schemes were diverted and then expanded.

Two-seat Sea Fury G-BCOW at Blackbushe in April 1976, prior to its sale to Spencer.

Red Hunter

As a Hawker product, Sea Fury *Oscar-Whisky* was very welcome at the annual Hawker Siddeley Families Day at Dunsfold in Surrey. It was there that Spencer met with Bob Coles and the conversation turned to another ambition – to own and fly a jet fighter. Parked on the airfield were some former Danish Air Force Hunters and they had caught Spencer's eye. It had been hoped these machines would be refurbished for export for foreign air arms but HSA's priorities had changed and instead they were in the process of being passed on to museums and similar organisations. Bob explained that one might be available; he knew that a south coast society could no longer take on the example offered to them. (More on Bob in Chapter 9.)

In May 1978 Hunter F.51 E-418 arrived on the back of a lorry at Elstree. Heading the volunteer restoration team from that summer was Eric Hayward, who worked at Dunsfold as a senior airframe inspector and had encyclopaedic knowledge of Sir Sydney Camm's jet fighter. Retired in the early 1970s, E-418 had clocked up 3,574 hours. In *Hawker Hunter – Biography of a Thoroughbred* author Francis K Mason noted this was "believed to be the highest number of flight hours by a Hunter F.4 derivative." It had been one of Eric's tasks to inspect the Danish machines and he was impressed by their condition; hence their arrival at Dunsfold.

Hunter F.51s of Eskadrille 724, Royal Danish Air Force, in 1961. Furthest from the camera is E-418 which became G-HUNT. *RDanAF*

G-HUNT at Biggin Hill on 17th May 1980, its airshow debut.

As the project gained momentum, it became apparent that the 2,135ft east-west runway at Elstree would probably be too short and that the disruption of a move to another airfield for flight test was necessary. Spencer had befriended Stefan Karwowski, a New Zealand-born son of a Polish World War Two fighter pilot and a talented display and fast jet pilot. Mild mannered-Stefan had no worries that what was now G-HUNT would have no problems with Elstree's runway. He was happy to conduct the first flight from its 'native' aerodrome, while the remainder of the shake-down would take place at Cranfield, Bedfordshire.

Came the day, 20th March 1980, and G-HUNT was positioned on the very end of Elstree's runway, to give Stefan every available inch! The Hunter was off with space to spare and returned for a victory roll before positioning to Cranfield. As charted in Chapter 17 at Carlisle 33 days earlier de Havilland Vampire T.11 G-VTII had flown, becoming the first privately operated and restored, Permit to Fly, former military jet. (Note: 1980 was a Leap year!) With the debut of G-HUNT, the Vampire's glory was short-lived; here was a single-seat swept-wing jet fighter – a very different beast. Spencer had familiarised himself with the Hunter courtesy of a T.8 two-seater of the Fleet Requirements and Air Direction Unit at Yeovilton, Somerset. He went on to fly G-HUNT on July 28, 1980.

In Spencer's 'house colours' of overall gloss red with white and blue trim G-HUNT was a sensation at airshows. Some rapidly deployed pens decried the lack of authentic, or at least appropriate, colour scheme but Spencer was not concerned. Talking about his red Spitfire, he noted: "It's mine, it flies, it turns heads and that's what it's supposed to do." Two other Danish Air Force airframes had been acquired to help with spares for G-HUNT; elements of two-seater ET-272 moved with Eric Hayward's crew to nearby Leavesden where they worked on Brian Kay's two-seater T.7 G-BOOM which first flew on 24th April 1981. (Brian had supplied his Lear Jet 35A G-ZOOM as chase-plane for G-HUNT's first flight. Both Eric and G-BOOM went on to join Hunter One – see Chapter 23.) Also in use as a 'Christmas tree' was F.51 E-423 and Spencer presented this to Bob Coles as a 'thank you' – see Chapter 9.

(Stefan Karwowski went on to display Folland Gnat G-GNAT, owned by Arnold Glass, with incredible style and also flew with great panache the warbirds of Stephen Grey, particularly the Grumman Bearcat. Tragically, Stefan was killed while displaying a Pitts Special in New Zealand in April 1985.)

If in doubt: 'Plan B'

By the time G-HUNT took to the air, another red beauty was rapidly taking form inside the workshop, Sea Fury FB.11 G-FURY. This was Spencer's *third* Fury; his second one never made it to Elstree. With the sad death of Ormond Haydon-Baillie (Chapter 12) Spencer acquired FB.11 G-AGHB from his estate. *Hotel-Bravo* had been left at Osnabruck in West Germany following an engine failure. Spencer and good friend and skilled engineer and pilot Mike Searle commuted across to carry out a powerplant change. Work complete, Mike carried out a test flight on 24th June 1979 but there was a serious fuel problem and in the ensuing forced-landing he was very lucky to get away with minor injuries. *Hotel-Bravo* was a write-off and was consigned to supplying parts to Spencer's "Plan B".

The machine that became all-red G-FURY was acquired from a barn in Kent and prior to that had been a founder member of the museum at Southend – see Chapters 5 and 7. In June 1980 *Romeo-Yankee* thundered down Elstree's runway and also became an instant air show star. Later G-FURY was fitted with a pair of Sanders Smokewinder smoke generators under the wing tips to add to the aircraft's already impressive aerobatic routine.

Sea Fury FB.11 WJ288 lying forlorn in the long grass at Southend. It was to be resurrected as G-FURY.

Space was then available for project No.3 and Mike Searle had tracked this down, pointing out an advert for Spitfires available at Strathallan (Chapter 10) and in January 1979 a deal was concluded for Griffon-engined Spitfire XIV NH904. With G-HUNT and then G-FURY, Spencer applied for the out-of-sequence registration G-SPIT on March 21 but was mortified to discover that Doug Arnold (Chapter 13) had snapped that up 19 days before! Spencer settled for G-FIRE – a very apt identity for something destined to be all red. Spitfire maestro Ray Hanna carried out the first flight on 14th March 1981. Spencer now had a red trio – but not for long.

Spitfire G-FIRE prior to start up at Abingdon, 1985.

Flying G-FURY, with drop tanks fitted, on 2nd August 1981 Spencer encountered severe problems. Out of the corner of his eye he saw the long runway at Waddington, Lincs, and hoped he could get there. Alas, on long finals the engine failed completely and as those five big blades stopped so did the aerodynamics. The naval fighter came down in a potato field not far from the end of the runway. *Romeo-Yankee* disintegrated, but the cockpit area stayed more or less integral... and a fire was raging. The canopy would not roll back, but quickly Spencer realised that an adrenalin-pumped head and a 'bone-dome' could be used to smash a way out. In hospital on the way to recovery Spencer reverted to his ironic self and out of the accident arose an oft-quoted line: "Someone asked me what *sort* of potato field [I'd come down in]... I told him, 'after I'd finished with them, they were mashed, baked *and* roasted!'"

After much reflection Spencer decided that it was "time to put the train set away". Arrangements were made to dispose of the 'Elstree Air Force' and G-HUNT went on to become founder member of Mike Carlton's Hunter One organisation – see Chapter 23.

It can't be red

But there was still an unticked box on Spencer's 'things to do' list... So it was not surprising when on 22nd June 1987 North American P-51D Mustang N1051S '511371' *Sunny VIII* landed at Southend having flown the Atlantic, fresh from an exacting restoration in Texas. Before long Spencer's was piloting it to air races, fly-ins and just where-ever he needed to be. It wore the colours of the 336th Fighter Squadron of the Debden-based 4th Fighter Group – 'The Eagles'. This got the pundits going: why was it not all-red; had Spencer finally got the message about colour schemes? When I asked, the answer came: "Can't do that – it's leased!"

There is another quote from Spencer that arose from a post-race conversation. He felt that there were a number of pilots who thought that success came from cutting corners – sometimes literally. "You don't have to be brave to take unnecessary risks, just stupid. The brave take *necessary* risks." The Mustang went home in 1994 and after *Red Baron* G-FLAK, came another carefully honed Baron 58, N951SF.

Then came news that he had been killed in a race. Not the flying kind, but another of his passions; 'heritage' motor racing. On 23rd February 2002, in his 59th year, he had been competing in a 1950s BRM in Australia and his car and another had 'clipped'. A life brim full of challenge, experience and determination was brought to an end while doing what Spencer was best at, striving for that all-important edge.

'Race 51' Baron N951SF, with Spencer at the helm, ready to power away at the start of another air race. *Ken Ellis*

Spencer Flack

Type	Identity	Built	Arrived	Background / current status, or fate
Hawker Sea Fury FB.11 *	G-FURY	1952	9 Apr 1978	ex Southend – see Chapter 7, Biggin Hill, Dunsfold, WJ244, Fleet Requirements Unit, 801 Sqn. *Crashed Waddington 2nd Aug 1981*
Hawker Sea Fury FB.11	WH589	1951	1979	G-AGHB, ex Ormond Haydon-Baillie – see Chapter 12, Southend – see Chapter 7, ex Canada CF-CHB, Cold Lake, Australia, WH589, Royal Aus Navy 724 Sqn. *Crashed on air test 24 Jun 1979. Part of a composite rebuild in the USA, airworthy in Seattle, USA as N4434P*
Hawker Sea Fury T.20S *	G-BCOW	1949	Feb 1977	ex Warbirds of Great Britain – see Chapter 13, West Germany D-CACO, Hawker G-9-64, Fleet Air Arm VX281, 738 and 736 Sqns. *To USA as N8476W Jul 1980, then to N281L; airworthy with Royal Navy Historic Flt, Yeovilton as G-RNHF*
Hawker Hunter F.51 *	G-HUNT	1956	May 1978	ex Dunsfold, G-9-440, Danish Air Force E-418. *Airworthy with AirVenture Museum, Oshkosh, USA, marked as 'WB188', registered as N611JR*
Hawker Hunter F.51	E-423	1956	1979	ex Bitteswell, Dunsfold G-9-444, Dan AF, Esk 724. Used for spares – see Chapter 9. *Stored, Enstone, Oxfordshire*
North American P-51D Mustang *	N1051S	1945	22 Jun 1987	ex USA N751CB, N1051S, N12067, Nicaraguan Air Force GN-121, USAAF 45-11371. *Returned to USA Jan 1994 – became N51KF, fatal crash USA 2 Jul 1995*
Supermarine Spitfire FR.XIV	G-FIRE	1945	Mar 1979	ex Strathallan – see Chapter 10, Flimwell, Henlow, Valley, Belgian Air Force SG-108, RAF NH904, 610, 414 Sqns. *Airworthy in the USA as N114BP*

Note: * – Illustrated in the colour sections.

CHAPTER 19

Marauders
Rebel Aircraft Museum and the
Earls Colne Aviation Museum
1978 to 1997

One of the smallest museums to feature within the main body of this book, the Rebel Air Museum punched above its weight. Its story is essentially that of a father and son team who could trace their enthusiasm back to enlisting with the supporter society backing the British Historic Aircraft Museum at Southend (Chapter 7). Avid collectors, they were especially galvanised when talking about the USAAF in Essex and all the more so when they were face-to-face with veterans. Their Essex locale meant that the prime target of their passions was the Ninth Air Force and the Martin B-26 Marauder, or 'Widow Maker'.

The airfield at Great Saling, near Stebbing, was the first in the UK to be constructed by a US Army team. Always intended for a US outfit, it was renamed – uniquely as it transpired – on 21st May 1943 as Andrews Field. American air bases were often named after prominent airmen and in this case it was to honour Lt Gen Frank Maxwell Andrews, Commander European Theatre of Operations, killed in a flying accident in Iceland on 3rd May 1943. Perhaps realising there was no mileage in such remembrance at a base that would be only temporary, the USAAF dropped the 'naming' of airfields in the ETO. To make amends, in 1947 Camp Springs Field in Maryland became Andrews Air Force Base and went on to gain fame as the home of *Air Force One*. As USAAF Station 485, Andrews Field received the B-26s of the 322nd Bomb Group from June 1943.

In 1979 Stan Brett and his son, David, negotiated the use of a building at Andrewsfield to house their collection and items from friends and colleagues. (These days, it's one word and a pleasant grass strip aerodrome within the boundaries of the original bomber base.) They also put their name down for a former French Air Force, but US-funded, Mystère IVA which the USAF was loaning out to UK museums. The pair settled on the name Rebel Air Museum, mostly to underline their attitudes to 'established' collections.

Above: A B-26 flying over Earls Colne in 1944. *via Dave Brett*

Ninth Air Force relics

Their greatest treasure had come from Duxford where it was surplus to requirements and Stan and Dave just had to have it. This was the rear fuselage of B-26C 41-35253 that flew with the 454th Bomb Squadron of the 323rd BG, based not far away at Earls Colne. This machine was struck off charge on 1st June 1945 and joined many others at the huge base at Burtonwood. Eventually it, and probably that of many others, was taken to a scrapyard in the nearby town of Warrington. On a tip-off, a team from the Liverpool-based Merseyside Aviation Society – including the author – found the substantial remains of the fuselage in 1974 amid a huge heap of salvage. Contact was made with the East Anglian Aviation Society and a lorry load of USAAF-related material headed for Duxford. By the time that Stan and Dave got their hands on it, only the rear fuselage was available – nevertheless it represents the largest surviving morsel of B-26 in the UK. Today, this artefact is with the Boxted Airfield Historical Group Museum, at another former USAAF Essex airfield.

The displays put together were little short of shrines to the USAAF and the Ninth Air Force in particular. Regular visits were made by former B-26 aircrew and they were always made very welcome. Robs Lamplough (Chapter 16) allowed one of the North American P-51D Mustangs his team had salvaged from Israel to go on show and a Fairchild Cornell project, previously at Southend, also lodged at Andrewsfield.

In August 1986 Stan Brett died and Dave had to come to terms with the loss of a father and fellow enthusiast. In late 1986 the Rebel Air Museum had to vacate Andrewsfield. Dave vowed that the set-up would relocate and quickly announced the new venue was Earls Colne. Hopes were that it would be up and running by 1988, but there was so much to do that it was not until the early summer of 1991 that RAM was fully open again. At the same name, it was decided to add another name, to emphasize the new location: Earls Colne Aviation Museum.

As with Andrewsfield, Earls Colne was – and remains – a light aviation centre on the site of the former wartime airfield. There is also another great use of the available land, a thriving golf and country club and all elements get on well with one another. Earls Colne was another Ninth Air Force base, Station 358, and in July 1943 the 323rd BG arrived – the B-26C rear fuselage had come 'home'. Tragically, Dave Brett died in mid-1993 and all involved at Earls Colne found this almost too great to bear. The doors finally shut in mid-1997 and the extensive collection was dispersed. Despite the relatively short time 'in action' at both sites, for veterans and visitors alike, the 'Rebels' had made a lasting impression.

Inside the museum hangar at Andrewsfield. In the left foreground is the Meteor nose, with the Cornell in the centre. *Ken Ellis*

Stan (left) and Dave Brett with the recently-arrived B-26C rear fuselage, at Andrewsfield. *Ken Ellis*

Proudly 'flying' the Confederate flag, the Rebel Air Museum at Andrewsfield, 1982. *Ken Ellis*

Rebel Aircraft Museum

Type	Identity	Built	Arrived	Background / *current status, or fate*
Dassault Mystère IVA	315	1957	1980	ex Sculthorpe, French Air Force. *Remained at Andrewsfield; in open store*
Fairchild PT-26 Cornell	N9606H	1942	1983	ex Southend – see Chapter 7, USA, RCAF FJ662, USAAF 42-15491. *Under restoration as G-CEVL in Lincolnshire*
Gloster Meteor F.3	EE425	1946	1981	cockpit, ex Foulness, 206, 210 and 206 Advanced Flg Schs, 63, 266, 1 and 222 Sqns. *Jet Age Museum, Staverton, Glos*
Mignet HM.14 'Flying Flea'	G-ADXS	1935	1983	ex Southend – see Chapter 7, Staverton – see Chapter 4, Southend. *Real Aeroplane Co, Breighton, Yorks*
Mignet HM.14 'Flying Flea'	-	c 1936	1980	ex Balham and 'South Wales'. *Norfolk and Suffolk Aviation Museum, Flixton, Suffolk*
NAA P-51D Mustang	146	c 1945	1981	ex Duxford, Israel, Israeli Air Force/Defence Force, ?, USAAF. On loan, returned to Duxford 1985. *Last noted stored at North Weald, Essex, 1991*

ONES THAT GOT AWAY

Saunders-Roe Princess, 1967

Doubtless costing a fortune and representing a huge logistics operation and a nightmare to house, that the Saro Princess slipped the preservation net is still deeply regretful. Work stopped on the uncompleted G-ALUO and 'P in March 1952 and they were towed to Calshot Spit in February. (G-ALUN and the incomplete G-ALUO illustrated on the slipway outside the Columbine hangar at East Cowes.) These two made one more move in 1965, going up the Solent to a breaker's yard in Southampton. In June 1954 G-ALUN made its last flight, its 47th, and was cocooned for storage. It was kept at East Cowes until May 1966 when it was towed across the River Medina and beached in a yard at Cowes. On 12th April 1967 G-ALUN was towed to Southampton and was scrapped over the next six months. Some sections of the leviathan's fuselage remained in the yard for another two years and then vanished.

CHAPTER 20

East Midlands Migrants
Loughborough Leicestershire Aircraft Museum and the
Bruntingthorpe Aviation Collection
1979 to 1986

Visitors today to Nottingham East Midlands Airport can have a fabulous view of the comings and goings at the busy airport, thanks to the Aeropark on the north-west boundary, adjacent to the threshold of Runway 09. Due to the many endeavours of the East Midlands Airport Volunteers Association there is an impressive park of historic aircraft including an Armstrong Whitworth Argosy, Avro Vulcan and a Vickers Varsity. As discussed in several chapters, airports are not renowned for a burning desire to foster the nation's aviation heritage, but there are a couple of shining examples where good observation facilities and preserved airframes go hand-in-hand, East Midlands and Manchester spring immediately to mind.

Above: Sqn Ldr Neil McDougall DFC handing over documentation for Vulcan B.2 XM575 after delivery, 28th January 1983. In 1982, Neil and his crew of Vulcan XM597 'Black Buck 6' hit the headlines when they landed in Brazil after a raid on the Falkland Islands encountered in-flight refuelling problems.

The present day set-up at East Midlands is not the first attempt to establish an aircraft exhibition at the airport. That prototype was initiated by the Loughborough Leicestershire Aircraft Museum and Preservation Society and it opened to the public on 27th May 1979. The site for this was on hard standings on the south side, to the east of the terminal building, close to the expanding freight sheds. As we have seen in Chapter 8, land priorities can change rapidly at an airport and the late 1970s and early 1980s were times of massive growth for EMA.

Founder LLAM airframe was a former French Air Force Super Sabre that arrived in April 1978 and was restored to high standards by willing hands on the airport. The remaining exhibits, some on loan and most acquired by individual LLAM members, arrived in short order over the next three years. Final inmate was an Avro XIX that had been with the Strathallan Collection (Chapter 10) and was showing the stresses and strains of external storage in Scotland and at Thruxton in Hampshire before that. Two aircraft took advantage of EMA's runway; the Varsity in November 1979 and the Vulcan on its last flight from Waddington in January 1983. Manoeuvring the big delta to its position took considerable man-power and planning.

Change of plans

During 1983 the airport management, in a joint venture with Leicestershire Museum of Technology, announced the launch of the East Midlands Aero Park (later to become just one word) to be built on the south-eastern boundary. Phase 1, a visitor centre and raised spectator viewing platform, was to open in 1984. These plans did not involve LLAM and its members were faced with finding a new home, followed by dismantling the airframes, transporting them, and starting all over again. And all by November....

While being close to Derby, East Midlands Airport is firmly in Leicestershire and after contact with the Walton family LLAM was offered space at Bruntingthorpe in the south of the county. The bulk of aircraft left over a frenetic weekend, 19-20th November. Left behind was the Vulcan and for a while the prospect of preparing the delta for a one-shot ferry flight to the new home was examined. To this end, the civil registration G-BLMC was allocated, and even painted on the tail, but in the end the paperwork was not taken up. To roam off on a 'what if' filibuster, that would have put a Vulcan down at

The author trying out the P1 position in Graham Vale's Varsity T.1 WL626 at East Midlands, 1986. *Alan Curry*

Mystère IVA 85 during re-assembly at East Midlands, July 1980. Behind is Whirlwind HAR.3 XG577. *Ken Ellis*

Bruntingthorpe long before XH558 arrived – apparently on its last-ever flight – on 23rd March 1993. If, XM575 had been in resident, would David Walton have put in a bid for XH558? Having rethought the possibilities of flying the Varsity, Graham Vale and family, who had set up the East Midlands Historic Flying Group by May 1982, decided to let it join the new venture and, when all options for moving the Vulcan were exhausted, these two became the first airframes at the new facility.

LLAM changed its name to the Bruntingthorpe Aviation Collection but by mid-1985 all of this had ground to a halt and, in the face of finding yet another home, it petered out. Briefly the Hinckley-based Phoenix Aviation Museum attempted to save what it could but, all of the airframes needed to leave the site by 1986 and that too withered. For a while, both the Mystère and F-100 were reportedly to be taken on by the Bader Wing of the Confederate Air Force at their planned base at Coventry Airport, but that came to nought. As both airframes were on loan from the USAF Museum at Dayton, Ohio, they required a 'keeper' and the Super Sabre was 'repatriated' to West Germany for Air Force use while the French jet gravitated to what became the resident Cold War Jets Collection looked after by C Walton (Aviation Division) Ltd.

As a reminder of the ever-changing nature of an airport, in April 1996 it was announced that the Aeropark was going to close as building developments were going to swallow up the current site. There followed a considerable period of uncertainty where it seemed that scrapping was the only option for the larger airframes. However, eyes turned to the north and thanks to the airport authorities, several resident major operators and the Volunteers Association, the migration was made to the impressive facilities now occupied.

Loughborough Leicestershire Aircraft Museum and the Bruntingthorpe Aviation Collection

Type	Identity	Built	Arrived	Background / *current status, or fate*
Avro XIX Series 2	G-AGWE	1946	May 1983	ex Strathallan – Chapter 10, Thruxton, RAF TX201 – no service. # *Last reported in Florida, USA, 1998*
Avro Vulcan B.2 *	XM575	1964	28 Jan 1983	G-BLMC, ex 44 Sqn, Waddington, Scampton, 617 Sqn. *Transferred to Aeropark, 1984*
Blackburn Buccaneer S.1	XN964	1963	27 Oct 1982	ex Brough, Pershore, Royal Radar Est, Royal Aircraft Est, 803, 736 and 801 Sqns. # *Newark Air Museum, Notts*
Dassault Mystère IVA	85	1955	Jul 1980	ex Sculthorpe, French Air Force. # *Cold War Jets, Bruntingthorpe, Leics*
De Havilland Vampire T.11	WZ553	1953	10 Mar 1979	ex Speke, Woodford, St Athan, 4 and 7 Flg Tng Schs, 202 Advanced Flg Sch. # *Became G-DHYY, pod with private owner, Warks*
DH Canada Chipmunk T.10	WB624	1950	1980	on loan, ex Wigan, Durham and Aberdeen Univ Air Sqns, Henlow Stn Flt, St Athan, 22 Group Comm Flt, Debden and Jurby Stn Flts, 8 Flg Tng Sch, 18 Reserve Flg Sch. *Newark Air Museum, Notts*
Hawker Hunter F.51	E-407	1956	Jul 1980	ex Dunsfold, HSA G-9-435, Danish Air Force E-407. # *Exported to the USA, 1990*
NAA F-100D Super Sabre	42239	1954	21 Apr 1978	ex Sculthorpe, French Air Force, USAF 54-2239. # *Returned to the custody of the USAF and moved to West Germany Jun 1988*
Percival Provost T.1	XF914	1956	24 Oct 1979	ex Barton, Connah's Quay, Shawbury, Flg Tng Command Comm Flt, Central Flg Sch, Glasgow and London Univ Air Sqns. See also Chapter 17. *To the USA 1993*
Vickers Varsity T.1	WL626	1953	8 Nov 1979	G-BHDD, ex Baginton, 6 Flg Tng Sch, 1 and 2 Air Nav Schs, 201 Advanced Flg Sch. *Transferred to Aeropark, 1984*
Westland Whirlwind HAR.3	XG577	1955	21 May 1980	ex Duxford, Lee-on-Solent, Arbroath A2571, 705, 737, 815, 705 and 701 Sqns, *Albion* Flt. *To fire dump at Leconfield, Yorks, as 9050M; scrapped in 2001*

Note: * – Illustrated in the colour sections. # Moved from East Midlands to Bruntingthorpe.

CHAPTER 21

Gentleman's Relish
Patrick Lindsay
1971 to 1986

Not to include the informal but wonderfully eclectic collection of the Honourable Patrick Lindsay would render great injustice to a man who brought to these shores some real gems. As with many owners of wonderful aircraft, Patrick ensured that his treasures were flown as often as was practical so that others could get the same enjoyment from them that he did. The son of an earl, Patrick was a classic car and motor racing owner-driver who readily took to aircraft of similar style and potency. His tastes and knowledge extended to works of art of the canvas and oil variety and he became the senior director of auction house Christie's paintings department.

As an aviator, he also presided over several prestigious sales for Christie's, including the contents of the Strathallan Aircraft Collection in 1981 (Chapter 10) and the Wings and Wheels Museum of Orlando, Florida, in 1982. At the Duxford auction of 14th April 1983 Patrick tried the market with three from his own collection: the Siemens SH14A-powered Sopwith Triplane replica, built by Personal Plane Services at Booker; the Morane-Saulnier-built Fieseler Fi 156 Storch powered by an Argus As 10C-3; and the delightful 1929 Great Lakes biplane.

Above: Patrick Lindsay's Spitfire Ia AR213 in mid-1986.
Left: Patrick poised to 'hammer' Hurricane G-AWLW for £260,000 at the Strathallan sale, 14th June 1981. *Peter Green*

French-built Stampe SV-4C G-AZGC visiting Old Warden in 1976.

While it is the Spitfire Ia, previously owned and flown by Allen Wheeler, that many people associate with Patrick, his love of biplanes provided restoration workshops with several important commissions and allowed some precious types to fly in the UK again. When in the early 1980s Patrick invited Viv and Rod Bellamy of Westward Airways at Land's End to build a replica Hawker Fury biplane, it was believed that the type was 'extinct'. What resulted was an impressive and challenging project, complete with a Rolls-Royce Kestrel V. Since that time, Guy Black and his team have tracked down a former South African Fury and, as G-CBZP; it is nearing first flight at the Retrotec workshop in Sussex.

As well as wielding the gavel at the Wings and Wheels sale in Florida, Patrick was also tempted to deploy the cheque book. He came away with a Royal Aircraft Factory SE.5 rebuilt and re-engined by Eberhart Steel Products at Buffalo, New York, in 1921 as an SE.5E to serve with the United States Army Air Service. It was later flown in the Howard Hughes extravaganza, the 1930 movie *Hell's Angels*. Restoration of this was entrusted to Personal Plane Services (PPS), the company that looked after all of his collection, at Booker, Buckinghamshire.

By 1985, Patrick was very ill and at Land's End and Booker there was a determination to give this great patron of classic aircraft the satisfaction of the maiden flights of both projects. SE.5E G-BLXT took to the air at Booker on 18th November 1985 and Fury G-BKBB did likewise the following day at Land's End. Aged just 57, Patrick died on January 11, 1986. His family kept several of his aircraft and cars in running trim for some time afterwards, eventually all finding their way to other appreciative owners. The world of fine art, classic cars and aircraft, lost a dedicated and highly individual benefactor in Patrick. At his funeral, Spitfire Ia AR213, gracefully flown by Tony Bianchi of PPS, paid fitting tribute.

Great Lakes 2T-1A G-BIIZ at Duxford in April 1983 ready for the Christie's sale. *Alan Curry*

Argus-engined 'Storch' G-AZMH displaying in September 1984.

Patrick Lindsay

Type	Identity	Built	Arrived	Background / *current status, or fate*
Fiat G.46-3B *	G-BBII	1950	Sep 1973	ex Italy I-AEHU, Italian Air Force MM52801. *Airworthy, London-based owner*
Great Lakes 2T-1A	G-BIIZ	1929	Apr 1981	ex USA N603K, NC603K. *Airworthy, Colchester owner*
Hawker Fury I replica	G-BKBB	1982	Apr 1982	'K1930'. *Sold in Belgium as OO-HFU Jan 1991, returned to UK; current status unknown*
Morane-Saulnier MS.230 *	G-AVEB	1949	Jun 1967	ex France F-BGJT. *Sold in the USA as N230EB Jun 1996, returned to UK and sold again in the USA Mar 2011*
Morane-Saulnier Criquet	G-AZMH	1951	Jan 1972	ex *The Eagle has Landed* film, Ireland EI-AUU, French F-BJQG, French military No.637. See also Chapter 26. *Sold in West Germany Jun 1997*
Royal Aircraft Factory SE.5E	G-BLXT	1919	Oct 1985	'B4863', ex USA, Wings and Wheels, Orlando, Tallmantz Collection, N4488, *Hell's Angels* film, USAAS 22-296. *Believed stored in the UK*
Stampe (SNCAN) SV-4C	G-AZGC	1946	Oct 1971	ex France F-BCGE. *Under restoration, Berkshire workshop*
Sopwith Triplane replica *	G-BHEW	1979	Oct 1979	'N5430'. *Sold in the USA as N5460 Jan 1986*
Supermarine Spitfire Ia	AR213	1941	Jun 1974	G-AIST, ex *Battle of Britain* film, Old Warden, Little Rissington, 53 and 57 Oper Tng Units. *Airworthy, based at Kemble, Glos*

Note: * – Illustrated in the colour sections.

CHAPTER 22

Maintenance Unit
Cotswold Aircraft Restoration Group
1979 to 2007

Here is another organisation that blows a huge hole in the catch-all of 'collection'. The Cotswold Aircraft Restoration Group was *not* a collection, nor was it a museum, or a 'squadron' of historic aircraft. Yet, without CARG, collections, museums and owner-operators across the world would be all the worse. The brainchild of former Skyfame Aircraft Museum volunteer Tony Southern, CARG was born out of the demise of that pioneering museum. Tony realised that a group of able people were without an outlet and that this was a shame from a social point of view, let alone the potential loss to aviation heritage. But there was no mileage in a museum or similar venture.

What evolved was a unique organisation acting as a 'maintenance unit' for others. So, the workshop would restore items large or small; seek out airframes or components and find them a good 'home', or store them until one could be found. It was all ear-to-the-ground stuff and Tony and his team excelled at it. CARG started off on its novel task in April 1979 and carried on its vital, if largely unsung, work until 2007, when a replacement for its workshop proved to be impractical. To provide an instant purpose for members, former Skyfame Auster AOP.9 XR267 was to be restored to flying condition. Pivotal to CARG's existence was the Officer Commanding RAF Innsworth, a non-airfield station just short distance away from Staverton aerodrome where Skyfame had been. Workshop space within the camp was readily granted and subsequent 'Bosses' proved equally as encouraging and enlightened, until such time as RAF presence ceased. As time went on the AOP.9 became less and less of a priority as what Tony called "supply missions" grew and grew. One of these might constitute working on the restoration of Miles Messenger G-AJOE – a project that got CARG second place in the 1990 Transport Trust awards – or sending a package of radio fittings to help complete the interior of the Yorkshire Air Museum's Handley Page Halifax *Friday 13th*. By the time that CARG celebrated its 25th anniversary in 2004, it had clocked up an amazing 750 'missions'.

Above: Loading the fuselage of Monospar VH-UTH at Newark ready for the journey to Innsworth for restoration by CARG in April 1998. *Newark Air Museum*

Unpainted Messenger G-AJOE at Staverton, February 1990. *Scania (Great Britain) Ltd*

Wonderful 'see-through' Tiger Moth 'G-MAZY' at the Newark Air Museum. *Ken Ellis*

Airframe 'missions'

The Messenger was an early inmate at the CARG workshop, the task being carried out on behalf of a group called Classic Messenger. On 16th August 1987, *Oscar-Echo* moved to Staverton for flight test. A series of problems, none of CARG's making, meant that it was not until 22nd November 1997 that the Messenger got airborne. As a 'thank you' and a 'reason' for CARG personnel to be working within RAF Innsworth, early Gloster Meteor T.7 VW453 arrived in late 1981, for painstaking restoration so that it could become a 'gate guardian'. The completed aircraft was handed over on 14th November 1991, allowing the previous 'guardian', the far rarer Javelin FAW.9 XH903, to join the nascent Jet Age Museum in October 1993.

An astounding piece of 'scrounging' was the discovery of the substantial cockpit section of former 10 Squadron Handley Page Halifax II R9371 in a local scrapyard. Initially, this did not find a home, so CARG carried out another one of its purposes and stored it carefully until such time as the RAF Museum decided to take it on.

Two restorations were undertaken for the Newark Air Museum, the first being a composite Tiger Moth designed to show off its construction, with the port side fuselage, wings and tail surfaces uncovered. Carrying out much of this brilliant work was Harry Hodgson BEM. When the restoration was returned to Newark on 25th June 1995, the blue fabric carried a 'registration' in honour of Harry's wife – 'G-MAZY'. The space previously occupied by the Tiger was taken up by the large outer wings of another Newark machine, General Aircraft ST-12 Monospar VH-UTH. In 1998 the remainder of this 1935-built twin also made the move to Innsworth. Restored so that it could be shown off completely uncovered, *Tango-Hotel* was the last major project completed by CARG, returning to Newark on 2nd October 2007.

After that CARG wound down. The workshop was lost with the redevelopment of Innsworth and besides, as Tony noted: "we none of us are getting any younger". Sadly, this was all too prescient; the quiet, caring and meticulous Tony Southern died in late October 2008. He had an unrivalled ability to 'ferret' and his extensive knowledge of 'the business' meant that he could place an item with the best possible recipient, almost before a CARG team had travelled out to fetch it! As this book was turning from a huge pile of paper into pixels in a processor another CARG stalwart passed away – Steve Thompson in only his 55th year. There was nothing like CARG before it came along and I doubt there will ever be anything like it again – much though we need one.

Cotswold Aircraft Restoration Group

Type	Identity	Built	Arrived	Background / *current status, or fate*
Auster AOP.6	TW536	1946	18 Nov 1980	ex Bristol, Compton Abbas, Middle Wallop 7704M, Army Air Corps, 652 Sqn, 1912 Flt, 657 Sqn, Eastern Sector Flt. *Airworthy as G-BNGE, Swindon owner*
Auster AOP.9	XN412	1962	1 Jun 1986	ex Swindon, Dorchester, Middle Wallop, 20 Flt, 656 Sqn, Seletar, Handling Sqn. *Last noted stored near Melton Mowbray, Leics, 2008*
Auster AOP.9	XR267	1965	Apr 1979	ex Staverton – see Chapter 4, Bristol, Congresbury, Army Air Corps/RAF, St Athan, no service. *Airworthy, Hucknall, Notts as G-BJXR*
De Havilland Tiger Moth	'G-MAZY'	1940	1987	composite, ex Newark. *Newark Air Museum, Notts*
Edwards Gyrocopter	G-ASDF	1962	29 Apr 1995	ex Woking, Coulsdon. *Private owner, Herefordshire*
English Electric Lightning F.1	XG331	1959	23 Oct 1986	cockpit, ex Dowty, Staverton, Foulness, Aeroplane & Armament Exp Est. *Gloucester Aviation Club, Gloucester, Glos*
Fairey Ultra-Light Helicopter	G-AOUJ	1957	7 Nov 1999	ex Weston-super-Mare, Harlow, White Waltham, XJ928. *The Helicopter Museum, Weston-super-Mare, Somerset*
General Aircraft ST-12 Monospar	VH-UTH	1935	Apr 1998	ex Newark, Booker, Croydon, Panshanger, Biggin Hill, Australia – New England Airways. *Newark Air Museum, Notts*
Gloster Meteor T.7	VW453	1948	11 Nov 1981	8703M, ex Salisbury Plain, Aston Down, Ta Qali Stn Flt, 604 Sqn, 226 Oper Conv Unit, 203 Advanced Flg Sch. *Held at Imjin Barracks, Innsworth, move pending*

Type	Identity	Built	Arrived	Background / *current status, or fate*
Handley Page Halifax II	R9371	1941	1982	cockpit section, ex local scrapyard, 10 Sqn – crashed 9 Mar 1942. *RAF Museum, stored Stafford, Staffs*
Hawker Siddeley Harrier T.2	XW264	1970	8 Nov 1986	forward fuselage, ex Dowty, Staverton, Aeroplane & Armament Exp Est – damaged 11 Jul 1970. *Stored for the Jet Age Museum, Gloucestershire Airport, Glos*
Miles Messenger 2A	G-AJOE	1947	25 Jan 1980	ex 'RH378'. *Airworthy, Reading owner*
Mignet HM.14 'Flying Flea'	'G-ADRG'	1974	1981	ex Staverton – see Chapter 4. *Stondon Transport Museum, Lower Stondon, Beds*

Notes: Most of the above were worked on, or looked after on behalf of others; details of main examples in the text. As well as the above, CARG briefly had the following airframes for use as spares: Auster AOP.9 XK421 1982; and Messenger G-AIDK 1985. The wings of Monospar VH-UTH arrived in the workshop in 1995, date given in the table is for the fuselage

CHAPTER 23

Jet Stable
Hunter One and Jet Heritage
1981 to 1999

In Chapter 17 Sandy Topen and his team succeeded in putting UK 'warbirds' into the 'jet age' with the first flight of de Havilland Vampire T.11 G-VTII at Carlisle on 17th February 1980. Thirty-three days later, Spencer Flack watched as Hawker Hunter F.51 G-HUNT blasted down the short runway at Elstree. Within the space of just over a month, Permit to Fly jet flight had been pioneered. (Take a look at Chapters 17 and 18 respectively.) After Spencer's miraculous escape from the burning hulk of Hawker Sea Fury FB.11 G-FURY on the approach to Waddington on 2nd August 1981, he took the decision to wind-down his collection. Britain's first privately-owned swept-wing, single-seat jet fighter was probably going abroad...

Above: Having acquired Hunter G-BOOM, Mike Carlton decided to paint it overall bright red to match the new scheme he gave G-HUNT. *Hunter One*

Having learned to fly on a DH Tiger Moth at Biggin Hill and gone on to clinch a series of British and one world glider flying records, 38-year old Michael Richard Carlton was then piloting 1941-built North American Harvard IIA G-TEAC, painted in RAF colours as 'MC280'. He was the managing director of the Brencham Group, owning a diverse range of properties and companies. Among the portfolio was Trans European Air Charter – hence the Harvard's registration – with a Cessna Citation executive jet at Biggin Hill. The allure of G-HUNT was powerful and Spencer and Mike came to a deal. One of the companies that Brencham had an interest in was Glos-Air at Bournemouth Airport and in September 1981 the red Hunter was ferried from Stansted to its new Dorset home.

Mike Carlton getting out of G-HUNT after a display at Biggin Hill in May 1983.

There was a compelling reason why *November-Tango* went to Bournemouth, when Biggin Hill was a more obvious location. No longer working for Hawker Siddeley, living in Dorset and working for Airwork looking after the company's

significant holding of Hunter spares was Eric Hayward. As Chapter 18 explains, it was Eric's intimate knowledge of the type that has made G-HUNT's existence as a flying machine possible. (Eric and his team had gone on to do the same for Brian Kay's two-seater G-BOOM.) When approached, Eric was keen, but would not relocate – hence Bournemouth!

While an accomplished flyer, Mike knew the transition from Harvard to single-seat Hunter was a leap too far. He had befriended jet pilot Adrian Gjertsen, who had exceptional experience and was a qualified flying instructor. Brian Kay was persuaded to allow Adrian to teach Mike how to fly a Hunter on *Oscar-Mike*. Brian then offered to sell the two-seater to Mike and the Harvard was put on the market. Within the blink of an eye, Mr Carlton had a 'stable' of thoroughbreds, a chief pilot and chief engineer. Even though he had *two* jets, the call-sign *Hunter One* had always appealed to Mike and it was taken as the name for the collection. That general sequence of events can be found elsewhere in this book and is the 'critical path' by which many collections come into being – they seem to take on their own pace.

To launch Hunter One, Brencham Ltd produced a lavish brochure – complete with thread and tassel binding and appliqué prints. The final page was this tongue-in-cheek view of the ultimate in wing-walkers! Left to right: Adrian Gjertsen, Eric Hayward and Geoff Roberts. Mike Carlton is perched astride the canopy. *Arthur Gibson via Hunter One*

From two Hunters to an 'air force'

G-HUNT was registered on 2nd October 1981 to Mike in his own name, but as his stable grew, machines were then placed on Brencham's books. As a shrewd businessman, he decided that a separate concern should be created for his new-found 'hobby' and so the Brencham Historic Aircraft Company (BHAC) came about in June 1983. (Later still, some were re-registered to another entity, Berowell Management.) By this time, Mike was tracking down a pair of Hunting Jet Provosts previously with the Singapore Air Defence Command at Seletar. He was also tempted by a Gloster Meteor and a Hawker Sea Hawk on offer at the wind-up auction of the Historic Aircraft Museum at Southend – Chapter 7. Eric Hayward gave up his post with Airwork and came to work for BHAC full time. Flying aircraft were based at Biggin Hill and maintenance and restoration work was carried out at Bournemouth.

Eric tracked down the single-seat nose of a Hunter F.6 and mated it up with the centre section and other elements of former Danish Air Force two-seater ET-272 – used as a source of spares in the restoration of G-BOOM – to create a flightless Hunter to serve as 'gate guardian' outside the Brencham hangar at Biggin Hill from 1985. While this hybrid was being created, the engineering team paid honour to their boss by painting the 'registration' 'G-ERIC' on its side. This monument was later to make the move to Bournemouth. In another tribute to the Hunter maestro, when the Swiss government presented a Hunter to the Jet Heritage Charitable Foundation in June 1995 it was registered as G-EGHH. There are two ways of interpreting this, the first being that EGHH is the ICAO designator for Bournemouth Airport. The author was told that it actually stood for Eric G Hayward's Hunter!

G-PROV one of a pair of former Singapore Air Defence Command Jet Provost T.52s. *Hunter One*

Meteor TT.20 G-LOSM getting airborne for a display at Woodford. *Alan Curry*

While on holiday in Zimbabwe, Mike and his wife Kathy took a flight as passengers in a Republic Seabee amphibian from the waters near the Kariba Dam on 31st August 1986. The aircraft crashed on take-off, killing all on board. Suddenly, Hunter One looked very vulnerable. In due course Brencham ceased trading and auction house Christie's was brought in to oversee the sale at Bournemouth on October 1, 1987 with Robert Brooks presiding. On offer were Jet Provosts G-JETP and G-PROV, Meteor T.7 G-JETM, Meteor TT.20 G-LOSM, Sea Hawks G-JETH and G-SEAH, Hunters G-HUNT and G-BOOM. It was a disappointing process, as only G-HUNT sold on the day, 'hammered' for £150,000 – around £600,000 in present-day values. Several deals were conducted afterwards, one of which was to prove crucial...

Syndicates, regular work and museum

When a patron leaves his (or her) pride and joy for whatever reason – new passions, sudden impoverishment, or leaving the mortal coil – seldom, if ever, do things go on as before. We have seen this phenomenon already in this book. Hunter One was about to become Jet Heritage and while several aircraft stayed on, giving the appearance of sameness, it was not to be. To continue, it needed to be a *business*, not a hobby. Two brothers, Ian and Douglas Craig-Wood, were at the Christie's sale and were very taken with the Jet Provosts. Adrian Gjertsen had been considering how things might be able to continue; doubting he'd find someone with a *very* large wallet, he developed a business plan to widen the activities of the collection. In the Craig-Woods, he found determined people who felt they could invest and keep the 'stable' running. In July 1988 Jet Heritage Ltd was inaugurated with Hunter Wing Ltd as its holding organisation. Hunter G-BOOM, 'JPs' G-JETP and G-PROV and Meteor G-LOSM would form the caucus of the fleet. As well as running these machines for airshow, film and promotional work, JHL would specialise in the maintenance of classic jets and operate similar aircraft for third parties.

There was also an intention to establish a museum, so that the *working* collection could be enjoyed by not just airshow audiences. This was inspired by the Battle of Britain Memorial Flight Visitor Centre at RAF Coningsby, Lincs. Hangar 600 at Bournemouth lent itself to this concept, with a bay for static museum exhibits and next door as an active maintenance centre. To prevent the public getting in the way of work-in-hand, an elevated observation gallery would give great views and a picnic area outside would do likewise. To this end, the already mentioned Jet Heritage Charitable Foundation was established in 1994.

The Jet Heritage Aviation Museum

Located at Bournemouth International Airport. Information and directions overleaf

In the summer of 1995 Adrian gave up his post as chief pilot and established his own operation, Classic Jets at Biggin Hill. For Adrian the emphasis had come off airshow flying and was increasingly centred upon syndicate ownership of jet trainers and fighters. Owing a Hunter outright was then, and remains, an expensive venture. With JHL providing the means for acquiring, say, a tenth share, the company was allowing far more people to get a foot up the ownership ladder. In February 1997 Mike Giles and Jonathon 'Flapjack' Whaley took over the operation of JHL and in that year a fond farewell was bade to Eric Hayward, retiring the tender age of 71. Jonathon had established Heritage Aviation Developments Ltd and had acquired former Swiss Air Force Hunter F.58A G-PSST which JHL were going to look after. This machine was shortly to be rolled out in the fantastic 'space re-entry' colour scheme that never ceases to stop the audience in its tracks where-ever Jonathon displays it.

A major boost was a contract to overhaul, restore and initially operate Hunters and Vampires acquired by consultancy RV Aviation on behalf of the nascent Royal Jordanian Air Force Historic Flight. After a season display flying within the UK and Europe, the Flight moved to its base at Marka in Jordan. Most of the aircraft relocated in 1997, with the final example heading east in 1999.

By 1998 both Mike and Jonathon stood down from JHL with another management team stepping in. Both wanted to follow their own passions more fully; as was so often the case running a business was getting in the way flying! Before they left the Jet Heritage Aviation Museum was opened to the public on 17th May 1998, another goal achieved. Sadly, JHL ceased trading on 19th August 1999 and a pioneering jet venture stretching all the way back to Spencer Flack and G-HUNT nearly two decades before came to a halt. Thankfully, thanks to the trust fund, the museum element survived and on 27th August the Bournemouth Aviation Charitable Foundation Ltd arose, ultimately taking the form of the Bournemouth Aviation Museum. Hunter One and Jet Heritage had proven that flying former military jets was no different in concept to running Spitfires, or indeed Tiger Moths.

Hand-out for the Jet Heritage Aviation Museum.

Hunter One and Jet Heritage

Type	Identity	Built	Arrived	Background / *current status, or fate*
De Havilland Vampire FB.6	G-SWIS	1952	May 1991	HW – ex Swiss Air Force J-1149. *Exported to New Zealand 2001*
De Havilland Sea Vixen FAW.2	G-VIXN	1965	Aug 1985	BHAC – ex Fleet Air Arm XS587, Flight Refuelling Ltd, 8828M, Royal Aircraft Est – Llanbedr, FRL, Fleet Requirements and Air Direction Unit, FRU, 899 and 893 Sqns. *Gatwick Aviation Museum, Charlwood, Surrey*
De Havilland Vampire T.11	XD599	1953	1984	ex Blackbushe – Chapter 13, Staverton, Stroud, Central Air Traffic Control Sch, RAF College, 1 Sqn. *Sywell Aviation Museum, Northants*
De Havilland Vampire T.11	XH328	1956	Dec 1990	ex Cranfield – Chapter 17, Hemel Hempstead, Croxley Green, Bushey, Keevil, 3 Civilian Anti-Aircraft Co-op Unit, 14 Sqn RNZAF, 60 Sqn. *Norfolk owner, stored*
De Havilland Vampire T.11	XK623	1956	1984	ex Moston, Woodford, Hawarden, St Athan, 5 Flg Tng Sch. *Caernarfon Airport Airworld Museum*
De Havilland Vampire T.11	G-HELV	1958	28 Aug 1991	HW – ex Swiss Air Force U-1215. *Airworthy as 'XJ-771' with Aviation Heritage Ltd, Coventry*
Folland Gnat T.1	G-NAAT	1961	Dec 1989	HW – ex Woking, RAF XM697, Aeroplane & Armament Exp Est. *Displayed at Reynard Nursery, Carluke, Scotland*
Folland Gnat T.1	G-NATY	1963	Mar 1990	JH – ex Cosford 8642M, RAF XR537, Central Flg Sch, 4 Flg Tng Sch, CFS, 4 FTS. *Airworthy with DS Aviation, Bournemouth*
Gloster Meteor T.7	G-JETM	1949	Nov 1983	BL / BHAC – ex Southend – Chapter 7, RAF VZ638, Kemble, College of Air Warfare, RAF College, 237 Op Conv Unit, 501 Sqn, Biggin Hill Stn Flt, Fighter Command Comm Sqn, 85, 54, 25 and 500s Sqns. *Gatwick Aviation Museum, Charlwood*
Gloster Meteor TT.20 *	G-LOSM	1952	Jun 1984	BHAC – ex Blackbushe – Chapter 13, WM167, Royal Aircraft Est – Llanbedr, Farnborough, RAF 228 Sqn, Colerne St Flt, 228 Oper Conv Unit. *Airworthy as G-LOSM with Air Atlantique at Coventry*
Hawker Sea Hawk FB.5	G-SEAH	1954	Oct 1983	BHAC, ex Southend, Swansea, Cranfield – Chapter 3, Fleet Air arm WM994, Arbroath, Hal Far Search and Rescue Flt, 806, 767 and 800 Sqns. *Amjet, USA, registered as N994WM*
Hawker Sea Hawk FGA.6	WV795	1954	Oct 1989	ex Bath, Cardiff, Culdrose, Halton 8151M, Sydenham, 738, 806, 700 Sqns. *Displayed at Aces High at Dunsfold, Surrey*
Hawker Sea Hawk FGA.6	G-JETH	1955	20 May 1967	BL / BHAC, ex Southend – Chapter 7, XE489, Fleet Requirements Unit, 806 Sqn. *Majority sold in Netherlands Aug 1989*
Hawker Hunter F.4	G-HHUN	1955	Sep 1989	HW – ex East Kirkby, Loughborough – Chapter 2, HSA Dunsfold, RAF XE677, 229 Op Conv Unit, 111, 93 and 4 Sqns. *Registered G-HHUN, destroyed in fatal crash 5 Jun 1998.*

Type	Identity	Built	Arrived	Background / *current status, or fate*
Hawker Hunter T.7	G-BXFI	1955	11 Aug 1997	JH – ex Transair – North Weald, Fleet Air Arm WV372, Culdrose, Fleet Requirements and Air Direction Unit, RAF WV372, 237 Oper Conv Unit, 208 Sqn, 4 Flg Tng Sch, 222 Sqn. *Airworthy, Hunter Flying Ltd, Exeter*
Hawker Hunter T.7	G-HNTR	1958	Oct 1988	HW – ex Cosford 8834M, RAF XL572, 1 Tactical Weapons Unit, 2 TWU, 229 Oper Conv Unit. *Painted as 'XL571', Yorkshire Air Museum, Elvington*
Hawker Hunter T.7	G-VETA	1958	Jun 1996	JH – ex Southall G-BVWN, XL600, Scampton, Laarbruch Stn Flt, 237 Oper Conv Unit, 4 Flg Tng Sch, 111 and 65 Sqns. *Airworthy, Viper Classics Ltd, Exeter*
Hawker Hunter T.7	G-HHNT	1958	Oct 1988	HW – ex Cosford 8837M, RAF XL617, 1 Tactical Weapons Unit, 229 Oper Conv Unit, Gütersloh and Jever Stn Flts, 4 Sqn. *Sold in USA Nov 1989 as N617NL*
Hawker Hunter T.7 *	G-BOOM	1958	Sep 1982	BL / BHAC, ex Brian Kay, Leavesden – see Chapter 18, HSA Hatfield, Dunsfold G-9-432, Danish Air Force ET-274, Netherlands Air Force N-307. *To Royal Jordanian Air Force Historic Flight as '800' Jun 1997*
Hawker Hunter F.51 *	G-HUNT	1956	Sep 1981	BHAC – ex Spencer Flack – Chapter 18, Dunsfold, G-9-440, Danish Air Force E-418. *Airworthy with AirVenture Museum, Oshkosh, USA, marked as 'WB188', registered as N611JR*
Hawker Hunter F.58	G-EGHH	1959	16 Jun 1995	JHCF – ex Swiss Air Force J-4083. *Stored for Heritage Aviation Developments*
Hawker Hunter *	-	1958	May 1985	composite, centre section of ET-272, nose of XJ690 – 'gate guardian' at Biggin Hill and then Bournemouth. *Stored at Bournemouth Airport*
Hunting Jet Provost T.52A	G-JETP	1962	Nov 1983	BL / BHAC, ex Singapore Air Defence Command 355, Yemen Air Force 104, BAC G-27-7, RAF XP666, 7 Flg Tng Sch. *Sold in Cyprus mid-1993*
Hunting Jet Provost T.52	G-PROV	1964	Nov 1983	BL / BHAC, ex Singapore Air Defence Command 352, Yemen Air Force 107, BAC G-27-92, RAF XS228 – no service. *Airworthy, The Provost Group, North Weald*
Percival Provost T.1	G-AWVF	1955	Dec 1990	JH / HW, ex RAF XF877, Central Navigation and Control Sch, RAF College. *Sold in Cyprus, May 1993*
Supermarine Swift F.7	G-SWIF	1956	19 Jan 1989	JH, ex RAF XF114, Connah's Quay, Aston Down, Cranfield. *In store at Solent Sky, Southampton*

Note: * – Illustrated in the colour sections. Column 4 starts with a registered owner code (for civil machines) as follows: BHAC – Brencham Historic Aircraft Co; BL – Brencham Ltd; HW – Hunter Wing Ltd; JH – Jet Heritage Ltd; JHCF – Jet Heritage Charitable Foundation. Hunter One, Jet Heritage etc maintained and/or operated aircraft for other individuals/organisations – these are not listed here. Also not included are airframes acquired for short-term use for spares recovery, for example Jet Provost T.5 XS231 in mid-1988.

CHAPTER 24

Curtain Up!
Whitehall Theatre of War and the
London War Museum
1983 to 1985

During the early 1980s a new character appeared on the UK aviation heritage scene and he raised more than few eyebrows. The idea of Paul Raymond, the so-called 'King of Soho', wanting to open a museum seemed bizarre in the extreme. Short-lived it may have been, but he carried out his wishes.

Born in Liverpool in 1925 as Geoffrey Anthony Quinn, he served in the RAF as a switchboard operator for his National Service. He rose to fame via his 'Revuebar' and a string of Soho strip joints, not to mention founding *Men Only* magazine in 1971. Alongside the 'exotic entertainment' business, he also became a property tycoon. He died on 3rd March 2008 a very rich man.

Amid much glitz, the impresario opened his new attraction – the Whitehall Theatre of War just off Trafalgar Square – on 1st August 1983. Above the entrance to the former theatre was a board that proclaimed the exhibition was: "dedicated to the fighting people of all nations from World War Two". A billboard explained that the venue showed: "aircraft vehicles and equipment in action scenes from some of the famous theatres of war". Punters were invited to: "See the daring rescue of Mussolini by the Germans and the famous Fieseler Storch". A banner summed it all up: "A dramatic spectacular – theatrical entertainment."

Above: The former Italian Air Force instructional Mustang with the Spanish-built Bf 109 inside the Whitehall Theatre of War. *Phillips*

Transformed impresario

Paul Raymond had acquired the Whitehall Theatre in the mid-1960s and it hosted a series of sleazy farces, including *Yes, We Have No Pyjamas*. Clearly, he was looking for other avenues in the early 1980s and the theatre was re-launched in its guise as a museum and a *lot* of money had been spent on the transformation. The entrance was 'guarded' by 'Military Police', complete with 'snowball' helmets, and very probably they had served as 'bouncers' at other Raymond palaces of pleasure.

I visited this emporium twice and the first time I remember walking around in disbelief – a state that I seemed to share with the handful of other 'punters' during my stay. I have an enduring memory of thinking that it was an incredible waste of a theatre. I also couldn't help speculating that a lot of faithful, mackintosh-clad, Raymond clients must have been *extremely* disappointed by what they found within! Then again, anyone looking for the events of 1939 to 1945 presented in a careful, balanced and sympathetic manner was equally in for a let-down. The Imperial War Museum had nothing to fear!

At the same time as planning the transformation of the Whitehall Theatre, Paul Raymond was hoping to open a similar venture in another of the many properties in his portfolio. This was the London War Museum, intended for railway arches in Crucifix Lane, near London Bridge. This never opened its doors to the public and the hoped-for exhibits remained in storage, mostly in a country retreat in deepest Hertfordshire.

It was not long before it became apparent that Madame Tussauds, the Natural History Museum and the 'conventional' theatres of the capital had far greater 'pull' than Mr Raymond's diversion. The curtain came down on the Whitehall Theatre of War for the last time in early 1985. Planning problems, not dwindling attendances, were given for the reason for the demise.

Bought and sold

With Raymond's 'museum period' over, the contents of the Whitehall Theatre and would-be exhibits for the London War Museum were disposed of with speed. The showman turned to auctioneers Phillips, and a sale was staged on 5th June 1985. And that was the occasion for my *second* visit... The catalogue was extensive, ranging from a box crammed full of model gliders – unsold from the box office shop and going at £35; an *apparently* original Bazooka anti-tank weapon (£40) and a Daimler Dingo II scout car (£2,000). Then, of course, there were the airframes – column three of the table shows the high bids received at the auction.

Mr Raymond invested seriously in exhibits for his sortie into history and culture. The main source of his aeroplanes was the closure of the Historic Aircraft Museum at Southend, Essex – see Chapter 7. It is quite possible that the very availability of these machines spurred the decision to change the Whitehall Theatre's role. Raymond spent £58,200 on four Southend inmates – a Spanish-built Heinkel, North American Harvard, Percival Proctor and a Fieseler Storch – of which only the latter ever went on show. This sum may not seem much, but in 2011 values this would have been close on a quarter of a million pounds.

'Max' the Storch 'flying' over a Special Air Service jeep. *Phillips*

To represent the Great War, a formerly airworthy Sopwith Pup replica was acquired. A Supermarine Spitfire XIV, salvaged from India, in the mid-1970s, headed an impressive World War Two trio. Mr Raymond acquired two types from well-known warbird operator Robs Lamplough. One of these was a North American Mustang that had served with the Italian Air Force and served out its time as an instructional airframe. The other was a former film star.

Above what had been the stage a Sopwith Pup replica was suspended. Below it is a mock-up German tank on a French AMX chassis and to the right the M5 half-track from which the auction was conducted. *Phillips*

Harvard LN-BNM in USAF markings at the Historic Aircraft Museum, Southend, 1969. It was not auctioned in June 1985, having been secured by the RAF Museum previously. *Alan Curry*

On 3rd April 1982 Merlin-engined Hispano Buchón *Yellow 14* took to the air at Duxford, Cambs, following a four-year restoration. Like the Heinkel, this was a veteran of the 1969 film *Battle of Britain*, and had been imported from the USA following a ground-loop in Texas in October 1977. Sadly, the Spanish-built Messerschmitt Bf 109 suffered *another* ground-loop during the Biggin Hill Air Fair, just 43 days after its UK maiden flight. Both the Buchón and the Mustang were patched up for there new theatrical careers.

At the sale, the auctioneer presided from the back of an International Harvester Company-built M5 'half-track' perched on the stage above what had been the orchestra pit in another era. This armoured personnel carrier was 'guarded' by a mannequin of General George Smith Patton ᴊɴʀ toting Colt .45 revolvers. (Patton reached £420, but Lot 108A was the runaway success of the dummies – Adolph Hitler hitting £700. The M5, sold literally from under the auctioneer, was a snip at £2,100.) All of this provided a suitably dramatic setting for the hammer to crash down on the gavel for the final time on Lot 195 – the Storch. The crowd wended its way out into Whitehall, many to find a tavern to mark the end of an extraordinary episode in Britain's aviation heritage.

Whitehall Theatre of War and London War Museum

Type	Identity	Built	Auctioned for	Background / *current status, or fate*
Fieseler Fi 156C-3 Storch	D-EKMU	1943	£16,000	ex Southend – see Chapter 7, D-EKMU, OE-ADR, Swedish AF Fv3812, Luftwaffe. *Fantasy of Flight, USA* [2]
Heinkel He 111 (CASA 2-111B)	G-AWHB	1951	£24,000	ex Southend – see Chapter 7, *Battle of Britain* film, Spanish AF B2I-57. *Flying Heritage Collection, USA* [1]
Messerschmitt Bf 109 (Buchón) *	G-BJZZ	1958	£34,000	ex Duxford, N48157, *Battle of Britain* film, Spanish AF C4K-235. Became G-HUNN – Chapter 25. *Cavanaugh Flight Museum, USA, registered N109GU* 2]
North American Harvard IIB	LN-BNM	1943	not entered	ex Southend – see Chapter 7, LN-BNM, Danish AF 31-329, RCAF, 41 SFTS, FE905, USAAF 42-12392. *Royal Air Force Museum, Hendon* [1] [2]
North American P-51D Mustang	MM4292	c 1944	£9,000	ex Fowlmere, Rome, Italian AF, USAAF. *USA, current status uncertain* [2]
Percival Proctor IV	NP303	1944	£500	ex Southend, G-ANZJ, RAF NP303, 23 Group Comm Flt, 4 Radio Sch. *UK, current status uncertain* [1]
Sopwith Pup replica	N6452	1983	£19,000	ex G-BIAU. *Fleet Air Arm Museum, Yeovilton* [2]
Supermarine Spitfire XIV	MV370	1945	£30,000	G-FXIV, ex St Leonards On Sea, Henfield, Indian AF inst T44, IAF, RAF MV370, no service – see Chapter 12. *Luftfahrtmuseum, Germany* [2]

Notes: Note: * – Illustrated in the colour sections. [1] Intended for the London War Museum. [2] Displayed at the Whitehall Theatre of War.

CHAPTER 25

Warbird Patron
Charles Church (Spitfires) Ltd
1984 to 1989

Charles Church houses are an established and renowned brand. In 1965 Charles and his wife Susanna built their first home and this became the launch pad for a vibrant business, Charles Church Developments plc, creating homes of quality design and character. This success provided Charles with the wherewithal to indulge in his two great passions and both of these he managed to combine on the family estate near Winchester in Hampshire. Charles enjoyed shooting, both target and game, and the estate was acclaimed for its terrain and birds. Gaining his private pilot's licence in 1984, Charles had a generous airstrip laid down and a modern hangar and workshop built. Here he planned not only to house his airworthy aircraft, but to establish a restoration centre of the highest quality.

His first aircraft was a former Swiss Air Force Pilatus P.2 acquired from Warbirds of Great Britain (Chapter 13) in July 1984; two Spitfire IX restoration projects also arrived during the year. Also making the journey from Blackbushe was Dick Melton who quickly established a major restoration workshop, including substantial jigs for Spitfires. At this point Charles Church (Spitfires) Ltd was set up and in due course another concern, Charles Church Displays Ltd, was initiated. The first machine to fly was a former Israeli Spitfire IX that had been salvaged by Robs Lamplough (more on him in Chapters 16 and 24) and completed as a Tr.9 two-seater. G-CTIX first flew from the Hampshire airstrip on 25th July 1987. It was exported to the USA in 1994, becoming N462JC but returned to the UK in April 1998. Since then it has been owned and flown by North Wales-based Anthony Hodgson. Also rolling out of the workshop in 1987 was another former Robs Lamplough aircraft, Spanish-built Messerschmitt Bf 109 G-HUNN. This took to the air on 15th August, having last been on show inside the Whitehall Theatre of War. By 1987 a total of five Spitfire projects were in hand.

Above: Spitfire V EE606 taxying out amid the lush surroundings of the Charles Church estate near Winchester.
Duncan Cubitt – Key Publishing www.flypast.com

P-51D 'Susie' in the colours worn during July 1989 for the filming of 'Memphis Belle'.

Ambitious Lancaster

On 28th November 1987 an airworthy North American P-51D touched down at the airstrip. Registered G-SUSY in honour of his wife, it was not the only acquisition late that year. Charles had bought the Fairey Battle restoration project from the former Strathallan Aircraft Collection but in a dramatic departure from his previous single-engined acquisitions he decided to purchase the Avro Lancaster X from the same source. Moving with the 'Lanc' to oversee its restoration and later to become manager of Popham aerodrome, was Dick Richardson. (More on the Lancaster and Dick in Chapter 10.) Charles had contracted with no less an organisation that British Aerospace to restore G-BCOH to airworthy condition. To this end, it arrived by road at Woodford, near Manchester – on 9th April 1987. On 9th January 1941 the prototype Lancaster, BT308, first flew from Woodford and in addition to three prototypes, 3,670 were built by Avro – the bulk of these first flying at Woodford.

Lancaster KB976 dismantled and trestled ready for restoration to commenced at Woodford, mid-1987.
Charles Church (Spitfires) Ltd

The Lancaster cockpit, guillotined by the roof collapse of 12th August 1987. *Charles Church (Spitfires) Ltd*

On 12th August 1987 disaster struck when the roof of the production shed the Lancaster was in collapsed, badly damaging it. Negotiations with BAe were lengthy and on 10th May 1989 a press conference was held where it was announced that Charles Church (Spitfires) Ltd had issued a high court writ that day to the tune of £4 million. Charles explained: "Discussions with British Aerospace to repair the Lancaster to its pre-accident condition at their expense and to complete the work contracted by BAe have proved fruitless." He enoted that he was not seeking to profit from the writ, merely to get the project back on line: "We even went to great lengths to obtain spare parts from around the world so that BAe could complete the repairs."

In October 1988 the Lancaster project was moved to Exeter initially, before moving to Cranfield, Bedfordshire, in December. Cranfield Institute of Technology was to take over the ambitious restoration and to that end fuselage sections from Mk.X KB994 had arrived from Canada and substantial elements of former Cranfield test-bed Avro Lincoln 2 G-29-1 arrived from North Weald, Essex. (For more on this aircraft, see Chapters 7 and 13.)

Spitfire tragedy

Determined to prove that it was possible to build a Spitfire effectively from new, the next product from the workshop and maiden flight from the airstrip was of Mk.V EE606 (G-MKVC). Based upon salvage of a former RAAF aircraft, it was regarded as a 'series prototype' and Charles believed that there was a market for effectively new-build examples. (This was a prescient viewpoint, since then Yakovlev World War Two fighters have been produced in the former Soviet Union, Flug Werk has built Focke-Wulf FW 190 new-builds and there has been the US-built Messerschmitt Me 262s.) *Victor-Charlie* first took to the air on 20th November 1988. With Charles at the controls, a local flight went tragically wrong on 1st July the following year. Encountering engine problems, Charles announced on the radio that he was attempting to make an emergency landing at Blackbushe, but was unable to do this. The Spitfire came down close to the aerodrome, crashed and burst into flames, killing Charles.

In the year he died, Charles had finalised the acquisition of Popham aerodrome, adjacent to his estate. As noted earlier, this is run with great energy by Dick Richardson on behalf of Charles Church (Spitfires) Ltd and Susanna Church. Popham is a vibrant aviation centre and a lasting tribute to the endeavours of Charles. The Spitfire workshop had been transferred to Dick Melton and was trading as Dick Melton Aviation. It went on to complete further Spitfires and a Hurricane, but its activities are beyond the scope of this book. The Lancaster project did not re-start and it was acquired by Florida-based pilot and restorer Kermit Weeks and has been in store ever since.

In Charles, Britain's aviation heritage had lost a great patron, a man who put unstinting efforts into each of his ventures. In the catalogue of the Sotheby's sale that handled the disposal of some of his aeroplanes, a touching tribute was made: "Charles Church was a man of boundless energy who totally committed himself to every project he undertook. He was a highly successful businessman who was keen that all those who were employed by him enjoyed their work and where therefore motivated to create a product of the highest quality, be it an aircraft restoration or a new house."

Charles Church (Spitfires) Ltd

Type	Identity	Built	Arrived	Background / *current status, or fate*
Avro Lancaster Mk.10(AR)	KB976	1945	Dec 1986	G-BCOH, ex Strathallan – Chapter 10, CF-TQC, RCAF KB976, RAF, 405 Sqn. See also main text. *Shipped to the USA Apr 1993, stored Fantasy of Flight Museum, Florida*
Fairey Battle I	1899	1940	1987	ex Strathallan – Chapter 10, Canada, RAF R3950 – no service. *Brussels Museum, Belgium*
Hawker Hurricane XII	G-ORGI	1942	mid-1986	ex Canada, RCAF 5481. *Exported to USA as N678DP Mar 1992, Museum of Flying, Santa Monica*
Messerschmitt Bf 109 (Buchón)	'14'	1958	1986	G-HUNN, ex Duxford, Whitehall Theatre of War – Chapter 24, G-BJZZ, Duxford, N48157, *Battle of Britain* film, Spanish AF C4K-235. *Cavanaugh Flight Museum, USA, registered N109GU*
NAA P-51D Mustang	472773	1944	28 Nov 1987	G-SUSY, ex USA N12066, Nicaragua Air Force GN-120, USAAF 44-72773. *Became G-CDHI, exported to Germany Nov 2007, airworthy aas D-FPSI*
Pilatus P.2-05 *	'CC+43'	1950	Jul 1984	G-CJCI, ex Warbirds of Great Britain – Chapter 13, Swiss Air Force U-143. *Sold in Germany Aug 2008*
Supermarine Spitfire V *	EE606	1942	1987	G-MKVC, ex Australia, RAAF A58-106, RAF EE606 – no service. *Fatal crash near Blackbushe, Hampshire, 1st Jul 1989*
Supermarine Spitfire IX	PL344	1944	1985	G-IXCC, Netherlands, RAF 129, 130, 401, 442 and 602 Sqns. *Exported to USA as N644TB, returned to UK, exported again to the USA Nov 2010*
Supermarine Spitfire IX	RR232	1943	13 Jan 1987	ex Australia, South Africa, SAAF 5632, RAF R232, Empire Central Flg Sch. *Became G-BRSF, under restoration by Martin Philips, Exeter*
Supermarine Spitfire IX	TE517	1945	Aug 1984	G-CCIX, ex G-BIXP, Duxford, Israel, Israeli Air Force/Defence Force, Czechoslovakia Air Force, RAF TE517, 313 Sqn. *Became G-JGCA, under restoration at Booker, Bucks*
Supermarine Spitfire Tr.9	PT462	1944	6 Apr 1985	G-CTIX, ex Nailsworth, Duxford – Robs Lamplough, Israel, Israeli Air Force/Defence Force 2067, Italian Air Force MM4100, RAF PT662, 73 and 253 Sqns. *Airworthy with Anthony Hodgson, North Wales*
Supermarine Spitfire XIV	MV262	1945	7 Aug 1986	G-CCVV, ex The Fighter Collection – Duxford, Warbirds of Great Britain – Chapter 13, OHB – Chapter 12, India, Indian Air Force, RAF MV262 – no service. *Under restoration at Booker, Bucks, as N808U*
Supermarine Spitfire XIV	SM832	1945	1988	G-WWII, ex Warbirds of Great Britain – Chapter 13, OHB – Chapter 12, India, Indian Air Force, RAF SM832. *Airworthy with Chino Warbirds as N54SF, USA*

Note: * – Illustrated in the colour sections.

ONES THAT GOT AWAY

Bristol 170 Freighter Mk.31M, 1996

When Instone Airline imported Bristol Freighter G-BISU from New Zealand in early 1981 a lot of enthusiasts must have breathed a sigh of relief that a much-deserving type had returned to the fold in the UK. An example of this wonderful machine should have found its way into a museum many a year before. Built for the Royal New Zealand Air Force as NZ5912, this machine was delivered in March 1955 and served on until the early 1960s. It was leased to famous New Zealand operator Straits Air Freight Express as ZK-BVI during 1957 and 1958 by the air force. Instone flew the aircraft for a couple of years and (as illustrated) there was the tantalising prospect of seeing it on the flightline at Duxford in June 1981. It was sold on to a Canadian concern, becoming C-FDFC in December 1988 but remained in the UK. On 18th July 1996 it was wrecked when it crashed on take-off at Enstone, Oxfordshire. The flight deck is preserved as a plaything at a private house in Fleet, Hampshire. Another one slipped the net...

CHAPTER 26

Wind in the Wires
Wessex Aviation and Transport Collection
1985 to 2002

Several collections of classic aircraft owned by an individual could have merited a major mention in this book, but most were essentially private endeavours, purely for the pleasure of the owner and friends. That could not be said of the de Havilland 'Moth' biased fleet assembled by businessman Brian Douglas Woodford in the mid-1980s. He delighted in attending fly-ins, airshows and especially the de Havilland Moth Club gathering at Woburn Abbey. Particularly at the latter, it would be a case of blazers, boaters and a fine picnic hamper – Brian enjoyed sharing his pride and joy with others.

First member of the collection was not a Moth, it was Argus As 10C-3 engined Morane-Saulnier MS.500 Criquet G-AZMH, once owned by the Hon Patrick Lindsay – see Chapter 21. Brian co-owned this machine with the Earl of Suffolk and Berkshire and it was registered to the pair on 24th January 1984. During that year, Brian set up Wessex Aviation and Transport Ltd and his rapidly expanding 'squadron' was established under this banner. There was a strip in the grounds of his home at Chalmington Manor, near Dorchester in Dorset, but his aircraft could also be found at Henstridge in Somerset, where a more generous runway was available.

The first de Havilland type, Leopard Moth G-AIYS – once with the Strathallan Collection, see Chapter 10 – followed in December 1984. After that, Brian wasted no time in gathering as many DH classics as he could, but others also took his fancy. In 1985 no less than seven aircraft were registered to 'Wessex'; with three more in 1986 and another trio the following year. This represented the zenith of Brian's acquisition 'surge', but he did top-up in the early 1990s with a second Tiger Moth, a Polish-built Antonov An-2 and a DH.2 replica – although this did not fly during its time with the fleet.

Another that remained on the ground was Spanish-built Junkers Ju 52 G-BFHD (imported by Warbirds of Great Britain, see Chapter 13) which was stored at Bournemouth Airport and was eventually traded to Aces High who supplied it to the National Air and Space Museum in the USA during 1987. Acquired in early 1985, the Westland Lysander was restored by Personal Plane Services at Booker, Buckinghamshire, and flew again on 18th September 1987.

Above: Superb DH Dragonfly G-AEDT of Wessex Aviation and Transport at a fly-in at Badminton in July 1988. It carried the winged sword of 601 (County of London) Squadron, Auxiliary Air Force on the fin. *Sam Tyler*

DH Moth G-ABEV in September 1980, not long after it had been used in a film about Amy Johnson, hence the name 'Jason' on the cowling. *Roy Bonser*

Squadron patron

Probably the most eyebrow-raising member of Brian's fleet was DH.90 Dragonfly G-AEDT which was brought in from the USA. It was painted in medium blue and silver colours and carried the winged sword badge of 601 (County of London) Squadron, Auxiliary Air Force, on the fin. In this guise, the Dragonfly was flown by Sir Philip Sassoon who ordered it new from de Havilland production and took delivery at Hatfield, Herts, in June 1936. While based it at Lympne in Kent, G-AEDT was frequently to be seen at Hendon, Middlesex, where 601 was based. Sir Philip became the unit's commanding officer in 1931 but when he was appointed, for the second time, as Under Secretary of State for Air, he had to relinquish the reservist post. Sir Philip maintained strong links with 601, presenting the unit with Spartan Three-Seater G-ABZI as a 'runabout' in 1935 – hence the winged sword emblazoned proudly on the fin of his Dragonfly.

By June 1993 the level of flying activity by Wessex Aviation and Transport had reduced considerably and on the 19th Brooks auctioneers offered the Criquet, Lysander, Stampe and 'Stearman' for disposal. The Lysander was withdrawn before the auction came around, and the other three failed to reach their reserve. Brian is reported to have bought US-built Moth G-AAVJ at the sale; though it was never registered to him and returned to the USA in the spring of 1994. With much of the fleet out of permit, in 1996 it was announced that all were available for offers. Last to leave the nest is thought to have been Moth Minor G-AFOB which changed owner on 5th February 2002. Lycoming IO-360-B2F engined Stampe SV-4 G-BMNV is still registered to Wessex Aviation and Transport, but is thought to be under restoration to fly again in South Wales, having left Dorset in 1999.

Hornet Moth G-ADUR at Old Warden, 1977. *Roy Bonser*

Wessex Aviation and Transport Collection

Type	Identity	Built	Arrived	Background / current status, or fate
Antonov An-2T *Cub*	G-BTCU	1964	25 Feb 1991	ex Poland SP-FDS, Polish Air Force. *Sold in Nicaragua Sep 1998*
BA Swallow II	G-ADPS	1935	18 Sep 1985	ex Hungerford, Strathallan – see Chapter 10, Sandown. *Airworthy, Devon owner*
Boeing PT-13D Kaydet	N4712V	1942	Sep 1985	ex USAAF 42-16931. *Airworthy, Norfolk owner*
CASA 352L (Junkers Ju 52)	G-BFHD	1951	7 Mar 1985	ex Warbirds of GB – Blackbushe – see Chapter 13, Spanish Air Force T2B-255. *National Air and Space Museum, Udvar Hazy Center, Dulles, USA*
De Havilland DH.2 replica	'5894'	1978	13 May 1991	G-BFVH, ex Duxford, Land's End, Leisure Sport – Chertsey. *Airworthy, Lincolnshire owner*
De Havilland DH.60G Moth	G-ABEV	1930	20 May 1985	ex USA N4203E, G-ABEV, Swiss HB-OKI and CH-217. *Airworthy, Somerset owner*
De Havilland DH.60GM Moth	G-AAVJ	1929	Sep 1993	ex USA N573N, NC573N. *Sold in the USA Mar 1994*
De Havilland Tiger Moth	GANLH	1941	10 Jan 1992	ex Hamble, USA N3744F, Belgium OO-EVO, G-ANLH, RAF PG637 1 Reserve Flg Sch, Honiley Stn Flt. *Sold in New Zealand Aug 2004*
De Havilland Tiger Moth	T5672	1940	28 May 1985	G-ALRI, ex New Zealand ZK-BAB, G-ALRI, RAF T5672, 7 Flying Tng Sch, 21 Elementary FTS, 7 FTS, RAF College, 4 EFTS. *Sold in Thailand Nov 2009*
De Havilland Fox Moth	G-ADHA	1934	15 Apr 1985	ex USA N83DH, New Zealand ZK-ASP, RNZAF NZ566, ZK-ADI. *Sold in New Zealand Feb 2007*
De Havilland Hornet Moth	G-ADUR	1936	16 Jun 1986	ex Cuckfield, USA N9026Y, G-ADUR. *Sold in Australia Nov 2010*
De Havilland Leopard Moth *	G-AIYS	1935	17 Dec 1984	ex Strathallan – Chapter 10, Iraq YI-ABI, Egypt SU-ABM. *Airworthy, Hertfordshire owner*
De Havilland Moth Minor	G-AFOB	1939	23 Mar 1987	ex Shuttleworth – Old Warden, RAF X5117, 10 Overseas Aircraft Ferry Unit, St Andrews Univ Air Sqn, 613 Sqn, G-AFOB. *Airworthy, Hertfordshire owner*
De Havilland Dragon Rapide *	G-ACZE	1940	23 Jan 1985	ex G-AJGS, G-ACZE, RAF Z7266, 3 Ferry Pool, 6 Air Observers Navigation Sch, G-ACZE. *Airworthy, Isle of Wight owner*
De Havilland Dragonfly	G-AEDT	1936	27 Apr 1987	ex Southampton, USA N2034, G-AEDT, Australia VH-AAD, G-AEDT. *Sold in New Zealand Mar 1998*
Morane-Saulnier Criquet	G-AZMH	1951	24 Jan 1984	ex Booker, Ireland EI-AUU, French F-BJQG, French military No.637. See also Chapter 21. *Sold in West Germany Jun 1997*
Piper J3F-50 Cub	G-AGAT	1939	17 Jul 1987	ex USA NC26126. *Airworthy, Edinburgh owner*
Stampe (SNCAN) SV-4L	G-BMNV	1946	14 Mar 1986	ex Booker, French F-BBNI. *Believed under restoration in South Wales*
Westland Lysander IIIa	V9281	1942	20 Feb 1985	G-BCWL, ex Booker, Hamble, Blackbushe – see Chapter 13, Booker, Canada, RCAF. *Fantasy of Flight, Florida, USA*

Note: * – Illustrated in the colour sections.

CHAPTER 27

Island Heritage
Island Aeroplane Company and the
Front Line Aviation Museum
1995 to 1999

Given the exceptional aeronautical heritage of the Isle of Wight, it is surprising that it was not until the autumn of 1995 that a serious attempt was made to establish a dedicated museum there. In October and November of that year the first wave of an 'invasion' from Germany took place as no less than eight aeroplanes touched down at Sandown aerodrome and taxied over to an extensive hangar on the north-western perimeter. This had been in use as the production facility for Island Aircraft's ARV-1 two-seater, but this project came to a halt at Sandown in 1991.

The arrivals had made the journey in stages from Augsburg, Germany, and constituted part of the 'oldtimer' collection of Josef Maximilian Koch. Josef had established his fleet of classics at Augsburg Airport, but infrastructure developments there meant that he had to vacate during 1995. His search was not limited to Germany's boundaries. Sandown on the Isle of Wight offered a receptive grass aerodrome, a very suitable building and potentially a good 'footfall' of tourists, both through the main gate and by pilots visiting from the mainland. Most of the Augsburg-based fleet had been prepared for their new life in the UK by Bitz Flugzeugbau, a specialist replica-building concern, which had also made the metal components for Josef's full-scale Fokker Dr.I.

Above: Commissioned by Josef Koch himself, the Fokker Dr.I replica on display at the Front Line Aviation Museum, Sandown, 1998. *Ken Ellis*

Blériot replica (left) and Miles Magister at Sandown, 1998 . *Ken Ellis*

Howard Shore's superb 'Flying Flea', fitted with a period Douglas flat twin, on show at Sandown. *Ken Ellis*

By the end of 1996 a total of 20 aircraft, the majority airworthy and some on loan, had arrived at Sandown. What was known as the Island Aeroplane Company opened to the public during that summer. For the enthusiast, Josef's selection included some rarities: a Czechoslovakian Sokol tourer of 1947, a German Klemm Kl 35 trainer, a French Morane-Saulnier MS.317 parasol, a Swiss-built Mignet 'Flea' with tricycle undercarriage and enclosed cockpit, and a Polish PZL Gawron utility type. As well as his Fokker, Josef brought a Blériot XI replica. There were also more familiar types, including a Canadian-remanufactured Harvard, a Tiger Moth and a Dragon Rapide.

Rethink and revival

By the spring of 1998 some of Josef's aircraft started to head eastwards, either by air or by road. Visitor numbers were not reaching expectations and there was speculation that the museum was going to receive a revamp. This came in the form of three friends, Mark Kirby, John Tickner and Steve Vizard and they provided items from their extensive collections to add a much-needed dimension to what was on offer. While the aircraft of the Island Aeroplane Company were of great interest, the exhibition was lacking *detail*, and the trio provided visitors with fascinating wartime artefacts to study up-close and enhanced information panels. Steve, managing director of Airframe Assemblies Ltd, a specialist 'warbird' restoration workshop in Sandown, managed to bring in more airframes on loan from colleagues, including a Bristol F.2b Fighter restoration courtesy of Guy Black's Aero Vintage, and a Hunter and Meteor from the Duxford-based Old Flying Machine Company. Re-branded as the Front Line Aviation Museum, hopes were high that this would reverse the downward trend of visitors.

All of this was to no avail, and on 14th November 1999 the doors for the last time. Aircraft and supporting exhibits, large and small, were dispersed. In Germany, Josef Koch continued to search for a new venue for his collection and settled on Grossenhain, near Dresden, in 2002 where plans to open it to the public have yet to reach fruition. In late 2003 Airframe Assemblies re-located from an industrial unit on the edge if the town to Sandown aerodrome and continues to work wonders on Spitfire projects and much more.

The roll-out of Meteor F.8 'WF714' after completion by the Medway Aircraft Preservation Society, at Rochester, Kent, October 1983. It was displayed at Sandown during 1998 and 1999. *Medway APS via Lewis Deal*

Island Aeroplane Company and the Front Line Aviation Museum

Type	Identity	Built	Arrived	Background / current status, or fate
Aeronca K	G-ONKA	1938	1996	ex US N19870, NC19870. Airworthy, Buckinghamshire-based owner
Antonov An-2T Cub	12802	1962	5 Feb 1996	D-FOFM, ex East German Air Force. To Germany Apr 1998
Bell P-39Q Airacobra	–	c 1941	14 Jul 1999	substantial wreckage, ex Russia, Soviet AF, USAAF. To the USA Sep 200
Benes-Mraz M.1D Sokol	G-BWRG	1947	8 Oct 1995	ex German D-EGWP, Swiss HB-TBG, Czech OK-DIX. To Germany May 2000
Blériot XI replica	G-BWRH	1960	Oct 1995	ex German D-EFTE, US N25WM. To Germany Sep 1999
Bristol F.2b Fighter	D7889	1917	7 Jan 1999	on loan from Aero Vintage, ex St Leonards-on-Sea, Old Warden, Weston-on-the-Green. To Canada Dec 2006
Bücker Bü 131 Jungmann	D-EAZO	1938	1996	ex Swiss HB-UTK, Swiss Air Force A-41. To Germany Oct 1997
Cessna 195	D-EFTH	1949	1996	ex US N195MN. To Germany 1999
Curtiss P-40E Warhawk	41-13570	1941	26 Aug 1998	substantial wreckage, ex Russia, Soviet AF, USAAF. To the USA Jun 200
De Havilland Tiger Moth	T6390	1941	8 Oct 1995	G-ANIX, ex German D-EFTF, D-ELOM, G-ANIX, RAF T6390, 1 Glider Unit, 6 Elementary Flg Tng Sch. To Germany Aug 1998
De Havilland Dragon Rapide	G-AMAI	1945	Oct 1995	ex Germany D-ILIT, Spain EC-AGP, G-AMAI, RAF Dominie NR803, Transport Command Comm Flt, Valley Stn Flt, Dunkeswell Stn Flt, Talbenny Stn Flt. To Germany Apr 1998
Fokker Dr.I replica	425/17	1988	1 Nov 1995	G-BWRJ, ex German D-EFTN. To Germany Oct 1999 as D-EFTN
Gloster Meteor F.8	'WF714'	1952	5 Aug 1998	WK914. On loan, ex Duxford, Rochester, Manston, 85 Sqn, College of Air Warfare, 5 Civilian Anti-Aircraft Co-op Unit, 19 Sqn. Private owner, Hooton Park, Cheshire
Grunau Baby III glider	CRM	1939	28 Mar 1997	ex Nympsfield, RAF Gliding and Soaring Assoc RAFGSA.361, German D-8061. Believed stored in Gloucestershire
Hawker Hurricane IIb	BH238	1942	26 Aug 1998	substantial wreckage, ex Russia, Soviet AF, RAF – no service. Stored on the Isle of Wight
Hawker Hunter F.4	WV276	1955	5 Aug 1998	ex Duxford, Farnborough, 1 Sch of Tech Trg – Halton 7847M, Horsham St Faith, Boscombe Down, Rolls-Royce. To Germany Jul 2005
Hawker Hunter F.51	'XF314'	1956	16 Nov 1998	ex Tangmere, Dunsfold, Hawker Siddeley G-9-439, Danish Air Force E-412. Brooklands Museum, Weybridge, Surrey
Klemm L.25a-1a	G-AAHW	1929	1997	ex German D-ELFK, G-AAHW To Germany, Jun 1998 as D-EFTE
Klemm Kl 35D	G-BWRD	1939	8 Oct 1995	ex German D-EFTG, D-EHUX, Sweden SE-AIP, Swedish Air Force Fv5081, SE-AIP. To Germany 1998 as D-EFTY
Mignet HM.14 'Flying Flea'	'G-ADZW'	1994	27 Feb 1996	on loan. Ex Sussex. Solent Sky, Southampton
Mignet HM.19C	G-BWRI	1959	30 Jan 1996	ex Swis HB-SPG. To Germany Oct 1999

Type	Identity	Built	Arrived	Background / *current status, or fate*
Miles Magister	V1075	1938	20 Jul 1996	on loan. Ex Shoreham, RAF V1075, 16 Elementary Flg Tng Sch. *Airworthy, based at Old Warden.* See Note [1]
Morane-Saulnier MS.317	F-BBQE	1946	6 Nov 1995	ex La Ferte Alais, France F-BCNL. *To Germany Oct 1997*
Morane-Saulnier Criquet	G-BWRF	1946	8 Oct 1995	ex German D-EFTY, France F-BAUV, French military No.73. *To Germany 1997*
NAA (CCF) Harvard IV	28578	c 1944	1996	D-FABE, ex West German Air Force AA+624, USAAF 52-8578. *To Germany May 1998*
Percival Provost T.1	XF877	1955	25 Nov 1996	G-AWVF, ex RAF XF877, Civilian Air Traffic Controller Sch, Central Nav and Controller Sch, RAF College. *Airworthy, Reading-based owner*
Ryan PT-21 Recruit	G-AGYY	1941	1996	on loan. Ex US N56792, USAAF 41-1942. *Airworthy, Netherlands-based owner*
PZL Gawron	SP-CHD	c 1960	6 Nov 1995	ex Poland. *To Germany circa 1999*
Stampe SV-4A	No.396	1947	8 Oct 1995	G-BWRE, ex German D-EJKA, France F-BDOT, French Air Force No.396. *To Germany Sep 1999*
Supermarine Spitfire replica	'K5054'	1984	22 Jul 1999	ex Keevil. *Solent Sky, Southampton.* See Note [2]
UFM Easy Riser ultra-light	–	?	1997	Moved on by 1999.

Notes: All initially ex-Augsburg, unless noted. [1] Composite airframe from rebuild in mid-1950s, centre section of G-AIUA, fuselage from G-ANLT, wings from G-AHYL; rebuilt again 1970s including parts from G-AKPF – flies today as N3788, the RAF serial of G-ANLT. Additionally, a mock-up Spitfire cockpit and V-1 'Doodlebug' were displayed during 1998 to the closure. [2] Full-scale replica but with airframe built of wood and powered by a converted Jaguar V-12.

Appendix

50 Years – 22 Covers

**WRECKS
and
RELICS
1961**

A Merseyside Aviation Society Publication

While celebrating the half-century, we thought that readers might like to see all of the covers – how many do *you* have? Compiling the 1st and 2nd Editions (1961 and 162 respectively) was David J Stephens and even the current editor does not have a 1st Edition so we show the reprinted edition of 1974. Edition 3 was compiled by S George Jones and appeared in 1968. In 1974 the 4th Edition appeared, edited by Ken Ellis. Since then, a new edition has been published every 'even' year and the 23rd is due in 2012.

The 20th, 21st and 22nd Editions of *Wreck & Relics* are still available, contact the good people at Crécy Publishing on **0161 499 0024** or take a look at **www.crecy.co.uk**

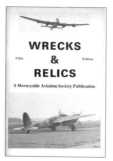

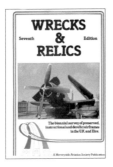

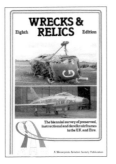

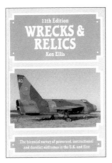

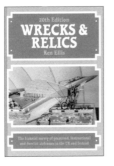

BIBLIOGRAPHY

Books

Action Stations Revisited 4 – South West England, David Berryman, Crécy Publishing, Manchester, 2009
Adventure with Fate, Harald Penrose, Airlife, Shrewsbury, 1984
Aircraft of the Royal Air Force since 1918, Owen Thetford, Putnam Aeronautical Books, London, ninth edition, 1995
Armstrong Whitworth Aircraft since 1913, Oliver Tapper, Putnam, London, second edition, 1978
Aviation in Leicestershire and Rutland, Roy Bonser, Midland Publishing, Hinckley, 2001
Avro Aircraft since 1908, A J Jackson, Putnam, London, second edition, 1990
Avro Lancaster – The Definitive Record, Harry Holmes, Airlife, Shrewsbury, 2001
Blackburn Aircraft since 1909, A J Jackson, Putnam, London, second edition, 1989
Bristol Aircraft since 1910, C H Barnes, Putnam, London, third edition, 1988
British Aviation – The Adventuring Years 1920-1929, Harald Penrose, Putnam, London, 1973
British Civil Aircraft since 1919, Volumes 1, 2 and 3, A J Jackson, Putnam & Co, London, second Editions, 1973, 1973 and
    1974 respectively
British Civil Aircraft Registers 1919 to 1999, Michael Austen, Air-Britain, Tunbridge Wells, 1999
British Independent Airlines 1946-1976, Tony Merton Jones, The Aviation Hobby Shop, West Drayton, combined volume edition, 2000
British Museum Aircraft, Ken Ellis and Phil Butler, Merseyside Aviation Society, Liverpool, 1977
Canadair Sabre, Larry Milberry, CANAV Books, Toronto, Canada, 1986
Cierva Autogiros – The Development of Rotary-Wing Flight, Peter W Brooks, Smithsonian Institution, Washington DC, USA, 1988
English Electric Canberra, Ken Delve, Peter Green, John Clemons, Midland Counties Publications, Earl Shilton, 1992
English Electric Lightning – Birth of a Legend, and English Electric Lightning – The Lightning Force, Stewart A Scott, GMS
    Enterprises, Peterborough, 2000 and 2004
Fairey Aircraft since 1915, H A Taylor, Putnam & Co, London, 1974
Fleet Air Arm Fixed-Wing Aircraft since 1946, Ray Sturtivant, Air-Britain, Tunbridge Wells, 2004
Gloster Aircraft since 1917, Derek N James, Putnam, London, second edition, 1987
Hawker Hunter – Biography of a Thoroughbred, Francis K Mason, Patrick Stephens, Bar Hill, 1981
Hunter One – The Jet Heritage Story, Mike Phipp with Eric Hayward, Amberley Publishing, Stroud, 2009
In Uniform – Britain's Airworthy Warbirds, Ken Ellis, Merseyside Aviation Society, Liverpool, 1983
The K File – The Royal Air Force of the 1930s, James J Halley MBE, Air-Britain, Tunbridge Wells, 1995
RAF Flying Training and Support Units since 1912, Ray Sturtivant with John Hamlin, Air-Britain, Staplefield, 2007
RAF Squadrons, Wg Cdr C G Jefford MBE, Airlife, Shrewsbury, 1988
Spirit of Britain First, Graham Warner, Patrick Stephens Ltd, Sparkford, 1996.
Story of a 'Lanc' – NX611 Just Jane, Brian Goulding and Richard J A Taylor, self-published, East Kirkby, 2010
Survivors, Roy Blewett, Gatwick Aviation Society with Aviation Classics, Croydon, 2007
Vampires and Fleas – A History of British Aircraft Preservation, Alec Brew, Crowood Press, Marlborough, 2003
Veteran and Vintage Aircraft, Leslie Hunt, self-published, Leigh-on-Sea, 1965; also the 1968, 1970 and 1974 editions
War Prizes – An Illustrated Survey of German, Italian and Japanese Aircraft Brought to Allied Countries during and after the
    Second World War, Phil Butler, Midland Counties Publishing, Earl Shilton, 1994
Warbirds Directory, 4th Edition in print and CD, Geoff Goodall, Derek McPhail (publisher), New Gisborne, Australia, 2008
Westland Aircraft since 1915, Derek N James, Putnam, London, 1991

and, of course...
Wrecks & Relics, all 22 editions: 1st and 2nd editions by D J Stephens, published in 1961 by the Merseyside Group of Aviation
Enthusiasts, Liverpool and in 1962 by the Merseyside Society of Aviation Enthusiasts, Liverpool. 3rd edition by S G Jones,
published by MSAE in 1968. 4th edition onwards by Ken Ellis; published 1974 and each 'even' year thereon. Publishers were
as follows: 4th by MSAE, 5th to 10th by Merseyside Aviation Society, Liverpool. 11th to 13th Midland Counties Publications,
Earl Shilton. 14th to 20th Midland Publishing, Earl Shilton. 21st and 22nd by Crécy Publishing Ltd, Manchester.

Magazines

Control Column, published initially by the Northern Aircraft Preservation Society, then by Neville Franklin, 1963 to 1988
Northern Aeronews, published by the Merseyside Group of Aviation Enthusiasts; in the early 1960s renamed Flypast, the
MGAE becoming the Merseyside Society of Aviation Enthusasts and then the Merseyside Aviation Society, 1956 to 1985
Vintage Aircraft, published by Gordon Riley, 1976 to 1982

and, of course...
FlyPast, published by Key Publishing from 1981, Britain's top-selling aviation monthly – **www.flypast.com**

INDEX

History is not what you thought
It is what you can remember

W C Sellar and R J Yeatman,
1066 and All That, 1930